MERRY CHRISTMAS!

Love,

MAD LIBS

Mad Libs
An Imprint of Penguin Random House

MAD LIBS
Penguin Young Readers Group
An Imprint of Penguin Random House LLC

Mad Libs format and text copyright © 1996, 2001, 2003, 2005, 2007, 2010, 2012, 2013, 2014, 2015, 2016 by Penguin Random House LLC. All rights reserved.

Concept created by Roger Price & Leonard Stern

Photo credit: page 193 (the title page of *History of the World Mad Libs*):
© Getty Images, photo by Niko Guido.

Merry Christmas! Love, Mad Libs published in 2017 by Mad Libs,
an imprint of Penguin Random House LLC,
345 Hudson Street, New York, New York 10014.
Printed in the USA.

Merry Christmas! Love, Mad Libs ISBN 9781524785079

1 3 5 7 9 10 8 6 4 2

MAD LIBS®

CHRISTMAS CAROL MAD LIBS

Mad Libs
An Imprint of Penguin Random House

INSTRUCTIONS

MAD LIBS® is a game for people who don't like games!
It can be played by one, two, three, four, or forty.

• RIDICULOUSLY SIMPLE DIRECTIONS

In this tablet you will find stories containing blank spaces where words are left out.
One player, the READER, selects one of these stories. The READER does not tell anyone
what the story is about. Instead, he/she asks the other players, the WRITERS, to give
him/her words. These words are used to fill in the blank spaces in the story.

• TO PLAY

The READER asks each WRITER in turn to call out a word—an adjective or a noun or
whatever the space calls for—and uses them to fill in the blank spaces in the story. The
result is a MAD LIBS® game.

When the READER then reads the completed MAD LIBS® game to the other players,
they will discover that they have written a story that is fantastic, screamingly funny,
shocking, silly, crazy, or just plain dumb—depending upon which words each WRITER
called out.

• EXAMPLE (*Before* and *After*)

"_____!" he said _____
      EXCLAMATION   ADVERB

as he jumped into his convertible _____ and
                                           NOUN

drove off with his _____ wife.
                           ADJECTIVE

"_____OUCH_____!" he said _____STUPIDLY_____
      EXCLAMATION   ADVERB

as he jumped into his convertible _____CAT_____ and
                                           NOUN

drove off with his _____BRAVE_____ wife.
                           ADJECTIVE

QUICK REVIEW

In case you have forgotten what adjectives, adverbs, nouns, and verbs are, here is a quick review:

An ADJECTIVE describes something or somebody. *Lumpy, soft, ugly, messy,* and *short* are adjectives.

An ADVERB tells how something is done. It modifies a verb and usually ends in "ly." *Modestly, stupidly, greedily,* and *carefully* are adverbs.

A NOUN is the name of a person, place, or thing. *Sidewalk, umbrella, bridle, bathtub,* and *nose* are nouns.

A VERB is an action word. *Run, pitch, jump,* and *swim* are verbs. Put the verbs in past tense if the directions say PAST TENSE. *Ran, pitched, jumped,* and *swam* are verbs in the past tense.

When we ask for A PLACE, we mean any sort of place: a country or city *(Spain, Cleveland)* or a room *(bathroom, kitchen).*

An EXCLAMATION or SILLY WORD is any sort of funny sound, gasp, grunt, or outcry, like *Wow!, Ouch!, Whomp!, Ick!,* and *Gadzooks!*

When we ask for specific words, like a NUMBER, a COLOR, an ANIMAL, or a PART OF THE BODY, we mean a word that is one of those things, like *seven, blue, horse,* or *head.*

When we ask for a PLURAL, it means more than one. For example, *cat* pluralized is *cats.*

MAD LIBS® is fun to play with friends, but you can also play it by yourself! To begin with, DO NOT look at the story on the page below. Fill in the blanks on this page with the words called for. Then, using the words you have selected, fill in the blank spaces in the story.

Now you've created your own hilarious MAD LIBS® game!

JINGLE BELLS

PLURAL NOUN _____

ANIMAL _____

NOUN _____

PLURAL NOUN _____

VERB ENDING IN "ING" _____

PLURAL NOUN _____

PLURAL NOUN _____

VERB _____

PLURAL NOUN _____

SAME PLURAL NOUN _____

VERB _____

SAME ANIMAL _____

MAD LIBS®
JINGLE BELLS

Dashing through the _____,
PLURAL NOUN

In a one-_____ open _____,
ANIMAL   NOUN

O'er the _____ we go,
PLURAL NOUN

_____ all the way.
VERB ENDING IN "ING"

_____ on bobtails ring,
PLURAL NOUN

Making _____ bright.
PLURAL NOUN

What fun it is to _____ and sing
VERB

A sleighing song tonight!

Jingle _____ , jingle _____ ,
PLURAL NOUN   SAME PLURAL NOUN

Jingle all the way!

Oh, what fun it is to _____
VERB

In a one-_____ open sleigh.
SAME ANIMAL

MAD LIBS® is fun to play with friends, but you can also play it by yourself! To begin with, DO NOT look at the story on the page below. Fill in the blanks on this page with the words called for. Then, using the words you have selected, fill in the blank spaces in the story.

Now you've created your own hilarious MAD LIBS® game!

GOING CAROLING

ADJECTIVE _____

ADJECTIVE _____

NUMBER _____

ADJECTIVE _____

PLURAL NOUN _____

PLURAL NOUN _____

ADJECTIVE _____

PLURAL NOUN _____

NOUN _____

PLURAL NOUN _____

VERB _____

NUMBER _____

NOUN _____

NUMBER _____

ADVERB _____

NOUN _____

PLURAL NOUN _____

VERB _____

MAD LIBS
GOING CAROLING

'Tis the _____ season for caroling! Here's how to make everyone's
         ADJECTIVE

Christmas a little more merry and _____:
                                      ADJECTIVE

- Gather _____ of your _____ friends and family
            NUMBER   ADJECTIVE

  _____ together. Pick out a few classic _____ to
  PLURAL NOUN   PLURAL NOUN

  sing, like "Have Yourself a/an _____ Little Christmas," "Silver
                                    ADJECTIVE

  _____," and "Frosty the _____-man."
  PLURAL NOUN   NOUN

- Put Santa _____ on everyone's heads and _____ to your
              PLURAL NOUN   VERB

  neighbor's house.

- Knock _____ times on the front _____. Nothing?
          NUMBER   NOUN

  Knock _____ more times _____.
          NUMBER   ADVERB

- When your neighbor answers the _____, ask if he or she
                                    NOUN

  would like to hear you sing a song. If your neighbor says yes, sing your

  _____ out. If your neighbor says no, _____
  PLURAL NOUN   VERB

  anyway!

MAD LIBS® is fun to play with friends, but you can also play it by yourself! To begin with, DO NOT look at the story on the page below. Fill in the blanks on this page with the words called for. Then, using the words you have selected, fill in the blank spaces in the story.

Now you've created your own hilarious MAD LIBS® game!

DECK THE HALLS

PLURAL NOUN _____

PLURAL NOUN _____

NOUN _____

ADJECTIVE _____

ADJECTIVE _____

ADJECTIVE _____

VERB ENDING IN "ING" _____

NOUN _____

ADJECTIVE _____

ADJECTIVE _____

MAD LIBS®
DECK THE HALLS

Deck the ___Shoes___ with boughs of ___Stockings___,
                PLURAL NOUN   PLURAL NOUN

Fa-la-la-la-la-la-la-la-la!

'Tis the ___Cat___ to be ___Furry___,
            NOUN   ADJECTIVE

Fa-la-la-la-la-la-la-la-la!

Don we now our ___Smelly___ apparel,
                  ADJECTIVE

Fa-la-la-la-la-la-la-la-la!

Troll the ancient ___Tasty___ carol,
                     ADJECTIVE

Fa-la-la-la-la-la-la-la-la!

See the ___Crawling___ Yule before us,
          VERB ENDING IN "ING"

Fa-la-la-la-la-la-la-la-la!

Strike the ___Dog___ and join the chorus,
              NOUN

Fa-la-la-la-la-la-la-la-la!

Follow me in ___Pricey___ measure,
                ADJECTIVE

Fa-la-la-la-la-la-la-la-la!

While I tell of ___Droops___ treasure,
                  ADJECTIVE

Fa-la-la-la-la-la-la-la-la!

From CHRISTMAS CAROL MAD LIBS® • Copyright © 2003, 2007 by Penguin Random House LLC.

MAD LIBS® is fun to play with friends, but you can also play it by yourself! To begin with, DO NOT look at the story on the page below. Fill in the blanks on this page with the words called for. Then, using the words you have selected, fill in the blank spaces in the story.

Now you've created your own hilarious MAD LIBS® game!

THE TWELVE DAYS OF CHRISTMAS, PART 1

NOUN _____

NOUN _____

NOUN _____

ADJECTIVE _____

NOUN _____

ADJECTIVE _____

ADJECTIVE _____

NOUN _____

PLURAL NOUN _____

ADJECTIVE _____

NOUN _____

On the first day of Christmas,

My true _____ gave to me
          NOUN

A partridge in a/an _____ tree.
                         NOUN

On the second _____ of Christmas,
                    NOUN

My _____ love gave to me
       ADJECTIVE

Two turtle doves

And a/an _____ in a/an _____ tree.
              NOUN   ADJECTIVE

On the third day of Christmas,

My _____ _____ gave to me
       ADJECTIVE   NOUN

Three French hens,

Two turtle _____,
              PLURAL NOUN

And a partridge in a/an _____ _____.
                           ADJECTIVE   NOUN

MAD LIBS® is fun to play with friends, but you can also play it by yourself! To begin with, DO NOT look at the story on the page below. Fill in the blanks on this page with the words called for. Then, using the words you have selected, fill in the blank spaces in the story.

Now you've created your own hilarious MAD LIBS® game!

THE TWELVE DAYS OF CHRISTMAS, PART 2

NOUN _____

NUMBER _____

ADJECTIVE _____

NOUN _____

ADJECTIVE _____

NOUN _____

PLURAL NOUN _____

PLURAL NOUN _____

ADJECTIVE _____

PLURAL NOUN _____

ADJECTIVE _____

PLURAL NOUN _____

NOUN _____

ADJECTIVE _____

NOUN _____

On the fourth day of Christmas,

My true __Paris__ gave to me

NOUN

Four calling birds,

__13__ French hens,

NUMBER

Two __gargantian__ doves,

ADJECTIVE

And a/an __Penguin__ in a pear tree.

NOUN

On the fifth day of Christmas,

My __Fluffy__ __Treehouse__ gave to me

ADJECTIVE · NOUN

Five golden __Beers__,

PLURAL NOUN

Four calling __Cussions__,

PLURAL NOUN

Three __White__ __Tables__,

ADJECTIVE · PLURAL NOUN

Two __gross__ __Books__,

ADJECTIVE · PLURAL NOUN

And a/an __Steak__ in a/an __Creepy__ __Tree__.

NOUN · ADJECTIVE · NOUN

MAD LIBS® is fun to play with friends, but you can also play it by yourself! To begin with, DO NOT look at the story on the page below. Fill in the blanks on this page with the words called for. Then, using the words you have selected, fill in the blank spaces in the story.

Now you've created your own hilarious MAD LIBS® game!

CHRISTMAS SHOPPING

ADJECTIVE _____

ADJECTIVE _____

PLURAL NOUN _____

NOUN _____

CELEBRITY _____

VERB (PAST TENSE) _____

VERB _____

ADJECTIVE _____

NOUN _____

TYPE OF LIQUID _____

ADJECTIVE _____

ADJECTIVE _____

NOUN _____

PLURAL NOUN _____

PLURAL NOUN _____

PLURAL NOUN _____

PLURAL NOUN _____

NOUN _____

VERB ENDING IN "ING" _____

MAD LIBS®
CHRISTMAS SHOPPING

When I was a/an _____ kid, I loved going to the _____ mall
                   ADJECTIVE   ADJECTIVE

at Christmastime. My parents would dress me and my _____ in our
                                                      PLURAL NOUN

cutest holiday outfits. Then we'd all pile into the family _____ and
                                                              NOUN

drive to the mall to sit on _____'s lap. As we _____ in the
                              CELEBRITY   VERB (PAST TENSE)

long line to Santa's _____-shop, we'd look around at all the
                        VERB

_____ lights strung around the _____, drink hot
   ADJECTIVE   NOUN

_____, and sing _____ carols. Then the _____
TYPE OF LIQUID   ADJECTIVE   ADJECTIVE

moment would arrive—we'd finally get to meet Santa and tell him what we

wanted to find under the _____ on Christmas morning. Of course,
                            NOUN

now that I'm older, I avoid the mall at all _____. It's so crowded that
                                             PLURAL NOUN

all the _____ push into one another. You can't even catch of glimpse
          PLURAL NOUN

of Santa and his _____. These days, I buy all my _____
                   PLURAL NOUN   PLURAL NOUN

online. With just a click of the _____, Christmas _____
                                  NOUN   VERB ENDING IN "ING"

couldn't be easier!

MAD LIBS® is fun to play with friends, but you can also play it by yourself! To begin with, DO NOT look at the story on the page below. Fill in the blanks on this page with the words called for. Then, using the words you have selected, fill in the blank spaces in the story.

Now you've created your own hilarious MAD LIBS® game!

THE CHRISTMAS PAGEANT

ADJECTIVE _____

A PLACE _____

PLURAL NOUN _____

PLURAL NOUN _____

ADJECTIVE _____

NOUN _____

NOUN _____

SILLY WORD _____

PERSON IN ROOM (MALE) _____

NOUN _____

ADJECTIVE _____

ADJECTIVE _____

COLOR _____

NOUN _____

ADJECTIVE _____

PART OF THE BODY (PLURAL) _____

PLURAL NOUN _____

SILLY WORD _____

MAD LIBS
THE CHRISTMAS PAGEANT

Every December, our school puts on a/an _____ holiday
ADJECTIVE

pageant. We decorate (the) _____ with snow-_____ and
A PLACE   PLURAL NOUN

red and green _____, and we perform a/an _____
PLURAL NOUN   ADJECTIVE

play and sing Christmas carols. This year, the _____ is set in the
NOUN

North Pole. Our music _____, Mrs. _____, cast
NOUN   SILLY WORD

my best friend, _____, as Santa. He will, of course,
PERSON IN ROOM (MALE)

be wearing a red _____ stuffed with a/an _____
NOUN   ADJECTIVE

pillow so he'll look really _____. I was cast as Rudolph the
ADJECTIVE

_____-nosed _____. I'll be wearing _____
COLOR   NOUN   ADJECTIVE

antlers on my _____. The rest of the class will be elves
PART OF THE BODY (PLURAL)

making _____ in Santa's workshop. It's going to be so much fun! Ho,
PLURAL NOUN

_____, ho!
SILLY WORD

MAD LIBS® is fun to play with friends, but you can also play it by yourself! To begin with, DO NOT look at the story on the page below. Fill in the blanks on this page with the words called for. Then, using the words you have selected, fill in the blank spaces in the story.

Now you've created your own hilarious MAD LIBS® game!

O CHRISTMAS TREE

NOUN _____

SAME NOUN _____

ADJECTIVE _____

SAME NOUN _____

SAME NOUN _____

ADJECTIVE _____

ADJECTIVE _____

PLURAL NOUN _____

ADJECTIVE _____

PLURAL NOUN _____

SAME NOUN _____

SAME NOUN _____

ADJECTIVE _____

MAD LIBS®
O CHRISTMAS TREE

O Christmas _____, O Christmas _____,
              NOUN   SAME NOUN

How _____ are your branches!
        ADJECTIVE

O Christmas _____, O Christmas _____,
           SAME NOUN   SAME NOUN

How _____ are your branches!
        ADJECTIVE

They're _____ when summer _____ are bright,
        ADJECTIVE   PLURAL NOUN

They're _____ when winter _____ are white.
        ADJECTIVE   PLURAL NOUN

O Christmas _____, O Christmas _____,
           SAME NOUN   SAME NOUN

How _____ are your branches!
        ADJECTIVE

MAD LIBS® is fun to play with friends, but you can also play it by yourself! To begin with, DO NOT look at the story on the page below. Fill in the blanks on this page with the words called for. Then, using the words you have selected, fill in the blank spaces in the story.

Now you've created your own hilarious MAD LIBS® game!

UP ON THE HOUSETOP

NOUN _____

ANIMAL (PLURAL) _____

ADJECTIVE _____

NOUN _____

ADJECTIVE _____

PERSON IN ROOM _____

PLURAL NOUN _____

EXCLAMATION _____

NOUN _____

VERB _____

PERSON IN ROOM _____

NOUN _____

SILLY WORD _____

SAME SILLY WORD _____

SAME SILLY WORD _____

ADJECTIVE _____

MAD LIBS
UP ON THE HOUSETOP

Up on the _____-top, _____ pause,
                   NOUN   ANIMAL (PLURAL)

Out jumps _____ old Santa Claus.
                   ADJECTIVE

Down through the _____ with lots of toys,
                        NOUN

All for the _____ ones, Christmas joys.
                ADJECTIVE

Ho, ho, ho! Who wouldn't go? Ho, ho, ho! _____ wouldn't go!
                                         PERSON IN ROOM

First comes the _____ of little Nell.
                   PLURAL NOUN

_____! Dear Santa, fill it well!
EXCLAMATION

Give her a/an _____ that laughs and cries,
                   NOUN

One that will _____ and shut its eyes.
                   VERB

Ho, ho, ho! Who wouldn't go? Ho, ho, ho! _____ wouldn't go!
                                         PERSON IN ROOM

Up on the _____-top, _____, _____,
                   NOUN   SILLY WORD   SAME SILLY WORD

_____!
SAME SILLY WORD

Down through the chimney with _____ Saint Nick.
                                  ADJECTIVE

MAD LIBS® is fun to play with friends, but you can also play it by yourself! To begin with, DO NOT look at the story on the page below. Fill in the blanks on this page with the words called for. Then, using the words you have selected, fill in the blank spaces in the story.

Now you've created your own hilarious MAD LIBS® game!

A CHRISTMAS SOLO

NOUN _____

ADVERB _____

ADJECTIVE _____

VERB ENDING IN "ING" _____

NUMBER _____

NOUN _____

VERB (PAST TENSE) _____

COLOR _____

PART OF THE BODY _____

PERSON IN ROOM _____

ADJECTIVE _____

PLURAL NOUN _____

ADJECTIVE _____

PLURAL NOUN _____

ADJECTIVE _____

VERB (PAST TENSE) _____

SAME VERB (PAST TENSE) _____

NOUN _____

ADJECTIVE _____

MAD LIBS®
A CHRISTMAS SOLO

A few years ago, my music _____ asked me to sing a Christmas
                          NOUN

solo at our holiday concert. At first I was _____ flattered, but the
                                           ADVERB

more I thought about it, the more _____ I became. Every time I
                                 ADJECTIVE

thought about _____ in front of _____ people,
              VERB ENDING IN "ING"   NUMBER

my whole _____ started to shake. What if I _____ or
         NOUN   VERB (PAST TENSE)

forgot the lyrics? What if I suddenly developed a/an _____ rash on
                                                    COLOR

my _____? My friend _____ suggested picturing
   PART OF THE BODY   PERSON IN ROOM

the audience as a bunch of _____ _____ to make it
                           ADJECTIVE   PLURAL NOUN

easier. That seemed like a/an _____ plan—until I worried I'd start
                              ADJECTIVE

laughing and all the _____ would think I was _____.
                     PLURAL NOUN   ADJECTIVE

Finally, the night of the concert arrived. I walked onstage, gathered all my

courage, and _____ like I'd never _____ before.
             VERB (PAST TENSE)   SAME VERB (PAST TENSE)

The song went off without a/an _____, and I received a standing
                               NOUN

ovation. It was the most _____ moment of my entire life!
                         ADJECTIVE

MAD LIBS® is fun to play with friends, but you can also play it by yourself! To begin with, DO NOT look at the story on the page below. Fill in the blanks on this page with the words called for. Then, using the words you have selected, fill in the blank spaces in the story.

Now you've created your own hilarious MAD LIBS® game!

AUNTIE'S CRAZY CHRISTMAS CLOTHING

PLURAL NOUN _____

PLURAL NOUN _____

ADJECTIVE _____

PERSON IN ROOM (FEMALE) _____

ADJECTIVE _____

PLURAL NOUN _____

PLURAL NOUN _____

PART OF THE BODY _____

PLURAL NOUN _____

COLOR _____

A PLACE _____

NOUN _____

PART OF THE BODY _____

VERB (PAST TENSE) _____

PART OF THE BODY _____

Every Christmas, my family gets together to exchange _____

PLURAL NOUN

and eat a big Christmas dinner of ham, mashed _____,

PLURAL NOUN

and all the _____ trimmings. For me, though, the

ADJECTIVE

highlight of every Christmas is seeing my aunt _____

PERSON IN ROOM (FEMALE)

make her _____ entrance. She always wears the craziest

ADJECTIVE

_____ on Christmas. You wouldn't believe it! For

PLURAL NOUN

example, last year she wore earrings that looked like giant Christmas

_____, a sweatshirt with Santa's _____ on the

PLURAL NOUN .... PART OF THE BODY

front, and socks with red-and-white candy _____ on them. She

PLURAL NOUN

also wore a snowflake pin with a flashing _____ light that

COLOR

played "Santa Claus Is Coming to (the) _____," and she

A PLACE

carried a/an _____ made out of tinsel. To top it all off,

NOUN

she tied bells to her _____ so she would jingle when she

PART OF THE BODY

_____! Gosh, that was almost as funny as the year she wrapped

VERB (PAST TENSE)

her entire _____ in Christmas lights! I can't wait to see what

PART OF THE BODY

she'll wear this year.

MAD LIBS® is fun to play with friends, but you can also play it by yourself! To begin with, DO NOT look at the story on the page below. Fill in the blanks on this page with the words called for. Then, using the words you have selected, fill in the blank spaces in the story.

Now you've created your own hilarious MAD LIBS® game!

'TWAS THE NIGHT BEFORE CHRISTMAS, PART 1

NOUN _____

ANIMAL _____

PLURAL NOUN _____

CELEBRITY (MALE) _____

ADJECTIVE _____

NUMBER _____

ADJECTIVE _____

ADJECTIVE _____

SAME CELEBRITY _____

PLURAL NOUN _____

VERB (PAST TENSE) _____

VERB (PAST TENSE) _____

PERSON IN ROOM _____

SILLY WORD _____

SILLY WORD _____

SILLY WORD _____

NOUN _____

VERB _____

VERB _____

VERB _____

'Twas the night before Christmas, when all through the _____ ,
                                                        NOUN

Not a creature was stirring, not even a/an _____ .
                                            ANIMAL

The _____ were hung by the chimney with care,
     PLURAL NOUN

In hopes that _____ soon would be there.
               CELEBRITY (MALE)

When, what to my wondering eyes should appear,

But a/an _____ sleigh and _____ _____
         ADJECTIVE   NUMBER   ADJECTIVE

reindeer.

With a little old driver, so _____ and quick,
                              ADJECTIVE

I knew in a moment it must be _____ .
                               SAME CELEBRITY

More rapid than _____ , his reindeer they came,
                 PLURAL NOUN

As he _____ and _____ and called them by name:
       VERB (PAST TENSE)   VERB (PAST TENSE)

"Now, _____ ! Now, Dancer! Now, _____ and Vixen!
       PERSON IN ROOM   SILLY WORD

On, _____ ! On, Cupid! On, _____ and Blitzen!
     SILLY WORD   SILLY WORD

To the top of the _____ ! To the top of the wall!
                   NOUN

Now _____ away! _____ away! _____ away, all!"
     VERB   VERB   VERB

MAD LIBS® is fun to play with friends, but you can also play it by yourself! To begin with, DO NOT look at the story on the page below. Fill in the blanks on this page with the words called for. Then, using the words you have selected, fill in the blank spaces in the story.

Now you've created your own hilarious MAD LIBS® game!

'TWAS THE NIGHT BEFORE CHRISTMAS, PART 2

NOUN _____

VERB ENDING IN "ING" _____

VERB ENDING IN "ING" _____

ADJECTIVE _____

SAME CELEBRITY (FROM PART 1) _____

PLURAL NOUN _____

PLURAL NOUN _____

VERB (PAST TENSE) _____

PLURAL NOUN _____

VERB (PAST TENSE) _____

PART OF THE BODY _____

NOUN _____

VERB (PAST TENSE) _____

ADJECTIVE _____

ADJECTIVE _____

And then in a twinkling, I heard on the _____,
NOUN

The _____ and _____ of each
VERB ENDING IN "ING"   VERB ENDING IN "ING"

_____ hoof.
ADJECTIVE

And down the chimney _____ came, amid
SAME CELEBRITY (FROM PART 1)

_____ and soot.
PLURAL NOUN

He was covered in _____ from his head to his foot.
PLURAL NOUN

He _____ not a word, but went straight to his work,
VERB (PAST TENSE)

And filled all the _____, then _____ with
PLURAL NOUN   VERB (PAST TENSE)

a jerk.

And laying his _____ aside of his nose,
PART OF THE BODY

And giving a nod, up the _____ he rose!
NOUN

But I heard him exclaim as he _____ out of sight,
VERB (PAST TENSE)

" _____ Christmas to all, and to all a/an _____ night!"
ADJECTIVE   ADJECTIVE

MAD LIBS® is fun to play with friends, but you can also play it by yourself! To begin with, DO NOT look at the story on the page below. Fill in the blanks on this page with the words called for. Then, using the words you have selected, fill in the blank spaces in the story.

Now you've created your own hilarious MAD LIBS® game!

TOYLAND

NOUN _____

NOUN _____

NOUN _____

VERB _____

ADJECTIVE _____

NOUN _____

ADJECTIVE _____

ADJECTIVE _____

PLURAL NOUN _____

MAD LIBS®
TOYLAND

Toyland, _____ -land,
             NOUN

Little _____ and _____ land,
             NOUN   NOUN

While you _____ within it,
                  VERB

You are ever _____ there.
                  ADJECTIVE

_____'s joy land,
        NOUN

_____, _____ Toyland!
   ADJECTIVE   ADJECTIVE

Once you pass its _____,
                        PLURAL NOUN

You can never return again.

MAD LIBS® is fun to play with friends, but you can also play it by yourself! To begin with, DO NOT look at the story on the page below. Fill in the blanks on this page with the words called for. Then, using the words you have selected, fill in the blank spaces in the story.

Now you've created your own hilarious MAD LIBS® game!

JOLLY OLD SAINT NICHOLAS

ADJECTIVE _____

PART OF THE BODY _____

NOUN _____

ADJECTIVE _____

NUMBER _____

NOUN _____

ADVERB _____

PLURAL NOUN _____

VERB ENDING IN "ING" _____

ADJECTIVE _____

PLURAL NOUN _____

NOUN _____

ADJECTIVE _____

VERB (PAST TENSE) _____

ADJECTIVE _____

MAD LIBS
JOLLY OLD SAINT NICHOLAS

Jolly _____ Saint Nicholas, lean your _____ this way!
          ADJECTIVE   PART OF THE BODY

Don't you tell a single _____ what I'm going to say.
                         NOUN

Christmas Eve is coming soon; now you dear _____ man,
                                            ADJECTIVE

Whisper what you'll bring to me; tell me if you can.

When the clock is striking _____, when I'm fast asleep,
                            NUMBER

Down the chimney with your _____, _____ you
                            NOUN   ADVERB

will creep.

All the _____ you will find, _____ in a row;
         PLURAL NOUN   VERB ENDING IN "ING"

Mine will be the _____ one—you'll be sure to know.
                  ADJECTIVE

Johnny wants a pair of _____, Susie wants a/an
                              PLURAL NOUN

_____,
  NOUN

Nellie wants a/an _____ book—one she hasn't _____.
                   ADJECTIVE   VERB (PAST TENSE)

Now I think I'll leave to you what to give the rest.

Choose for me, _____ Santa Claus. You will know the best.
                ADJECTIVE

MAD LIBS® is fun to play with friends, but you can also play it by yourself! To begin with, DO NOT look at the story on the page below. Fill in the blanks on this page with the words called for. Then, using the words you have selected, fill in the blank spaces in the story.

Now you've created your own hilarious MAD LIBS® game!

OVER THE RIVER AND THROUGH THE WOOD

CELEBRITY _____

NOUN _____

NOUN _____

ADJECTIVE _____

ADJECTIVE _____

NOUN _____

NOUN _____

VERB _____

PART OF THE BODY (PLURAL) _____

PART OF THE BODY _____

NOUN _____

NOUN _____

NOUN _____

PLURAL NOUN _____

SILLY WORD _____

Over the river and through the wood,

To _____'s house we go.
        CELEBRITY

The _____ knows the way to carry the _____
        NOUN   NOUN

Through the _____ and _____ snow.
            ADJECTIVE   ADJECTIVE

Over the _____ and through the _____,
          NOUN   NOUN

Oh, how the wind does _____.
                       VERB

It stings the _____ and bites the _____
              PART OF THE BODY (PLURAL)   PART OF THE BODY

As over the _____ we go.
            NOUN

Over the river and through the _____,
                              NOUN

To have a full _____ of play.
               NOUN

Oh, hear the _____ ringing _____-a-ling-ling,
             PLURAL NOUN   SILLY WORD

For it is Christmas Day!

MAD LIBS® is fun to play with friends, but you can also play it by yourself! To begin with, DO NOT look at the story on the page below. Fill in the blanks on this page with the words called for. Then, using the words you have selected, fill in the blank spaces in the story.

Now you've created your own hilarious MAD LIBS® game!

THE NAUGHTY LIST

ADJECTIVE _____

NOUN _____

ADJECTIVE _____

ADVERB _____

PLURAL NOUN _____

NOUN _____

PLURAL NOUN _____

ADJECTIVE _____

PLURAL NOUN _____

NOUN _____

PART OF THE BODY (PLURAL) _____

NOUN _____

NOUN _____

ADJECTIVE _____

SAME ADJECTIVE _____

MAD LIBS®
THE NAUGHTY LIST

Make sure you are always a/an _____ little girl or boy, or you might
                                    ADJECTIVE

get a lump of coal in your _____ at Christmas! Here is a list of
                                 NOUN

_____ things to do and *not* to do to stay off Santa's naughty list:
   ADJECTIVE

ALWAYS play _____ with your brothers and/or sisters and share
                      ADVERB

your _____ with them.
        PLURAL NOUN

NEVER make a mess and then blame it on your pet _____.
                                                           NOUN

ALWAYS eat your green _____—even if they taste like
                                PLURAL NOUN

_____ _____.
   ADJECTIVE   PLURAL NOUN

ALWAYS make your _____ and brush your
                              NOUN

_____ every morning.
PART OF THE BODY (PLURAL)

NEVER tell your teacher that your _____ ate your
                                              NOUN

homework—unless, of course, you can bring in a well-chewed

_____ as proof.
      NOUN

And always remember: Santa knows when you've been bad or

_____, so be _____, for goodness' sake!
   ADJECTIVE   SAME ADJECTIVE

MAD LIBS® is fun to play with friends, but you can also play it by yourself! To begin with, DO NOT look at the story on the page below. Fill in the blanks on this page with the words called for. Then, using the words you have selected, fill in the blank spaces in the story.

Now you've created your own hilarious MAD LIBS® game!

FAVORITE CHRISTMAS CAROLS

ADVERB _____

VERB ENDING IN "ING" _____

ADJECTIVE _____

ADJECTIVE _____

NOUN _____

CELEBRITY _____

COLOR _____

VERB _____

NOUN _____

NOUN _____

NOUN _____

COLOR _____

NOUN _____

Here's a list of the top ten most _____ played Christmas carols.
ADVERB

Which one is your favorite?

1. "The Christmas Song" ("Chestnuts _____ on a/an
VERB ENDING IN "ING"

   _____ Fire")
   ADJECTIVE

2. "Have Yourself a Merry _____ Christmas"
   ADJECTIVE

3. "_____ Wonderland"
   NOUN

4. "_____ Is Coming to Town"
   CELEBRITY

5. "_____ Christmas"
   COLOR

6. "Let It _____"
   VERB

7. "Jingle _____ Rock"
   NOUN

8. "Little Drummer _____"
   NOUN

9. "_____ Ride"
   NOUN

10. "Rudolph the _____-Nosed _____"
    COLOR   NOUN

MAD LIBS® is fun to play with friends, but you can also play it by yourself! To begin with, DO NOT look at the story on the page below. Fill in the blanks on this page with the words called for. Then, using the words you have selected, fill in the blank spaces in the story.

Now you've created your own hilarious MAD LIBS® game!

WE WISH YOU A MERRY CHRISTMAS

ADJECTIVE _____

SAME ADJECTIVE _____

SAME ADJECTIVE _____

ADJECTIVE _____

ADJECTIVE _____

PLURAL NOUN _____

ADJECTIVE _____

ADJECTIVE _____

ADJECTIVE _____

SAME ADJECTIVE _____

SAME ADJECTIVE _____

NOUN _____

VERB _____

SAME VERB _____

SAME VERB _____

VERB _____

We wish you a/an _____ Christmas,
ADJECTIVE

We wish you a/an _____ Christmas,
SAME ADJECTIVE

We wish you a/an _____ Christmas
SAME ADJECTIVE

And a/an _____ New Year.
ADJECTIVE

_____ tidings we bring
ADJECTIVE

To you and your _____ ,
PLURAL NOUN

_____ tidings for Christmas
ADJECTIVE

And a/an _____ New Year.
ADJECTIVE

Oh, bring us a/an _____ pudding,
ADJECTIVE

Oh, bring us a/an _____ pudding,
SAME ADJECTIVE

Oh, bring us a/an _____ pudding
SAME ADJECTIVE

And a cup of good _____ .
NOUN

We won't _____ until we get some,
VERB

We won't _____ until we get some,
SAME VERB

We won't _____ until we get some,
SAME VERB

So _____ some out here.
VERB

MAD LIBS® is fun to play with friends, but you can also play it by yourself! To begin with, DO NOT look at the story on the page below. Fill in the blanks on this page with the words called for. Then, using the words you have selected, fill in the blank spaces in the story.

Now you've created your own hilarious MAD LIBS® game!

A CHRISTMAS BLIZZARD

ADJECTIVE _____

ADJECTIVE _____

PLURAL NOUN _____

ADJECTIVE _____

VERB ENDING IN "ING" _____

ADJECTIVE _____

NOUN _____

NOUN _____

NOUN _____

NOUN _____

NOUN _____

NOUN _____

ADJECTIVE _____

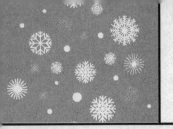

MAD LIBS
A CHRISTMAS BLIZZARD

Have you been dreaming of a/an _____ Christmas? Me too! But
                                        ADJECTIVE

what do you do when there is a/an _____ blizzard and you and your
                                        ADJECTIVE

_____ get snowed in on Christmas? Here's a/an _____
   PLURAL NOUN   ADJECTIVE

list of classic Christmas movies that'll keep everyone _____
                                                       VERB ENDING IN "ING"

for hours.

1. *It's a/an* _____ *Life*
                 ADJECTIVE

2. *Miracle on 34th* _____
                         NOUN

3. *A Christmas* _____
                     NOUN

4. *How the* _____ *Stole Christmas*
                 NOUN

5. *Frosty the Snow-*_____
                         NOUN

So just grab some pop-_____, throw a few more logs on the
                          NOUN

_____, and keep dreaming of a/an _____ white
   NOUN   ADJECTIVE

Christmas!

MAD LIBS® is fun to play with friends, but you can also play it by yourself! To begin with, DO NOT look at the story on the page below. Fill in the blanks on this page with the words called for. Then, using the words you have selected, fill in the blank spaces in the story.

Now you've created your own hilarious MAD LIBS® game!

```
┌─────────────────────────────────────────────┐
│                                               │
│   HERE WE COME A-CAROLING                     │
│                                               │
│   PLURAL NOUN _____ │
│                                               │
│   ADJECTIVE _____ │
│                                               │
│   VERB ENDING IN "ING" _____ │
│                                               │
│   ADJECTIVE _____ │
│                                               │
│   PLURAL NOUN _____ │
│                                               │
│   ADJECTIVE _____ │
│                                               │
│   ADJECTIVE _____ │
│                                               │
│   ADJECTIVE _____ │
│                                               │
│   NOUN _____ │
│                                               │
└─────────────────────────────────────────────┘
```

MAD LIBS®
HERE WE COME A-CAROLING

Here we come a-caroling among the _____ so _____.
                                              PLURAL NOUN   ADJECTIVE

Here we come a-_____ so _____ to be seen.
                  VERB ENDING IN "ING"   ADJECTIVE

Love and _____ come to you.
              PLURAL NOUN

And to you _____ Christmas, too.
                  ADJECTIVE

And we wish you and send you a/an _____ New Year.
                                          ADJECTIVE

And we wish you a/an _____ New _____.
                          ADJECTIVE   NOUN

MAD LIBS®

FIELD TRIP MAD LIBS

by Mickie Matheis

Mad Libs
An Imprint of Penguin Random House

INSTRUCTIONS

MAD LIBS® is a game for people who don't like games!
It can be played by one, two, three, four, or forty.

• RIDICULOUSLY SIMPLE DIRECTIONS

In this tablet you will find stories containing blank spaces where words are left out.
One player, the READER, selects one of these stories. The READER does not tell anyone
what the story is about. Instead, he/she asks the other players, the WRITERS, to give
him/her words. These words are used to fill in the blank spaces in the story.

• TO PLAY

The READER asks each WRITER in turn to call out a word—an adjective or a noun or
whatever the space calls for—and uses them to fill in the blank spaces in the story. The
result is a MAD LIBS® game.

When the READER then reads the completed MAD LIBS® game to the other players,
they will discover that they have written a story that is fantastic, screamingly funny,
shocking, silly, crazy, or just plain dumb—depending upon which words each WRITER
called out.

• EXAMPLE (*Before* and *After*)

"_____!" he said _____
　　　　EXCLAMATION　　　　　　　　　　　　ADVERB

as he jumped into his convertible _____ and
　　　　　　　　　　　　　　　　　　　NOUN

drove off with his _____ wife.
　　　　　　　　　ADJECTIVE

"_____OUCH_____!" he said _____STUPIDLY_____
　　　　EXCLAMATION　　　　　　　　　　　　ADVERB

as he jumped into his convertible _____CAT_____ and
　　　　　　　　　　　　　　　　　　　NOUN

drove off with his _____BRAVE_____ wife.
　　　　　　　　　ADJECTIVE

MAD LIBS®

QUICK REVIEW

In case you have forgotten what adjectives, adverbs, nouns, and verbs are, here is a quick review:

An ADJECTIVE describes something or somebody. *Lumpy, soft, ugly, messy,* and *short* are adjectives.

An ADVERB tells how something is done. It modifies a verb and usually ends in "ly." *Modestly, stupidly, greedily,* and *carefully* are adverbs.

A NOUN is the name of a person, place, or thing. *Sidewalk, umbrella, bridle, bathtub,* and *nose* are nouns.

A VERB is an action word. *Run, pitch, jump,* and *swim* are verbs. Put the verbs in past tense if the directions say PAST TENSE. *Ran, pitched, jumped,* and *swam* are verbs in the past tense.

When we ask for A PLACE, we mean any sort of place: a country or city *(Spain, Cleveland)* or a room *(bathroom, kitchen).*

An EXCLAMATION or SILLY WORD is any sort of funny sound, gasp, grunt, or outcry, like *Wow!, Ouch!, Whomp!, Ick!,* and *Gadzooks!*

When we ask for specific words, like a NUMBER, a COLOR, an ANIMAL, or a PART OF THE BODY, we mean a word that is one of those things, like *seven, blue, horse,* or *head.*

When we ask for a PLURAL, it means more than one. For example, *cat* pluralized is *cats.*

MAD LIBS® is fun to play with friends, but you can also play it by yourself! To begin with, DO NOT look at the story on the page below. Fill in the blanks on this page with the words called for. Then, using the words you have selected, fill in the blank spaces in the story.

Now you've created your own hilarious MAD LIBS® game!

I ♥ FIELD TRIPS

ADJECTIVE _____

A PLACE _____

VERB ENDING IN "ING" _____

NOUN _____

NOUN _____

PERSON IN ROOM _____

ADJECTIVE _____

NOUN _____

ANIMAL _____

VERB ENDING IN "ING" _____

NUMBER _____

PLURAL NOUN _____

VERB (PAST TENSE) _____

ADJECTIVE _____

PLURAL NOUN _____

ADJECTIVE _____

NOUN _____

MAD LIBS®
I ♥ FIELD TRIPS

I would rather go on a/an _____ field trip than go to school any day!
ADJECTIVE

Even just taking a trip to (the) _____ is better than being stuck
A PLACE

_____ in the classroom all day. One of my favorite parts about
VERB ENDING IN "ING"

field trips is riding in a/an _____ to our destination. I always choose my
NOUN

best _____, _____, to be my seatmate. We like to pass the time
NOUN   PERSON IN ROOM

playing a/an _____ game called Road Trip Scavenger Hunt. We make a
ADJECTIVE

list of items to look for during the drive, such as a/an _____ riding a
NOUN

motorcycle or a/an _____ _____ along the roadside.
ANIMAL   VERB ENDING IN "ING"

Field trips are fun because they teach us more about things we have already

learned in school, like how there are _____ _____ in our solar
NUMBER   PLURAL NOUN

system or how people cooked, farmed, and _____ back in the
VERB (PAST TENSE)

_____ days. But the best part about taking field trips is that our
ADJECTIVE

_____ usually don't assign any _____ homework that day. If we
PLURAL NOUN   ADJECTIVE

could take field trips every day, I'd be the happiest _____ in the world!
NOUN

MAD LIBS® is fun to play with friends, but you can also play it by yourself! To begin with, DO NOT look at the story on the page below. Fill in the blanks on this page with the words called for. Then, using the words you have selected, fill in the blank spaces in the story.

Now you've created your own hilarious MAD LIBS® game!

RULES OF THE RIDE

CELEBRITY (MALE) _____

ADJECTIVE _____

NOUN _____

VERB ENDING IN "ING" _____

VERB _____

ADVERB _____

ADJECTIVE _____

PLURAL NOUN _____

PLURAL NOUN _____

NUMBER _____

ADJECTIVE _____

COLOR _____

PART OF THE BODY (PLURAL) _____

PLURAL NOUN _____

PART OF THE BODY _____

MAD LIBS
RULES OF THE RIDE

Whenever our bus driver for field trips is _____, our class is in for
<u>CELEBRITY (MALE)</u>

a/an _____ time! This grumpy old _____ has strict rules to follow,
<u>ADJECTIVE</u>   <u>NOUN</u>

such as these:

- No running or _____ up and down the aisles of the
  <u>VERB ENDING IN "ING"</u>

  bus.

- Do not scream, yell, or _____ too loudly because it is _____
  <u>VERB</u>   <u>ADVERB</u>

  distracting for the driver. Use your _____ indoor voice.
  <u>ADJECTIVE</u>

- Eating any sort of _____ is expressly prohibited!
  <u>PLURAL NOUN</u>

- Do not throw anything, including paper _____.
  <u>PLURAL NOUN</u>

- Don't ask the bus driver every _____ minutes, "Are we _____
  <u>NUMBER</u>   <u>ADJECTIVE</u>

  yet?" This habit will make him scream and turn a bright shade of

  _____!
  <u>COLOR</u>

- Most importantly, keep your _____ and _____
  <u>PART OF THE BODY (PLURAL)</u>   <u>PLURAL NOUN</u>

  inside the bus at all times. Anyone caught sticking his or her

  _____ out the window will be immediately removed
  <u>PART OF THE BODY</u>

  from the bus.

MAD LIBS® is fun to play with friends, but you can also play it by yourself! To begin with, DO NOT look at the story on the page below. Fill in the blanks on this page with the words called for. Then, using the words you have selected, fill in the blank spaces in the story.

Now you've created your own hilarious MAD LIBS® game!

BUS BUDDY

ADJECTIVE _____

VERB ENDING IN "ING" _____

CELEBRITY _____

PART OF THE BODY _____

PLURAL NOUN _____

PLURAL NOUN _____

NOUN _____

VERB _____

ADJECTIVE _____

ANIMAL _____

ARTICLE OF CLOTHING _____

NOUN _____

A PLACE _____

VERB _____

PART OF THE BODY _____

MAD LIBS®
BUS BUDDY

Having a/an _____ buddy _____ next to you on the bus
    ADJECTIVE   VERB ENDING IN "ING"

is a good way to have a great field trip! First of all, I require my bus buddy to

know all the lines from every _____ movie ever made so we can recite
                        CELEBRITY

them throughout the entire bus ride, complete with random

_____ gestures. I also appreciate when my bus buddy packs
    PART OF THE BODY

snacks for the ride, especially things like chocolate-covered _____ and
                                                        PLURAL NOUN

salted _____. Of course, we have to be careful that the _____
        PLURAL NOUN   NOUN

driver doesn't see us, as we're not supposed to _____ when we're on the
                                                    VERB

bus! The best bus buddies also have _____ imaginations! We'll make up
                                        ADJECTIVE

stories about the flying _____ we wish we could have as a pet, or the
                        ANIMAL

sparkly _____ we'd wear as a superhero costume, or the giant
            ARTICLE OF CLOTHING

_____ we'd live in if we owned our own private island near
    NOUN

(the) _____. Perhaps the most important quality in a bus buddy is his/
        A PLACE

her size. After all, you don't want to _____ next to someone who has such
                                            VERB

a ginormous _____ that you keep falling off the seat!
                PART OF THE BODY

MAD LIBS® is fun to play with friends, but you can also play it by yourself! To begin with, DO NOT look at the story on the page below. Fill in the blanks on this page with the words called for. Then, using the words you have selected, fill in the blank spaces in the story.

Now you've created your own hilarious MAD LIBS® game!

PERMISSION SLIP

ADJECTIVE _____

VERB ENDING IN "ING" _____

NUMBER _____

NOUN _____

ADJECTIVE _____

PLURAL NOUN _____

A PLACE _____

CELEBRITY _____

PLURAL NOUN _____

PART OF THE BODY (PLURAL) _____

VERB ENDING IN "ING" _____

ADJECTIVE _____

NOUN _____

TYPE OF LIQUID _____

PLURAL NOUN _____

PLURAL NOUN _____

CELEBRITY _____

PLURAL NOUN _____

MAD LIBS®
PERMISSION SLIP

Dear Parents: Our class will be going on a/an _____ field trip to
<u>ADJECTIVE</u>

_____ Rivers State Park next Friday. The cost of the trip is
<u>VERB ENDING IN "ING"</u>

$_____, and we will be traveling to the park by _____. The purpose
<u>NUMBER</u>   <u>NOUN</u>

of this _____ trip is to support what we've been learning in science class
<u>ADJECTIVE</u>

about the flowers, wildlife, and _____ native to (the) _____.
                                        <u>PLURAL NOUN</u>   <u>A PLACE</u>

The trip will include a guided tour of the park by park ranger _____. Be
                                                                        <u>CELEBRITY</u>

sure to remind your child to wear comfortable _____ on his/her
                                                      <u>PLURAL NOUN</u>

_____ because he/she will be walking and
<u>PART OF THE BODY (PLURAL)</u>

_____ throughout the park the entire day. Also, please be sure
<u>VERB ENDING IN "ING"</u>

to pack a/an _____ lunch in a brown paper _____, including some
                <u>ADJECTIVE</u>   <u>NOUN</u>

bottled _____. We are asking for several _____ to serve as
          <u>TYPE OF LIQUID</u>   <u>PLURAL NOUN</u>

chaperones on this trip; you will oversee a group of six _____. If
                                                                       <u>PLURAL NOUN</u>

interested, please call Principal _____ at the school. Thank you in
                                              <u>CELEBRITY</u>

advance for encouraging your children to behave like young ladies and

_____.
<u>PLURAL NOUN</u>

MAD LIBS® is fun to play with friends, but you can also play it by yourself! To begin with, DO NOT look at the story on the page below. Fill in the blanks on this page with the words called for. Then, using the words you have selected, fill in the blank spaces in the story.

Now you've created your own hilarious MAD LIBS® game!

LET'S GROW TO THE FARM

NOUN _____

ANIMAL (PLURAL) _____

PERSON IN ROOM _____

EXCLAMATION _____

PART OF THE BODY _____

NOUN _____

CELEBRITY (MALE) _____

ADJECTIVE _____

NOUN _____

TYPE OF LIQUID _____

PLURAL NOUN _____

PLURAL NOUN _____

A PLACE _____

PLURAL NOUN _____

COLOR _____

PLURAL NOUN _____

NOUN _____

VERB ENDING IN "ING" _____

The moment I stepped onto the grass at Misty _____ Farm, I knew I was
_____ NOUN

going to like it there. Just listening to the sounds of _____
_____ ANIMAL (PLURAL)

mooing, _____ oinking, and sheep going "_____"
_____ PERSON IN ROOM _____ EXCLAMATION

put a smile on my _____. The _____ who ran the place
_____ PART OF THE BODY _____ NOUN

called himself Farmer _____. He showed my class how much
_____ CELEBRITY (MALE)

_____ work was required to run a farm. The first thing we learned was
ADJECTIVE

how to milk a/an _____. It was amazing to see _____
_____ NOUN _____ TYPE OF LIQUID

come out! Afterward, we visited the chicken coop and gathered up all the

_____ that the little feathered _____ had laid. Next, our class
PLURAL NOUN _____ PLURAL NOUN

climbed into a hay wagon and was pulled all around (the) _____ to check
_____ A PLACE

out the wheat, corn, and other _____ growing on the farm. Lastly, the
_____ PLURAL NOUN

farmer took us to his house, where we picked juicy _____ _____
_____ COLOR _____ PLURAL NOUN

from a tree in his yard and had cold glasses of _____ cider. If I can't do
_____ NOUN

_____ for a job someday, I'm going to farm!
VERB ENDING IN "ING"

MAD LIBS® is fun to play with friends, but you can also play it by yourself! To begin with, DO NOT look at the story on the page below. Fill in the blanks on this page with the words called for. Then, using the words you have selected, fill in the blank spaces in the story.

Now you've created your own hilarious MAD LIBS® game!

OVERNIGHT FIELD TRIPS

NUMBER _____

PLURAL NOUN _____

ADJECTIVE _____

PLURAL NOUN _____

VERB ENDING IN "ING" _____

ADJECTIVE _____

ADJECTIVE _____

PART OF THE BODY _____

NOUN _____

PLURAL NOUN _____

NOUN _____

NOUN _____

MAD LIBS®
OVERNIGHT FIELD TRIPS

Taking _____ school-age _____ on the road to a
         NUMBER   PLURAL NOUN

far-off location for a class trip is no small feat! Unlike trips that are close to

school, there's a whole other set of _____ rules for "away" trips, including
                                      ADJECTIVE

these:

- Remember to pack enough clean _____ to wear each day. After
                                   PLURAL NOUN

  all, if you're going to be _____ in a bus for hours, you
                              VERB ENDING IN "ING"

  should look and smell _____!
                         ADJECTIVE

- Exhibit _____ manners at meals. Be sure to neatly spread your
           ADJECTIVE

  napkin on your _____, and use your fork, knife, and
                  PART OF THE BODY

  _____ properly.
   NOUN

- Don't ruin your hotel room by cramming furniture and _____
                                                         PLURAL NOUN

  in the bathroom.

- Don't try to leave your hotel room after "lights out." While there may

  not be an armed _____ stationed outside your door, an exhausted
                   NOUN

  mom or _____ will be just as scary!
          NOUN

MAD LIBS® is fun to play with friends, but you can also play it by yourself! To begin with, DO NOT look at the story on the page below. Fill in the blanks on this page with the words called for. Then, using the words you have selected, fill in the blank spaces in the story.

Now you've created your own hilarious MAD LIBS® game!

WANTED:
PARENT CHAPERONES

ADJECTIVE _____

NOUN _____

PLURAL NOUN _____

PART OF THE BODY _____

ADJECTIVE _____

ANIMAL (PLURAL) _____

PLURAL NOUN _____

VERB _____

A PLACE _____

ADJECTIVE _____

NUMBER _____

PLURAL NOUN _____

ADJECTIVE _____

PART OF THE BODY (PLURAL) _____

ADJECTIVE _____

PART OF THE BODY (PLURAL) _____

ADJECTIVE _____

VERB _____

MAD LIBS
WANTED:
PARENT CHAPERONES

Are you daring, adventurous, and _____? Does the thought of driving in

ADJECTIVE

a stuffy, cramped _____ with a bunch of loud, boisterous _____

NOUN PLURAL NOUN

make your _____ beat with excitement? Can you picture

PART OF THE BODY

yourself herding rowdy, _____ children like a pack of pygmy

ADJECTIVE

_____? If so, then *you* could be a field trip chaperone! Join our

ANIMAL (PLURAL)

team of ultra-responsible adult _____ charged with making sure that

PLURAL NOUN

students *walk*, not _____, around a zoo, a museum, (the) _____,

VERB A PLACE

or whatever location their _____ teacher has selected for the field trip.

ADJECTIVE

While previous experience is not required, candidates who can manage up to

_____ _____ at any given time while maintaining a/an _____

NUMBER PLURAL NOUN ADJECTIVE

sense of humor are preferred. Those with eyes in the back of their

_____ will be given top consideration. And while there's no

PART OF THE BODY (PLURAL)

salary, the joy of seeing _____ expressions on the kids'

ADJECTIVE

_____ as they learn something new will be reward enough!

PART OF THE BODY (PLURAL)

If this sounds like a/an _____ job, _____ today for an application!

ADJECTIVE VERB

MAD LIBS® is fun to play with friends, but you can also play it by yourself! To begin with, DO NOT look at the story on the page below. Fill in the blanks on this page with the words called for. Then, using the words you have selected, fill in the blank spaces in the story.

Now you've created your own hilarious MAD LIBS® game!

FORGETTABLE FIELD TRIPS

ADJECTIVE _____

PART OF THE BODY _____

ADJECTIVE _____

VERB _____

PLURAL NOUN _____

PLURAL NOUN _____

ADJECTIVE _____

PART OF THE BODY (PLURAL) _____

ADVERB _____

NOUN _____

CELEBRITY _____

VERB ENDING IN "ING" _____

ADVERB _____

VERB (PAST TENSE) _____

PLURAL NOUN _____

VERB ENDING IN "ING" _____

ADJECTIVE _____

ADJECTIVE _____

MAD LIBS®
FORGETTABLE FIELD TRIPS

Not all field trips are fun, _____ adventures. Some have left me shaking
ADJECTIVE

my _____ and wondering what in the world my _____
PART OF THE BODY   ADJECTIVE

teacher was thinking. For example, one time my class had to _____ along
VERB

the highway, picking up crumpled _____, moldy _____, and
PLURAL NOUN   PLURAL NOUN

other _____ garbage that made us turn up our _____ in
ADJECTIVE   PART OF THE BODY (PLURAL)

disgust. It was _____ gross! Another time, we went to a/an _____
ADVERB   NOUN

hardware store where an employee wearing a name tag that said "Hi! My name

is _____" showed us pieces of wood, paint samples, and tools for
CELEBRITY

building, gardening, and _____. It was _____ boring!
VERB ENDING IN "ING"   ADVERB

And another time, we _____ for hours at a local funeral home
VERB (PAST TENSE)

and learned how dead _____ were prepared for burial. I still have
PLURAL NOUN

nightmares where I wake up trembling and _____! The next
VERB ENDING IN "ING"

time one of these _____ field trips is planned, I'll be calling in _____!
ADJECTIVE   ADJECTIVE

MAD LIBS® is fun to play with friends, but you can also play it by yourself! To begin with, DO NOT look at the story on the page below. Fill in the blanks on this page with the words called for. Then, using the words you have selected, fill in the blank spaces in the story.

Now you've created your own hilarious MAD LIBS® game!

BEST. FIELD TRIP. EVER.

A PLACE _____

CELEBRITY (MALE) _____

VERB _____

PLURAL NOUN _____

PART OF THE BODY _____

TYPE OF LIQUID _____

NUMBER _____

SILLY WORD _____

PART OF THE BODY (PLURAL) _____

ADJECTIVE _____

NOUN _____

NOUN _____

PLURAL NOUN _____

ADJECTIVE _____

PERSON IN ROOM _____

SAME PERSON IN ROOM _____

PART OF THE BODY _____

SILLY WORD _____

ADJECTIVE _____

MAD LIBS®
BEST. FIELD TRIP. EVER.

Our class was visiting the Bank of (the) _____ to learn about money. As

A PLACE

we stood there, waiting for security guard _____ to unlock the door

CELEBRITY (MALE)

to the vault so we could _____ inside, three masked _____ ran

VERB — PLURAL NOUN

into the bank. They blasted the guard squarely in the _____

PART OF THE BODY

with _____ from a water gun and knocked him to the ground. Then

TYPE OF LIQUID

they ran into the vault and stuffed bags full of $_____ bills. "_____!

NUMBER — SILLY WORD

Get down on your _____!" one of the _____ robbers

PART OF THE BODY (PLURAL) — ADJECTIVE

yelled at us. Then they ran out the front door, jumped into a getaway

_____, and sped off. Back inside the bank, the security _____

NOUN — NOUN

called the police to report the theft of thousands of _____. I could

PLURAL NOUN

hear the _____ sound of a police siren getting closer. "_____!

ADJECTIVE — PERSON IN ROOM

_____!" a voice said into my _____. "We're

SAME PERSON IN ROOM — PART OF THE BODY

here." _____, I had fallen asleep on the bus! The most exciting field trip

SILLY WORD

of my life had only been a/an _____ dream!

ADJECTIVE

MAD LIBS® is fun to play with friends, but you can also play it by yourself! To begin with, DO NOT look at the story on the page below. Fill in the blanks on this page with the words called for. Then, using the words you have selected, fill in the blank spaces in the story.

Now you've created your own hilarious MAD LIBS® game!

DREAM TRIPS

PERSON IN ROOM _____

PART OF THE BODY _____

ADJECTIVE _____

NOUN _____

A PLACE _____

NUMBER _____

CELEBRITY _____

VERB ENDING IN "ING" _____

PLURAL NOUN _____

TYPE OF LIQUID _____

NOUN _____

NOUN _____

A PLACE _____

TYPE OF FOOD _____

ANIMAL _____

A PLACE _____

TYPE OF FOOD _____

PLURAL NOUN _____

When the teacher asked for suggestions for class field trips, _____
PERSON IN ROOM

raised a/an _____ and proposed these far-fetched but
PART OF THE BODY

super-_____ ideas:
ADJECTIVE

- Charter a/an _____ to fly the class to (the) _____ for
NOUN   A PLACE

a/an _____-course meal prepared by _____.
NUMBER   CELEBRITY

- Go scuba-_____ with dolphins, stingrays, and other
VERB ENDING IN "ING"

undersea _____ in the crystal-clear _____ of the
PLURAL NOUN   TYPE OF LIQUID

_____ Ocean.
NOUN

- Travel to a private _____ off the coast of (the) _____
NOUN   A PLACE

where students could Jet Ski, yacht, and sip _____-flavored
TYPE OF FOOD

lemonade all day.

- Go _____-back riding around the remote jungles of (the)
ANIMAL

_____.
A PLACE

- Rent out the local ice-cream parlor and spend the afternoon eating

_____-flavored ice cream with whipped _____ and
TYPE OF FOOD   PLURAL NOUN

sprinkles on top.

MAD LIBS® is fun to play with friends, but you can also play it by yourself! To begin with, DO NOT look at the story on the page below. Fill in the blanks on this page with the words called for. Then, using the words you have selected, fill in the blank spaces in the story.

Now you've created your own hilarious MAD LIBS® game!

BROWN BAG LUNCH SPECIAL

NOUN _____

NOUN _____

PLURAL NOUN _____

TYPE OF FOOD _____

TYPE OF LIQUID _____

VERB _____

PART OF THE BODY _____

PLURAL NOUN _____

NOUN _____

ADJECTIVE _____

PERSON IN ROOM _____

NOUN _____

NOUN _____

NOUN _____

CELEBRITY _____

TYPE OF FOOD _____

ADJECTIVE _____

PART OF THE BODY _____

MAD LIBS®
BROWN BAG LUNCH SPECIAL

Remember to pack lunches in a brown paper _____ when your child is
_____NOUN

going on a field trip. One of the most popular bagged lunches is a peanut

butter and _____ sandwich, sliced _____, and
_____NOUN_____PLURAL NOUN

_____-chip cookies. A smart way to keep the lunch cold is to freeze a
TYPE OF FOOD

bottle of _____ the night before the trip. It serves as an ice pack
_____TYPE OF LIQUID

until it's time to _____. Don't forget to include a napkin so that your
_____VERB

child can wipe his or her _____. Some moms and _____
_____PART OF THE BODY_____PLURAL NOUN

like to make a packed lunch special for their little _____. You could tuck a
_____NOUN

small note in the bag that says "Have a/an _____ day, _____—
_____ADJECTIVE_____PERSON IN ROOM

I love you with all my _____!" Or you could liven up the lunch by drawing
_____NOUN

games of tic-tac-_____ on the bag or creating a lunch-themed word search
_____NOUN

with words like "sandwich," "drink," "_____," and more! Or, decorate
_____NOUN

the bag with pictures of _____ or stuff _____-scented stickers
_____CELEBRITY_____TYPE OF FOOD

inside. Any of these _____ ideas will bring a smile to your child's
_____ADJECTIVE

_____!
____PART OF THE BODY

MAD LIBS® is fun to play with friends, but you can also play it by yourself! To begin with, DO NOT look at the story on the page below. Fill in the blanks on this page with the words called for. Then, using the words you have selected, fill in the blank spaces in the story.

Now you've created your own hilarious MAD LIBS® game!

FIELD TRIP ETIQUETTE

ADJECTIVE _____

ADJECTIVE _____

PLURAL NOUN _____

VERB _____

NOUN _____

VERB ENDING IN "ING" _____

VERB _____

PART OF THE BODY _____

PLURAL NOUN _____

PART OF THE BODY (PLURAL) _____

NOUN _____

VERB _____

NOUN _____

NOUN _____

SILLY WORD _____

MAD LIBS
FIELD TRIP ETIQUETTE

Students are expected to be on their most _____ behavior during a field
$\quad$ ADJECTIVE

trip so a/an _____ time can be had by all. Our class rules are as follows:
$\quad$ ADJECTIVE

- Stay with the other _____ in your group as well as your chaperone.
  $\quad$ PLURAL NOUN

  When using the "buddy system," make sure you always _____
  $\quad$ VERB

  with your _____.
  $\quad$ NOUN

- No talking or _____ when the tour guide is trying to
  $\quad$ VERB ENDING IN "ING"

  _____.
  $\quad$ VERB

- If you have a question, raise your _____.
  $\quad$ PART OF THE BODY

- Don't touch any _____ on display unless you are given
  $\quad$ PLURAL NOUN

  permission.

- Keep your hands and _____ to yourself.
  $\quad$ PART OF THE BODY (PLURAL)

- If you get separated from your _____, don't panic. Calmly
  $\quad$ NOUN

  _____ where you are until an adult _____ comes to find
  $\quad$ VERB $\qquad\qquad$ NOUN

  you.

- Be courteous to the tour _____ and say things like "please," "thank
  $\quad$ NOUN

  you," and "_____."
  $\quad$ SILLY WORD

MAD LIBS® is fun to play with friends, but you can also play it by yourself! To begin with, DO NOT look at the story on the page below. Fill in the blanks on this page with the words called for. Then, using the words you have selected, fill in the blank spaces in the story.

Now you've created your own hilarious MAD LIBS® game!

THE NATURAL HISTORY MUSEUM

A PLACE _____

PLURAL NOUN _____

PLURAL NOUN _____

VERB ENDING IN "ING" _____

ANIMAL (PLURAL) _____

ADJECTIVE _____

PLURAL NOUN _____

ADJECTIVE _____

TYPE OF LIQUID _____

PART OF THE BODY _____

ANIMAL (PLURAL) _____

NUMBER _____

NOUN _____

A PLACE _____

PERSON IN ROOM _____

VERB _____

ADJECTIVE _____

VERB _____

MAD LIBS®
THE NATURAL
HISTORY MUSEUM

Teachers, one of the best places in all of (the) _____ to take your class on
                                                   A PLACE

a field trip is the Natural History Museum. The museum offers unique

experiences for _____ of all ages. Whether your students are learning
                   PLURAL NOUN

about the Earth, the solar system, dinosaurs, mammals, _____, or
                                                            PLURAL NOUN

_____ _____, the Natural History Museum
VERB ENDING IN "ING"   ANIMAL (PLURAL)

has _____ displays and interactive _____ to support your classroom
     ADJECTIVE   PLURAL NOUN

teachings. It's a one-of-a-kind environment to explore and learn about the

_____ natural world and our place in it. New exhibits include an actual
ADJECTIVE

working volcano from which _____ erupts, a hands-on enclosure
                              TYPE OF LIQUID

where you can come face-to-_____ with live _____,
                              PART OF THE BODY   ANIMAL (PLURAL)

a/an _____-year-old fossilized _____ found on an archaeological dig
      NUMBER   NOUN

in (the) _____, and _____, a skeleton of a three-million-year-
         A PLACE   PERSON IN ROOM

old human ancestor. Come to explore, stay to _____! You'll have such
                                                VERB

a/an _____ time visiting the Natural History Museum, you won't ever
      ADJECTIVE

want to _____!
        VERB

MAD LIBS® is fun to play with friends, but you can also play it by yourself! To begin with, DO NOT look at the story on the page below. Fill in the blanks on this page with the words called for. Then, using the words you have selected, fill in the blank spaces in the story.

Now you've created your own hilarious MAD LIBS® game!

THEATER ADVENTURES

ADJECTIVE _____

VERB ENDING IN "ING" _____

NOUN _____

NOUN _____

CELEBRITY (MALE) _____

NOUN _____

VERB _____

NUMBER _____

ADJECTIVE _____

ADJECTIVE _____

PART OF THE BODY (PLURAL) _____

VERB _____

NOUN _____

VERB (PAST TENSE) _____

PLURAL NOUN _____

VERB _____

PART OF THE BODY _____

ADJECTIVE _____

MAD LIBS
THEATER ADVENTURES

On the way to see the _____ stage musical _____ *in the*
            ADJECTIVE   VERB ENDING IN "ING"

Rain at the Little _____ Playhouse, our _____ teacher, Mr.
                        NOUN   NOUN

_____, quizzed the class on theater terms:
 CELEBRITY (MALE)

- To **audition** means to show the casting _____ how well you can
                                              NOUN

  _____. You'll recite up to _____ lines from a/an _____
      VERB   NUMBER   ADJECTIVE

  play while making _____ facial expressions and gesturing wildly
                      ADJECTIVE

  with your _____.
             PART OF THE BODY (PLURAL)

- A **callback** is the opportunity to _____ for the casting _____
                                        VERB   NOUN

  a second time because you _____ so well the first time.
                             VERB (PAST TENSE)

- A **curtain call** is when the _____ who acted in the play come
                                  PLURAL NOUN

  back out onto the stage and take bows while audience members clap and

  _____ with appreciation.
   VERB

- "**Break a/an** _____" is an odd but _____ way of saying
                   PART OF THE BODY   ADJECTIVE

  "good luck" to an actor.

MAD LIBS® is fun to play with friends, but you can also play it by yourself! To begin with, DO NOT look at the story on the page below. Fill in the blanks on this page with the words called for. Then, using the words you have selected, fill in the blank spaces in the story.

Now you've created your own hilarious MAD LIBS® game!

WELCOME TO WASHINGTON, DC

A PLACE _____

PLURAL NOUN _____

NOUN _____

ANIMAL (PLURAL) _____

NOUN _____

PLURAL NOUN _____

ADJECTIVE _____

CELEBRITY _____

VERB ENDING IN "ING" _____

PERSON IN ROOM _____

ADJECTIVE _____

NOUN _____

COLOR _____

PERSON IN ROOM _____

ADJECTIVE _____

VERB _____

PLURAL NOUN _____

MAD LIBS®
WELCOME TO
WASHINGTON, DC

Visiting (the) _____, the capital of the United States, is an amazing way
        A PLACE

to teach students about our country! This bustling city is home to many national

monuments, memorials, museums, and other _____ of historical
                                          PLURAL NOUN

significance. Get ready to explore the National Air and _____ Museum,
                                                         NOUN

which highlights America's journey of sending _____ into space.
                                               ANIMAL (PLURAL)

Pay your respects at the _____ War Memorial, which remembers the
                          NOUN

_____ that served in that _____ conflict. Grab photos at the
PLURAL NOUN   ADJECTIVE

_____ Memorial, which honors the leader of the _____
CELEBRITY   VERB ENDING IN "ING"

movement, and the _____ Monument, which commemorates
                   PERSON IN ROOM

the pioneering works of this _____ _____. The grand finale is a
                             ADJECTIVE   NOUN

private tour of the _____ House, led by the head of the Secret Service,
                     COLOR

Agent _____. Previous students have called this part of the trip
      PERSON IN ROOM

"unforgettable," "once in a lifetime," and "_____." Who knows? Maybe
                                            ADJECTIVE

someday you'll return to Washington, DC, to _____ there—as president
                                             VERB

of the United _____!
              PLURAL NOUN

MAD LIBS® is fun to play with friends, but you can also play it by yourself! To begin with, DO NOT look at the story on the page below. Fill in the blanks on this page with the words called for. Then, using the words you have selected, fill in the blank spaces in the story.

Now you've created your own hilarious MAD LIBS® game!

INTERVIEW WITH A ZOOKEEPER

PERSON IN ROOM (MALE) _____

PLURAL NOUN _____

PLURAL NOUN _____

NOUN _____

NOUN _____

COLOR _____

NOUN _____

CELEBRITY _____

NOUN _____

PLURAL NOUN _____

A PLACE _____

ADJECTIVE _____

NUMBER _____

PART OF THE BODY (PLURAL) _____

VERB _____

TYPE OF LIQUID _____

VERB _____

ADJECTIVE _____

This is Suzy Woods of ZOO-TV with _____, aka "Jungle
<u>PERSON IN ROOM (MALE)</u>

Genius," here at the _____ of the Wild Animal Park. He teaches facts
<u>PLURAL NOUN</u>

to kids about the different mammals, reptiles, and _____ from around
<u>PLURAL NOUN</u>

the world. I asked him to tell me which _____ at the park he liked best.
<u>NOUN</u>

Suzy: What's your favorite _____ here at the zoo?
<u>NOUN</u>

Genius: It's a two-ton _____ _____ named _____. It's a
<u>COLOR</u>   <u>NOUN</u>   <u>CELEBRITY</u>

rare species of _____ found only in the deepest, darkest _____ of
<u>NOUN</u>   <u>PLURAL NOUN</u>

(the) _____.
<u>A PLACE</u>

Suzy: What should we know about this _____ creature?
<u>ADJECTIVE</u>

Genius: It has gills, _____ legs, and wings resembling
<u>NUMBER</u>

_____, meaning it can _____ in
<u>PART OF THE BODY (PLURAL)</u>   <u>VERB</u>

_____, walk on the ground, and _____through the air!
<u>TYPE OF LIQUID</u>   <u>VERB</u>

Who needs a/an _____ dog or a cat when you can have one of these?
<u>ADJECTIVE</u>

MAD LIBS® is fun to play with friends, but you can also play it by yourself! To begin with, DO NOT look at the story on the page below. Fill in the blanks on this page with the words called for. Then, using the words you have selected, fill in the blank spaces in the story.

Now you've created your own hilarious MAD LIBS® game!

FIRE STATION FUN

NOUN _____

PERSON IN ROOM (MALE) _____

VEHICLE _____

PLURAL NOUN _____

ADVERB _____

PART OF THE BODY (PLURAL) _____

NOUN _____

PLURAL NOUN _____

ARTICLE OF CLOTHING _____

CELEBRITY (MALE) _____

VERB (PAST TENSE) _____

ADJECTIVE _____

PLURAL NOUN _____

TYPE OF LIQUID _____

NOUN _____

NOUN _____

VERB _____

ADJECTIVE _____

MAD●LIBS®
FIRE STATION FUN

When I was a little _____, my favorite field trip was visiting the fire
NOUN

station!

Firefighter _____ showed my class the big _____ that the
PERSON IN ROOM (MALE)   VEHICLE

firefighters drove. He turned on the flashing red _____ and even sounded
PLURAL NOUN

the alarm. It was so _____ loud that I had to cover my
ADVERB

_____! Another firefighter came out dressed in her
PART OF THE BODY (PLURAL)

_____-fighting gear, which included boots, a smoke mask, rubber
NOUN

_____, and a protective _____. Afterward, Chief
PLURAL NOUN   ARTICLE OF CLOTHING

_____ took us on a tour of the fire station. We saw where the
CELEBRITY (MALE)

firefighters ate, slept, and _____. There was an exercise room
VERB (PAST TENSE)

for the firefighters to use to stay strong and _____ in order to climb up
ADJECTIVE

_____ and haul the heavy hoses that spray _____. The chief
PLURAL NOUN   TYPE OF LIQUID

taught us to always make sure the _____ detectors in our houses worked
NOUN

and never play with a lighted _____. He also showed us how to stop, drop,
NOUN

and _____, because it's always better to be safe than _____!
VERB   ADJECTIVE

MAD LIBS® is fun to play with friends, but you can also play it by yourself! To begin with, DO NOT look at the story on the page below. Fill in the blanks on this page with the words called for. Then, using the words you have selected, fill in the blank spaces in the story.

Now you've created your own hilarious MAD LIBS® game!

AFTER THE AQUARIUM: A FIELD TRIP ESSAY

PERSON IN ROOM _____

A PLACE _____

TYPE OF LIQUID _____

VERB _____

ADJECTIVE _____

ADVERB _____

NOUN _____

PLURAL NOUN _____

PLURAL NOUN _____

COLOR _____

TYPE OF LIQUID _____

NOUN _____

TYPE OF LIQUID _____

PLURAL NOUN _____

PLURAL NOUN _____

NOUN _____

ADJECTIVE _____

VERB _____

MAD LIBS®
AFTER THE AQUARIUM:
A FIELD TRIP ESSAY

Ocean Life, by _____
PERSON IN ROOM

Oceans cover more than 70 percent of (the) _____'s surface and contain
A PLACE

about 97 percent of the Earth's supply of _____. There are many
TYPE OF LIQUID

fascinating creatures that _____ in the oceans, with _____ features
VERB　ADJECTIVE

and _____ amazing abilities. For example, the blue whale is the largest
ADVERB

_____ ever to have lived and weighs close to two hundred tons, which is
NOUN

roughly the equivalent of fifty full-grown African _____. The octopus
PLURAL NOUN

has eight long _____, called tentacles, and can shoot out _____
PLURAL NOUN　COLOR

_____ when a predator threatens it. A puffer-_____ is a fish that
TYPE OF LIQUID　NOUN

can quickly swallow enough _____ to inflate its own body so large,
TYPE OF LIQUID

no other _____ can eat it. Crabs are very lucky sea-_____
PLURAL NOUN　PLURAL NOUN

because whenever they lose a claw, another _____ grows in its place.
NOUN

These are just some of the _____ facts I learned about ocean life during
ADJECTIVE

my trip to the aquarium. I can't wait to _____there again!
VERB

MAD LIBS® is fun to play with friends, but you can also play it by yourself! To begin with, DO NOT look at the story on the page below. Fill in the blanks on this page with the words called for. Then, using the words you have selected, fill in the blank spaces in the story.

Now you've created your own hilarious MAD LIBS® game!

CHAPERONE SURVIVAL TIPS

NOUN _____

ADJECTIVE _____

PART OF THE BODY _____

VERB _____

PLURAL NOUN _____

PART OF THE BODY (PLURAL) _____

TYPE OF LIQUID _____

NOUN _____

PART OF THE BODY _____

NOUN _____

PART OF THE BODY _____

NUMBER _____

PART OF THE BODY _____

PERSON IN ROOM _____

NOUN _____

Any adult _____ who volunteers to chaperone a field trip is to be
        NOUN

congratulated for their _____ bravery. It's *not* a job for the faint of
                    ADJECTIVE

_____! Here are some tips from the pros to ensure you not only
PART OF THE BODY

survive, but _____!
          VERB

- Wear comfortable walking _____ on your
                          PLURAL NOUN

_____.
PART OF THE BODY (PLURAL)

- Stay hydrated with _____, and snack often.
                  TYPE OF LIQUID

- The bus ride will have the deafening noise level of a/an _____
                                                      NOUN

concert, and the seats will (literally) be a pain in your _____.
                                                   PART OF THE BODY

Take a headache pill in advance—or just plan to drive your own

_____.
   NOUN

- Do frequent _____-counts to ensure you start and
            PART OF THE BODY

finish with _____ kids.
          NUMBER

- Last but not least, keep a/an _____ on any student named
                            PART OF THE BODY

_____. A/An _____ with that name *always* seems
PERSON IN ROOM   NOUN

to be trouble!

MAD LIBS® is fun to play with friends, but you can also play it by yourself! To begin with, DO NOT look at the story on the page below. Fill in the blanks on this page with the words called for. Then, using the words you have selected, fill in the blank spaces in the story.

Now you've created your own hilarious MAD LIBS® game!

CLASSIC FIELD TRIP MOVIES

PLURAL NOUN _____

NOUN _____

ADJECTIVE _____

NOUN _____

PLURAL NOUN _____

ADJECTIVE _____

PERSON IN ROOM _____

ADJECTIVE _____

NOUN _____

CELEBRITY _____

VERB ENDING IN "ING" _____

PERSON IN ROOM (MALE) _____

TYPE OF FOOD _____

NOUN _____

NOUN _____

ADJECTIVE _____

NOUN _____

CELEBRITY (MALE) _____

MAD☺LIBS®
CLASSIC FIELD TRIP MOVIES

Let's grab a bucket of buttered _____ and curl up on the _____
                                   PLURAL NOUN   NOUN

to watch these _____ field trip movies that every school-age _____
                ADJECTIVE   NOUN

should see:

Prehistoric Park: A class of science-minded junior _____ visit an ancient
                                                        PLURAL NOUN

forest where _____ dinosaurs such as the _____-asaurus
               ADJECTIVE   PERSON IN ROOM

roam free.

Overnight at the _____ *Museum*: Students camp out at the Historical
                    ADJECTIVE

_____ Museum and discover that wax figures of famous historical people,
   NOUN

such as Pocahontas, Christopher Columbus, Teddy Roosevelt, and _____,
                                                                  CELEBRITY

come back to life at night and spend hours singing, dancing, and

_____ throughout the museum.
VERB ENDING IN "ING"

_____ *and the* _____ *Factory*: A young _____ finds a
PERSON IN ROOM (MALE)   TYPE OF FOOD   NOUN

winning golden _____ that allows him and his class to tour the elusive,
                 NOUN

_____ factory owned by an eccentric _____ named
 ADJECTIVE   NOUN

Mr. _____.
    CELEBRITY (MALE)

MAD LIBS® is fun to play with friends, but you can also play it by yourself! To begin with, DO NOT look at the story on the page below. Fill in the blanks on this page with the words called for. Then, using the words you have selected, fill in the blank spaces in the story.

Now you've created your own hilarious MAD LIBS® game!

FIELD TRIPPIN':
TEACHER FEEDBACK

PLURAL NOUN _____

VERB ENDING IN "ING" _____

PLURAL NOUN _____

PLURAL NOUN _____

NUMBER _____

ANIMAL (PLURAL) _____

TYPE OF FOOD (PLURAL) _____

NOUN _____

ADJECTIVE _____

VERB _____

NUMBER _____

TYPE OF LIQUID _____

PERSON IN ROOM (MALE) _____

TYPE OF LIQUID _____

PART OF THE BODY _____

PLURAL NOUN _____

VERB ENDING "ING" _____

ADJECTIVE _____

MAD LIBS®
FIELD TRIPPIN':
TEACHER FEEDBACK

Dear Parents:

I am sending home this note to tell you how proud I was of your _____
PLURAL NOUN

today on our field trip to the Science Museum! I was particularly impressed

with them during the Imagine an Invention exhibit. They put on their

_____ caps and came up with some genius _____! One
VERB ENDING IN "ING"   PLURAL NOUN

student used a spool of _____, _____ miniature _____,
                        PLURAL NOUN   NUMBER   ANIMAL (PLURAL)

paper clips, and some day-old _____ to fashion a
                              TYPE OF FOOD (PLURAL)

jet-propelled _____. And the students had a ton of _____ fun at
              NOUN   ADJECTIVE

the Ocean Exhibit, a giant tank where they could splash, play, and _____
                                                                   VERB

in over _____ gallons of _____. There was one minor
        NUMBER   TYPE OF LIQUID

mishap where _____ drenched the poor tour guide with
             PERSON IN ROOM (MALE)

a/an _____ cannon and soaked her from head to _____!
     TYPE OF LIQUID   PART OF THE BODY

Be sure to ask your _____ about the trip tonight when you're
                    PLURAL NOUN

_____ around the dinner table. They had a/an _____
VERB ENDING IN "ING"   ADJECTIVE

time!

MAD LIBS®

GIVE ME LIBERTY
OR GIVE ME MAD LIBS

Mad Libs
An Imprint of Penguin Random House

INSTRUCTIONS

MAD LIBS® is a game for people who don't like games!
It can be played by one, two, three, four, or forty.

• RIDICULOUSLY SIMPLE DIRECTIONS

In this tablet you will find stories containing blank spaces where words are left out. One player, the READER, selects one of these stories. The READER does not tell anyone what the story is about. Instead, he/she asks the other players, the WRITERS, to give him/her words. These words are used to fill in the blank spaces in the story.

• TO PLAY

The READER asks each WRITER in turn to call out a word—an adjective or a noun or whatever the space calls for—and uses them to fill in the blank spaces in the story. The result is a MAD LIBS® game.

When the READER then reads the completed MAD LIBS® game to the other players, they will discover that they have written a story that is fantastic, screamingly funny, shocking, silly, crazy, or just plain dumb—depending upon which words each WRITER called out.

• EXAMPLE (*Before* and *After*)

" _____ !" he said _____
     EXCLAMATION   ADVERB

as he jumped into his convertible _____ and
                           NOUN

drove off with his _____ wife.
          ADJECTIVE

" ___OUCH___ !" he said ___STUPIDLY___
     EXCLAMATION   ADVERB

as he jumped into his convertible ___CAT___ and
                           NOUN

drove off with his ___BRAVE___ wife.
          ADJECTIVE

QUICK REVIEW

In case you have forgotten what adjectives, adverbs, nouns, and verbs are, here is a quick review:

An ADJECTIVE describes something or somebody. *Lumpy, soft, ugly, messy,* and *short* are adjectives.

An ADVERB tells how something is done. It modifies a verb and usually ends in "ly." *Modestly, stupidly, greedily,* and *carefully* are adverbs.

A NOUN is the name of a person, place, or thing. *Sidewalk, umbrella, bridle, bathtub,* and *nose* are nouns.

A VERB is an action word. *Run, pitch, jump,* and *swim* are verbs. Put the verbs in past tense if the directions say PAST TENSE. *Ran, pitched, jumped,* and *swam* are verbs in the past tense.

When we ask for A PLACE, we mean any sort of place: a country or city *(Spain, Cleveland)* or a room *(bathroom, kitchen).*

An EXCLAMATION or SILLY WORD is any sort of funny sound, gasp, grunt, or outcry, like *Wow!, Ouch!, Whomp!, Ick!,* and *Gadzooks!*

When we ask for specific words, like a NUMBER, a COLOR, an ANIMAL, or a PART OF THE BODY, we mean a word that is one of those things, like *seven, blue, horse,* or *head.*

When we ask for a PLURAL, it means more than one. For example, *cat* pluralized is *cats.*

MAD LIBS® is fun to play with friends, but you can also play it by yourself! To begin with, DO NOT look at the story on the page below. Fill in the blanks on this page with the words called for. Then, using the words you have selected, fill in the blank spaces in the story.

Now you've created your own hilarious MAD LIBS® game!

AS AMERICAN AS . . .

ADJECTIVE _____

TYPE OF FOOD _____

SAME TYPE OF FOOD _____

ADVERB _____

ADJECTIVE _____

ADJECTIVE _____

NOUN _____

NOUN _____

NOUN _____

ADJECTIVE _____

NOUN _____

ADJECTIVE _____

A PLACE _____

ARTICLE OF CLOTHING _____

ADJECTIVE _____

PLURAL NOUN _____

TYPE OF FOOD _____

COLOR _____

Do you know the _____ saying "That's as American as
ADJECTIVE

_____ pie"? Well, _____ pie isn't the only thing
TYPE OF FOOD   SAME TYPE OF FOOD

that's _____ American! Here's a list of some of the most
ADVERB

_____ things that represent the _____ ole US of A!
ADJECTIVE   ADJECTIVE

• **Apple Pie:** There's nothing quite like biting into a forkful of

_____ pie to celebrate being a/an _____. Just don't
NOUN   NOUN

add _____ cream—à la mode makes it French!
NOUN

• **Baseball:** It's the _____ American pastime that dates all
ADJECTIVE

the way back to the 1700s! So, around the same time your mom and

_____ were in school!
NOUN

• **Blue Jeans:** These _____ pants can be worn all year round,
ADJECTIVE

for almost every occasion, like your next visit to (the) _____!
A PLACE

Matching denim _____ optional.
ARTICLE OF CLOTHING

• **Mad Libs:** There's nothing more _____ than playing Mad
ADJECTIVE

Libs with your _____! Just make sure to do it while eating
PLURAL NOUN

_____ pie and wearing your favorite _____ jeans!
TYPE OF FOOD   COLOR

MAD LIBS® is fun to play with friends, but you can also play it by yourself! To begin with, DO NOT look at the story on the page below. Fill in the blanks on this page with the words called for. Then, using the words you have selected, fill in the blank spaces in the story.

Now you've created your own hilarious MAD LIBS® game!

PATRIOTIC SONGS, PART 1

ADJECTIVE _____

NOUN _____

ADJECTIVE _____

NOUN _____

VERB _____

ADJECTIVE _____

ADVERB _____

NOUN _____

ADJECTIVE _____

NOUN _____

PLURAL NOUN _____

A PLACE _____

NOUN _____

VERB _____

NOUN _____

MAD LIBS®
PATRIOTIC SONGS, PART 1

There are tons of _____ songs that are perfect to listen to on the Fourth
  ADJECTIVE

of _____, or any day you want to get into a patriotic mood! Here's a list
  NOUN

of the most _____, complete with lyrics:
  ADJECTIVE

- **"The Star-Spangled _____"**: O say can you _____,
  NOUN VERB

  by the dawn's _____ light, what so _____ we hailed at the
  ADJECTIVE ADVERB

  _____'s last gleaming?
  NOUN

- **"Yankee Doodle"**: Yankee Doodle, keep it up. Yankee Doodle

  _____. Mind the music and the _____, and with the
  ADJECTIVE NOUN

  _____ be handy.
  PLURAL NOUN

- **"God Bless America"**: God bless (the) _____, _____
  A PLACE NOUN

  that I love. _____ beside her and guide her, through the night
  VERB

  with a/an _____ from above.
  NOUN

MAD LIBS® is fun to play with friends, but you can also play it by yourself! To begin with, DO NOT look at the story on the page below. Fill in the blanks on this page with the words called for. Then, using the words you have selected, fill in the blank spaces in the story.

Now you've created your own hilarious MAD LIBS® game!

PATRIOTIC SONGS, PART 2

PLURAL NOUN _____

VERB ENDING IN "ING" _____

NOUN _____

VERB _____

A PLACE _____

ADJECTIVE _____

NOUN _____

ADJECTIVE _____

VERB _____

PLURAL NOUN _____

PLURAL NOUN _____

PLURAL NOUN _____

PART OF THE BODY (PLURAL) _____

NOUN _____

NOUN _____

PLURAL NOUN _____

VERB (PAST TENSE) _____

ADJECTIVE _____

MAD LIBS

PATRIOTIC SONGS, PART 2

Here are more patriotic _____ that will have you
<u>PLURAL NOUN</u>

_____ a tune all day long!
<u>VERB ENDING IN "ING"</u>

- **"Stars and Stripes Forever":** Hurrah for the _____ of the free!
  <u>NOUN</u>

  May it _____ as our standard forever. The gem of the land and
  <u>VERB</u>

  (the) _____, the banner of the _____ .
  <u>A PLACE</u>   <u>ADJECTIVE</u>

- **"My Country, 'Tis of Thee":** My _____,'tis of thee, _____
  <u>NOUN</u>   <u>ADJECTIVE</u>

  land of liberty, of thee I _____. Land where my _____
  <u>VERB</u>   <u>PLURAL NOUN</u>

  died, land of the _____'(s) pride, from every mountainside,
  <u>PLURAL NOUN</u>

  let _____ ring.
  <u>PLURAL NOUN</u>

- **"The Battle Hymn of the Republic":** Mine _____
  <u>PART OF THE BODY (PLURAL)</u>

  have seen the glory of the coming of the _____ . He is trampling
  <u>NOUN</u>

  out the _____ where the _____ of wrath are stored. He
  <u>NOUN</u>   <u>PLURAL NOUN</u>

  hath _____ the fateful lightning of his _____ swift
  <u>VERB (PAST TENSE)</u>   <u>ADJECTIVE</u>

  sword.

MAD LIBS® is fun to play with friends, but you can also play it by yourself! To begin with, DO NOT look at the story on the page below. Fill in the blanks on this page with the words called for. Then, using the words you have selected, fill in the blank spaces in the story.

Now you've created your own hilarious MAD LIBS® game!

PARTY LIKE IT'S JULY FOURTH!

ADJECTIVE _____

A PLACE _____

NUMBER _____

ADJECTIVE _____

NOUN _____

ADJECTIVE _____

ADJECTIVE _____

ADJECTIVE _____

TYPE OF FOOD _____

COLOR _____

PART OF THE BODY _____

PLURAL NOUN _____

NOUN _____

ADJECTIVE _____

LETTER OF THE ALPHABET _____

VERB _____

PLURAL NOUN _____

NOUN _____

MAD LIBS®
PARTY LIKE IT'S JULY FOURTH!

The Fourth of July is right around the corner, and you want to throw the

most _____ party in all of (the) _____. It's as easy as 1, 2,
     ADJECTIVE   A PLACE

_____ if you follow this _____ guide! First, decide who you want to
 NUMBER   ADJECTIVE

invite. You can't invite every _____ on the block, so only invite the
                                 NOUN

most _____ (or the ones who will bring something _____ to eat!).
      ADJECTIVE   ADJECTIVE

Next, decide on a/an _____ menu. Wiggly _____ molds in the
                       ADJECTIVE   TYPE OF FOOD

shape of the American flag are sooo last year! Instead, find as many _____,
                                                                       COLOR

white, and blue _____-foods as you can, and spread them
                 PART OF THE BODY

out for your _____ to pick at. It doesn't hurt to ask your _____
              PLURAL NOUN   NOUN

to throw some burgers on the grill, too! Finally, don't forget about the music.

Put some _____ songs on your _____-pod for your
          ADJECTIVE   LETTER OF THE ALPHABET

guests to dance to. And make sure there are enough fireworks

for everyone to _____ once it gets dark outside! Follow these tips (and
                 VERB

ask for help from your _____), and it's sure to be a/an _____ to
                        PLURAL NOUN   NOUN

remember!

MAD LIBS® is fun to play with friends, but you can also play it by yourself! To begin with, DO NOT look at the story on the page below. Fill in the blanks on this page with the words called for. Then, using the words you have selected, fill in the blank spaces in the story.

Now you've created your own hilarious MAD LIBS® game!

DECLARATION OF INDEPENDENCE

NOUN _____

PLURAL NOUN _____

PLURAL NOUN _____

NOUN _____

ADJECTIVE _____

PLURAL NOUN _____

PLURAL NOUN _____

ADJECTIVE _____

PLURAL NOUN _____

PLURAL NOUN _____

VERB _____

PLURAL NOUN _____

PLURAL NOUN _____

DECLARATION OF INDEPENDENCE

You haven't read the Declaration of _____ until you've read it Mad Libs–
                                        NOUN

style!

We hold these _____ to be self-evident, that all _____ are created
              PLURAL NOUN   PLURAL NOUN

equal, that they are endowed by their _____ with certain _____
                                       NOUN   ADJECTIVE

Rights, that among these are Life, Liberty and the pursuit of _____.—
                                                              PLURAL NOUN

That to secure these _____, Governments are instituted among Men,
                     PLURAL NOUN

deriving their _____ powers from the consent of the governed,—That
               ADJECTIVE

whenever any Form of Government becomes destructive of these

_____, it is the Right of the _____ to alter or to _____ it,
PLURAL NOUN   PLURAL NOUN   VERB

and to institute new Government, laying its foundation on such principles and

organizing its _____ in such form, as to them shall seem most likely to
               PLURAL NOUN

effect their Safety and _____.
                        PLURAL NOUN

MAD LIBS® is fun to play with friends, but you can also play it by yourself! To begin with, DO NOT look at the story on the page below. Fill in the blanks on this page with the words called for. Then, using the words you have selected, fill in the blank spaces in the story.

Now you've created your own hilarious MAD LIBS® game!

ROAD TRIP!

ADJECTIVE _____

ADJECTIVE _____

PLURAL NOUN _____

NOUN _____

VERB ENDING IN "ING" _____

NOUN _____

NOUN _____

VEHICLE _____

SILLY WORD _____

PART OF THE BODY (PLURAL) _____

ADJECTIVE _____

COLOR _____

ADJECTIVE _____

NOUN _____

ADJECTIVE _____

MAD LIBS®
ROAD TRIP!

Pack your bags! It's time to take a/an _____ road trip across the United
                                        ADJECTIVE

States to visit some of the most _____ historical landmarks. First stop is
                                  ADJECTIVE

Philadelphia, where you can visit Independence Hall to see where the

Declaration of _____ was signed. After that, check out the Liberty Bell.
                PLURAL NOUN

It's the most famous cracked _____ in history, and a symbol of freedom
                             NOUN

across America. Then head on up to Boston, where you can check out the USS

Constitution, the oldest _____ naval vessel, and the _____
                           VERB ENDING IN "ING"   NOUN

Hill Monument. In New York, you can climb to the top of the _____ of
                                                            NOUN

Liberty (or take a/an _____ to check out the view from the harbor!).
                       VEHICLE

Now it's time to head west, where you can see famous landmarks like Mount

_____, which features carved statues of the _____ of
 SILLY WORD   PART OF THE BODY (PLURAL)

some of our most _____ presidents. Or check out _____-stone,
                  ADJECTIVE   COLOR

our first national park, which includes the famous geyser Old _____!
                                                              ADJECTIVE

Just don't forget to pack a/an _____—you'll want to take pictures to
                                NOUN

remember your _____ trip by!
               ADJECTIVE

MAD LIBS® is fun to play with friends, but you can also play it by yourself! To begin with, DO NOT look at the story on the page below. Fill in the blanks on this page with the words called for. Then, using the words you have selected, fill in the blank spaces in the story.

Now you've created your own hilarious MAD LIBS® game!

MOVIES TO GET YOU IN THE MOOD

ADJECTIVE _____

PLURAL NOUN _____

ADJECTIVE _____

ADJECTIVE _____

VERB _____

COLOR _____

CELEBRITY _____

ADJECTIVE _____

PLURAL NOUN _____

PERSON IN ROOM (MALE) _____

ADJECTIVE _____

OCCUPATION _____

OCCUPATION (PLURAL) _____

ADVERB _____

VEHICLE _____

PLURAL NOUN _____

TYPE OF FOOD _____

TYPE OF LIQUID _____

NOUN _____

MAD LIBS®
MOVIES TO GET YOU
IN THE MOOD

Fourth of July is right around the corner and you want to get in a/an _____
ADJECTIVE

mood to celebrate, so why not watch some of these classic _____?
PLURAL NOUN

- **Independence Day**: _____ aliens invade Earth in this sci-fi thriller.
  ADJECTIVE

  The aliens are so _____, they even _____ up the _____
  ADJECTIVE   VERB   COLOR

  House!

- **National Treasure**: _____ stars as a history buff who must find
  CELEBRITY

  the _____ lost treasure before his _____ get to it first.
  ADJECTIVE   PLURAL NOUN

- **The Patriot**: _____ Gibson is a war hero who just wants
  PERSON IN ROOM (MALE)

  to live a/an _____ life as a/an _____ on his farm when the
  ADJECTIVE   OCCUPATION

  American Revolution begins.

- **Apollo 13**: Three _____ try to get home _____ after
  OCCUPATION (PLURAL)   ADVERB

  their _____ malfunctions.
  VEHICLE

Now that you've got your _____ all picked out, don't forget your
PLURAL NOUN

_____ and _____. Just be sure to make enough for your little
TYPE OF FOOD   TYPE OF LIQUID

brother or _____!
NOUN

MAD LIBS® is fun to play with friends, but you can also play it by yourself! To begin with, DO NOT look at the story on the page below. Fill in the blanks on this page with the words called for. Then, using the words you have selected, fill in the blank spaces in the story.

Now you've created your own hilarious MAD LIBS® game!

RED, WHITE, AND BEAUTIFUL!

NOUN _____

ADJECTIVE _____

PERSON IN ROOM (FEMALE) _____

ADJECTIVE _____

A PLACE _____

PERSON IN ROOM (MALE) _____

NOUN _____

NUMBER _____

PLURAL NOUN _____

PLURAL NOUN _____

NUMBER _____

PLURAL NOUN _____

ADVERB _____

NOUN _____

NOUN _____

MAD LIBS®
RED, WHITE, AND BEAUTIFUL!

Sure, you pledge allegiance to the American _____ every morning
NOUN

when school starts, but do you know the history behind this _____
ADJECTIVE

flag? The legend goes that the first flag was made by

_____ Ross, a/an _____ seamstress
PERSON IN ROOM (FEMALE)   ADJECTIVE

who lived in (the) _____. In May 1776,
A PLACE

_____ Washington visited Ross at her shop and
PERSON IN ROOM (MALE)

asked her to sew a/an _____ based on the design he gave her. The
NOUN

stars in the flag originally had _____ points, but Ross changed
NUMBER

the design to five, which is how the flag still looks today! The first official flag

was known as the Stars and _____. The flag changed as more
PLURAL NOUN

_____ joined the Union, until Congress passed a law in 1818
PLURAL NOUN

that said the flag would always have _____ stripes, and stars
NUMBER

equal to the total number of _____ in the Union. The flag was
PLURAL NOUN

_____ completed in 1960, when Hawaii became the last state to join
ADVERB

the _____. Think about that next time you say, "I pledge allegiance
NOUN

to the _____"!
NOUN

MAD LIBS® is fun to play with friends, but you can also play it by yourself! To begin with, DO NOT look at the story on the page below. Fill in the blanks on this page with the words called for. Then, using the words you have selected, fill in the blank spaces in the story.

Now you've created your own hilarious MAD LIBS® game!

PATRIOTIC HOLIDAYS

ADJECTIVE _____

COLOR _____

ADJECTIVE _____

ADJECTIVE _____

PLURAL NOUN _____

ADJECTIVE _____

NOUN _____

PERSON IN ROOM (MALE) _____

PERSON IN ROOM (MALE) _____

VERB ENDING IN "ING" _____

NOUN _____

ADJECTIVE _____

ADVERB _____

NOUN _____

MAD LIBS
PATRIOTIC HOLIDAYS

The Fourth of July might be the most _____ patriotic holiday, but there
ADJECTIVE

are also many other times throughout the year that you can deck yourself out

in red, white, and _____, and show some _____ American pride! Here
COLOR   ADJECTIVE

are a few _____ holidays and their meanings:
ADJECTIVE

- **Martin Luther King Jr. Day:** Celebrates the life and _____
PLURAL NOUN

  of Martin Luther King Jr., a/an _____ civil rights activist, most
ADJECTIVE

  famous for his "I Have a/an _____" speech.
NOUN

- **Presidents' Day:** Celebrates the birthdays of both _____
PERSON IN ROOM (MALE)

  Washington and _____ Lincoln.
PERSON IN ROOM (MALE)

- **Labor Day:** Honors our country's hard-_____ people.
VERB ENDING IN "ING"

  It marks the end of the summer season and the beginning of a new

  _____ year for most students!
NOUN

- **Veterans Day:** This _____ holiday honors the veterans who
ADJECTIVE

  fought _____ for our _____.
ADVERB   NOUN

MAD LIBS® is fun to play with friends, but you can also play it by yourself! To begin with, DO NOT look at the story on the page below. Fill in the blanks on this page with the words called for. Then, using the words you have selected, fill in the blank spaces in the story.

Now you've created your own hilarious MAD LIBS® game!

FIREWORKS! FIREWORKS! FIREWORKS!

ADJECTIVE _____

NOUN _____

PLURAL NOUN _____

ADJECTIVE _____

PLURAL NOUN _____

PLURAL NOUN _____

ADVERB _____

ADJECTIVE _____

ADJECTIVE _____

ADJECTIVE _____

NOUN _____

EXCLAMATION _____

ADJECTIVE _____

ADJECTIVE _____

ADJECTIVE _____

NOUN _____

NOUN _____

MAD LIBS®
FIREWORKS! FIREWORKS! FIREWORKS!

Fireworks are a/an _____ way to celebrate the Fourth of _____!
ADJECTIVE   NOUN

But you probably didn't know that these explosive _____ have a long,
                                                   PLURAL NOUN

_____ history. In fact, some _____ believe that fireworks were
ADJECTIVE   PLURAL NOUN

invented by the Chinese in 200 BC. Chinese _____ _____ lit
                                            PLURAL NOUN   ADVERB

bamboo stalks on fire, and it caused a loud, _____ BANG! that scared
                                             ADJECTIVE

away the _____ mountain men nearby. That's how fireworks were born!
         ADJECTIVE

Even though they may seem like _____ magic, fireworks are actually just
                               ADJECTIVE

chemical reactions. Different _____ elements produce different colors of
                             NOUN

fireworks! _____—sure makes chemistry class a whole lot more
           EXCLAMATION

_____! Americans have been using _____ fireworks to celebrate
ADJECTIVE   ADJECTIVE

their independence since 1777, at least. So next time you want to celebrate the

_____ ole US of A, light up a sparkler or a Roman _____—with
ADJECTIVE   NOUN

your mom or _____'s permission, of course!
            NOUN

MAD LIBS® is fun to play with friends, but you can also play it by yourself! To begin with, DO NOT look at the story on the page below. Fill in the blanks on this page with the words called for. Then, using the words you have selected, fill in the blank spaces in the story.

Now you've created your own hilarious MAD LIBS® game!

HISTORY LESSON

NOUN _____

NOUN _____

NOUN _____

CELEBRITY _____

NUMBER _____

ADJECTIVE _____

NOUN _____

A PLACE _____

VERB (PAST TENSE) _____

ADJECTIVE _____

ADJECTIVE _____

OCCUPATION _____

ADVERB _____

VERB ENDING IN "ING" _____

NUMBER _____

ADJECTIVE _____

MAD LIBS®
HISTORY LESSON

Have you ever wondered why exactly we celebrate the Fourth of _____?
NOUN

The Fourth marks the day that the Continental _____ adopted the
NOUN

Declaration of _____ way back in 1776! The Declaration of Independence
NOUN

was originally written by _____. It stated that _____ North
CELEBRITY   NUMBER

American colonies planned to separate from Britain and become their own

_____ nation. The first ever Fourth of _____ celebration took place
ADJECTIVE   NOUN

in (the) _____ on July 8, 1776. On that day, the Declaration was read
A PLACE

aloud, city bells _____ loudly, and bands played _____ music.
VERB (PAST TENSE)   ADJECTIVE

Some towns even held a/an _____ fake funeral for the _____ of
ADJECTIVE   OCCUPATION

England! Independence Day was _____ declared an official holiday in
ADVERB

1870, but that didn't stop people from _____ every summer
VERB ENDING IN "ING"

on July _____! And now that you know your history, you can celebrate the
NUMBER

Fourth of July just like a/an _____ colonist would!
ADJECTIVE

MAD LIBS® is fun to play with friends, but you can also play it by yourself! To begin with, DO NOT look at the story on the page below. Fill in the blanks on this page with the words called for. Then, using the words you have selected, fill in the blank spaces in the story.

Now you've created your own hilarious MAD LIBS® game!

INTERVIEW WITH THE STATUE OF LIBERTY

PERSON IN ROOM (FEMALE) _____

PART OF THE BODY _____

NOUN _____

NOUN _____

A PLACE _____

ADJECTIVE _____

NUMBER _____

PLURAL NOUN _____

CELEBRITY _____

PLURAL NOUN _____

ADJECTIVE _____

ADJECTIVE _____

ADJECTIVE _____

SILLY WORD _____

NUMBER _____

ADJECTIVE _____

SAME ADJECTIVE _____

PERSON IN ROOM (MALE) _____

MAD LIBS®
INTERVIEW WITH THE
STATUE OF LIBERTY

Reporter: _____ Jones here, reporter for
PERSON IN ROOM (FEMALE)

_____-witness News. Today we're reporting live from Liberty
PART OF THE BODY

Island, where we scored an exclusive interview with the Statue of _____!
NOUN

So, tell us, what's it like to be the largest _____ in all of (the) _____?
NOUN   A PLACE

Statue of Liberty: It's _____! After all, I'm over _____ feet tall
ADJECTIVE   NUMBER

and weigh 450,000 _____. Nobody messes with me! Not even _____!
PLURAL NOUN   CELEBRITY

Reporter: Rumor has it that you're not originally from the United

_____. You were a gift from the _____ French! Can you
PLURAL NOUN   ADJECTIVE

confirm if this is true or _____?
ADJECTIVE

Statue of Liberty: Yes, it's totally _____! And it took the sculptor, Auguste
ADJECTIVE

_____, over _____ years to finish building me. That explains why
SILLY WORD   NUMBER

I'm so darn _____!
ADJECTIVE

Reporter: It's true; you're the most _____ statue ever built!
SAME ADJECTIVE

_____, now back to you in the studio with sports!
PERSON IN ROOM (MALE)

MAD LIBS® is fun to play with friends, but you can also play it by yourself! To begin with, DO NOT look at the story on the page below. Fill in the blanks on this page with the words called for. Then, using the words you have selected, fill in the blank spaces in the story.

Now you've created your own hilarious MAD LIBS® game!

APPLE PIE, SO DIVINE!

ADJECTIVE _____

VERB _____

PART OF THE BODY _____

TYPE OF FOOD _____

NOUN _____

PLURAL NOUN _____

NUMBER _____

PLURAL NOUN _____

ADJECTIVE _____

NOUN _____

ADJECTIVE _____

TYPE OF FOOD _____

NOUN _____

NUMBER _____

ADJECTIVE _____

MAD LIBS
APPLE PIE, SO DIVINE!

If you're looking for a/an _____ recipe to bring to your next Fourth of
                              ADJECTIVE

July celebration, _____ no further! Here's a/an _____-watering
                   VERB   PART OF THE BODY

recipe for the most American dessert of all, apple pie! First, gather your

ingredients. You will need the following:

- 2 premade _____ crusts
             TYPE OF FOOD

- 1/4 cup all-purpose _____
                       NOUN

- 3/4 cup sugar

- 1/2 teaspoon cinnamon

- 1/2 teaspoon _____
               PLURAL NOUN

- 2 tablespoons butter

- _____ cups thinly sliced _____
  NUMBER   PLURAL NOUN

To make this _____ recipe, first preheat the _____ to 425 degrees.
             ADJECTIVE   NOUN

Then mix together your _____ ingredients, and add in the apples. Pour
                       ADJECTIVE

the mixture into the _____ crust, dot with butter, and cover it with the
                     TYPE OF FOOD

other crust. Place it in the _____. Voilà! In just _____ short minutes,
                             NOUN   NUMBER

you'll have a/an _____ dessert that will impress all your friends!
                 ADJECTIVE

MAD LIBS® is fun to play with friends, but you can also play it by yourself! To begin with, DO NOT look at the story on the page below. Fill in the blanks on this page with the words called for. Then, using the words you have selected, fill in the blank spaces in the story.

Now you've created your own hilarious MAD LIBS® game!

CELEBRATE ACROSS AMERICA

ADJECTIVE _____

ADJECTIVE _____

NOUN _____

NOUN _____

ADJECTIVE _____

PERSON IN ROOM (MALE) _____

PLURAL NOUN _____

PLURAL NOUN _____

PLURAL NOUN _____

TYPE OF FOOD _____

ADJECTIVE _____

ADJECTIVE _____

TYPE OF FOOD _____

PLURAL NOUN _____

MAD LIBS

CELEBRATE ACROSS AMERICA

The Fourth of July is celebrated all across this _____
ADJECTIVE

nation of ours, but not every city honors America in the same way! Here's a list

of _____ cities and their favorite ways to celebrate the most
ADJECTIVE

patriotic _____ of the year!
NOUN

- The Boston _____ Orchestra holds a/an _____ concert on
NOUN ADJECTIVE

  the banks of the _____ River.
PERSON IN ROOM (MALE)

- _____ living in Philadelphia celebrate at Independence Hall, the
PLURAL NOUN

  place where the Declaration of _____ was first signed.
PLURAL NOUN

- In New York City, _____ flock to Coney Island to watch the
PLURAL NOUN

  annual _____ -eating contest.
TYPE OF FOOD

- In cities like Chicago and San Francisco, people cram together to watch

  the _____ fireworks shows that take place every year.
ADJECTIVE

- And in backyards all across this _____ country, people stuff their
ADJECTIVE

  faces with _____ , light sparklers, and spend quality time with
TYPE OF FOOD

  their friends and _____ !
PLURAL NOUN

MAD LIBS® is fun to play with friends, but you can also play it by yourself! To begin with, DO NOT look at the story on the page below. Fill in the blanks on this page with the words called for. Then, using the words you have selected, fill in the blank spaces in the story.

Now you've created your own hilarious MAD LIBS® game!

CELEBRATE WITH A BANG!

NOUN _____

PLURAL NOUN _____

NUMBER _____

A PLACE _____

NOUN _____

ADJECTIVE _____

PLURAL NOUN _____

VERB _____

VERB ENDING IN "ING" _____

NOUN _____

PLURAL NOUN _____

ANIMAL _____

EXCLAMATION _____

ADJECTIVE _____

ANIMAL (PLURAL) _____

ADJECTIVE _____

NUMBER _____

PLURAL NOUN _____

MAD LIBS®
CELEBRATE WITH A BANG!

Is your Fourth of July celebration feeling a little stale? Looking for some

excitement to liven up your boring _____? Want to impress
NOUN

your friends and _____? Well, we've got the solution for you!
PLURAL NOUN

Come on down to the Firework Warehouse, located right off exit

_____ in (the) _____ . We've got every type of
NUMBER   A PLACE

_____ imaginable—big ones, loud ones, _____
NOUN   ADJECTIVE

ones! If rockets are your thing, we've got a huge assortment of _____
PLURAL NOUN

that _____ off into the sky and make a loud_____
VERB   VERB ENDING IN "ING"

noise as they explode. We also carry a wide selection of _____
NOUN

spinners. These babies spray _____ everywhere as they spin on
PLURAL NOUN

the ground like a crazed _____ ! Can you say, "_____ !"?
ANIMAL   EXCLAMATION

We also carry a/an _____ assortment of sparklers, poppers, and
ADJECTIVE

caps for all the scaredy-_____ out there! But hurry, hurry, hurry!
ANIMAL (PLURAL)

Supply is limited, and this _____ deal won't last long! Offer
ADJECTIVE

valid until July _____ or until _____ run out!
NUMBER   PLURAL NOUN

MAD LIBS® is fun to play with friends, but you can also play it by yourself! To begin with, DO NOT look at the story on the page below. Fill in the blanks on this page with the words called for. Then, using the words you have selected, fill in the blank spaces in the story.

Now you've created your own hilarious MAD LIBS® game!

MEET UNCLE SAM

ADJECTIVE _____

NOUN _____

PERSON IN ROOM (MALE) _____

COLOR _____

ADJECTIVE _____

COLOR _____

PART OF THE BODY _____

ADJECTIVE _____

PERSON IN ROOM _____

OCCUPATION _____

ADVERB _____

PLURAL NOUN _____

VERB _____

NOUN _____

NUMBER _____

MAD LIBS
MEET UNCLE SAM

"Uncle Sam" is a/an _____ nickname for the US government that
          ADJECTIVE

became popular during the _____ of 1812. But there's so much more
              NOUN

about Uncle _____ that you don't know . . .
         PERSON IN ROOM (MALE)

Favorite Color: Red, white, and _____, of course!
                   COLOR

Favorite Article of Clothing: A toss-up between my _____ top
                                  ADJECTIVE

hat and my _____ bow tie. They both make my _____ look
      COLOR   PART OF THE BODY

_____!
ADJECTIVE

Favorite Phrase: I Want YOU! (Yes, you, _____!)
                             PERSON IN ROOM

Favorite Holiday: Talk like a/an _____ Day. Just kidding! It's
                         OCCUPATION

_____ Independence Day!
ADVERB

Favorite Band: The Rolling _____. Hey, even Uncle Sam likes to
                 PLURAL NOUN

_____ and roll sometimes!
VERB

Favorite Movie: Either *Born on the Fourth of* _____ or *Toy Story*
                           NOUN

_____.
NUMBER

MAD LIBS® is fun to play with friends, but you can also play it by yourself! To begin with, DO NOT look at the story on the page below. Fill in the blanks on this page with the words called for. Then, using the words you have selected, fill in the blank spaces in the story.

Now you've created your own hilarious MAD LIBS® game!

FOURTH OF JULY BLOOPERS

ADJECTIVE _____

PERSON IN ROOM (FEMALE) _____

PERSON IN ROOM (MALE) _____

ADJECTIVE _____

TYPE OF FOOD (PLURAL) _____

PLURAL NOUN _____

ADJECTIVE _____

NUMBER _____

CELEBRITY (MALE) _____

ADJECTIVE _____

EXCLAMATION _____

PART OF THE BODY _____

VERB _____

ADJECTIVE _____

VERB _____

PLURAL NOUN _____

TYPE OF LIQUID _____

ANIMAL _____

Our Fourth of July started out _____ enough. Aunt _____
                                  ADJECTIVE   PERSON IN ROOM (FEMALE)

and Uncle _____ were coming over to spend the day with my
             PERSON IN ROOM (MALE)

family. We had a really _____ barbecue set up in the backyard, with lots
                           ADJECTIVE

of _____ and _____ right off the grill. The trouble started
    TYPE OF FOOD (PLURAL)   PLURAL NOUN

when my aunt and uncle arrived and we found out they had brought along the

newest and most _____ member of their family: a/an _____-pound
                   ADJECTIVE   NUMBER

pet pig named _____! The pig looked _____ enough, and he
                 CELEBRITY (MALE)   ADJECTIVE

even made a noise that sounded like "_____!" when I petted him on
                                         EXCLAMATION

his _____. But when we put him in the backyard to _____,
     PART OF THE BODY   VERB

everything got totally out of hand! The pig took one sniff of all the _____
                                                                         ADJECTIVE

food and started to _____ around like crazy. He knocked over all the
                       VERB

tables and _____, destroyed my kid sister's playhouse, and took a swim in
              PLURAL NOUN

the _____. "That's it!" my father yelled. "Next time you bring a/an
     TYPE OF LIQUID

_____ to a barbecue, we're going to cook him!"
  ANIMAL

MAD LIBS® is fun to play with friends, but you can also play it by yourself! To begin with, DO NOT look at the story on the page below. Fill in the blanks on this page with the words called for. Then, using the words you have selected, fill in the blank spaces in the story.

Now you've created your own hilarious MAD LIBS® game!

BIRD OF PREY

ANIMAL _____

ADJECTIVE _____

PLURAL NOUN _____

NUMBER _____

ANIMAL _____

ADJECTIVE _____

TYPE OF LIQUID _____

ADJECTIVE _____

ADJECTIVE _____

VERB ENDING IN "ING" _____

TYPE OF LIQUID _____

NOUN _____

SAME NOUN _____

ADJECTIVE _____

ANIMAL _____

PART OF THE BODY _____

COLOR _____

PERSON IN ROOM (MALE) _____

ADJECTIVE _____

The bald eagle is famous for being the national _____ of the

ANIMAL

United States of America. You may have seen this _____ bird

ADJECTIVE

on the national seal, which is used on passports, _____, and

PLURAL NOUN

$_____ bills. But in the wild, the bald _____ is one of the most

NUMBER ANIMAL

ferocious and _____ birds of prey you can encounter. Bald eagles live

ADJECTIVE

near large bodies of _____ surrounded by lots of old _____

TYPE OF LIQUID ADJECTIVE

trees for nesting. If he's feeling hungry, the bald eagle swoops down and uses

his sharp, _____ talons to pick up fish _____ in the

ADJECTIVE VERB ENDING IN "ING"

nearby _____. Then he returns home to his _____, which

TYPE OF LIQUID NOUN

is the largest _____ built by any bird in North America. Talk about

SAME NOUN

living _____! And despite popular opinion, the bald _____ isn't

ADJECTIVE ANIMAL

actually bald. His _____ is simply covered with _____

PART OF THE BODY COLOR

feathers. So next time your uncle _____ complains about being

PERSON IN ROOM (MALE)

bald, tell him there's no shame in being _____. The bald eagle says so!

ADJECTIVE

MAD LIBS® is fun to play with friends, but you can also play it by yourself! To begin with, DO NOT look at the story on the page below. Fill in the blanks on this page with the words called for. Then, using the words you have selected, fill in the blank spaces in the story.

Now you've created your own hilarious MAD LIBS® game!

PATRIOTIC QUOTES

ADJECTIVE _____

VERB ENDING IN "ING" _____

OCCUPATION _____

ARTICLE OF CLOTHING _____

ADJECTIVE _____

A PLACE _____

ADJECTIVE _____

PART OF THE BODY _____

NOUN _____

VERB _____

The next time you really want to impress your parents at the dinner table,

recite one of these _____ quotes made famous by our _____
  ADJECTIVE   VERB ENDING IN "ING"

fathers! Even better, throw one into your next history paper to knock your

_____'s _____ off!
OCCUPATION ARTICLE OF CLOTHING

"History, in general, only informs us what _____ government is."
                                          ADJECTIVE

—Thomas Jefferson

"May the sun in his course visit no _____ more free, more happy, more
                                    A PLACE

_____, than this our own country!" **—Daniel Webster**
ADJECTIVE

"The cement of this Union is in the _____-blood of every
                                   PART OF THE BODY

American."**—Thomas Jefferson**

"Patriot: the _____who can _____the loudest without knowing what
             NOUN   VERB

he is hollering about."**—Mark Twain**

MAD LIBS® is fun to play with friends, but you can also play it by yourself! To begin with, DO NOT look at the story on the page below. Fill in the blanks on this page with the words called for. Then, using the words you have selected, fill in the blank spaces in the story.

Now you've created your own hilarious MAD LIBS® game!

DRESS UP!

ADJECTIVE _____

PLURAL NOUN _____

NOUN _____

PLURAL NOUN _____

COLOR _____

PART OF THE BODY _____

ADJECTIVE _____

EXCLAMATION _____

ADJECTIVE _____

COLOR _____

PERSON IN ROOM (MALE) _____

PERSON IN ROOM (FEMALE) _____

PLURAL NOUN _____

ADJECTIVE _____

ADJECTIVE _____

NOUN _____

PERSON IN ROOM (MALE) _____

MAD LIBS®
DRESS UP!

One _____ Fourth of July tradition in many towns
        ADJECTIVE

and _____ is dressing up for the annual _____ Day
        PLURAL NOUN   NOUN

Parade! There are tons of different patriotic _____ that you
                                               PLURAL NOUN

could wear. To dress up as the Statue of Liberty, wrap a/an _____
                                                              COLOR

bedsheet around your body and paint your _____ green. Borrow
                                          PART OF THE BODY

your _____ sister's tiara, and _____! You're Lady
      ADJECTIVE   EXCLAMATION

Liberty! Uncle Sam is another _____ costume choice. For this, you
                               ADJECTIVE

will need a red, white, and _____ suit. Borrow your uncle
                             COLOR

_____'s toupee and spray-paint it white for the perfect
   PERSON IN ROOM (MALE)

beard! A brother-and-sister duo can dress up as George and

_____ Washington. Just make sure the two
   PERSON IN ROOM (FEMALE)

_____ get along; otherwise they might start another
   PLURAL NOUN

_____ Revolutionary War! If all else fails, dress in all black, draw
   ADJECTIVE

a/an _____ beard on your face with _____ paint, and
      ADJECTIVE   NOUN

call yourself _____ Lincoln!
                 PERSON IN ROOM (MALE)

MAD LIBS® is fun to play with friends, but you can also play it by yourself! To begin with, DO NOT look at the story on the page below. Fill in the blanks on this page with the words called for. Then, using the words you have selected, fill in the blank spaces in the story.

Now you've created your own hilarious MAD LIBS® game!

I LOVE THE USA!

NOUN _____

ADJECTIVE _____

COLOR _____

ADJECTIVE _____

ADJECTIVE _____

ADJECTIVE _____

NOUN _____

NOUN _____

VERB _____

NOUN _____

PLURAL NOUN _____

ADJECTIVE _____

SAME ADJECTIVE _____

MAD LIBS
I LOVE THE USA!

Do you really love being an American _____? Then show your pride on
NOUN

the Fourth of July (or any _____ day!) by doing the following:
ADJECTIVE

- Wear red, white, and _____! Show off the colors of your country
COLOR

by wearing a/an _____ outfit that looks like it was designed from
ADJECTIVE

the American flag.

- Put a flag outside your home. Just make sure to take it down if it rains—

you don't want the flag to get _____!
ADJECTIVE

- Visit a/an _____ memorial and pay your respects. Chances are,
ADJECTIVE

there is a historical _____ a lot closer to your home than you think!
NOUN

- Do something artistic! Write a/an _____, _____ a song, or
NOUN   VERB

paint a/an _____ to show your love for your country!
NOUN

- Honor other people's _____ and beliefs. Be _____
PLURAL NOUN   ADJECTIVE

to everyone you meet, and they will be _____ to you
SAME ADJECTIVE

in return.

MAD LIBS®

GOBBLE GOBBLE MAD LIBS

Mad Libs
An Imprint of Penguin Random House

INSTRUCTIONS

MAD LIBS® is a game for people who don't like games!
It can be played by one, two, three, four, or forty.

• RIDICULOUSLY SIMPLE DIRECTIONS

In this tablet you will find stories containing blank spaces where words are left out.
One player, the READER, selects one of these stories. The READER does not tell anyone
what the story is about. Instead, he/she asks the other players, the WRITERS, to give
him/her words. These words are used to fill in the blank spaces in the story.

• TO PLAY

The READER asks each WRITER in turn to call out a word—an adjective or a noun or
whatever the space calls for—and uses them to fill in the blank spaces in the story. The
result is a MAD LIBS® game.

When the READER then reads the completed MAD LIBS® game to the other players,
they will discover that they have written a story that is fantastic, screamingly funny,
shocking, silly, crazy, or just plain dumb—depending upon which words each WRITER
called out.

• EXAMPLE (*Before* and *After*)

"_____!" he said _____
        EXCLAMATION   ADVERB

as he jumped into his convertible _____ and
                                 NOUN

drove off with his _____ wife.
                ADJECTIVE

"_____OUCH_____!" he said _____STUPIDLY_____
        EXCLAMATION   ADVERB

as he jumped into his convertible _____CAT_____ and
                                 NOUN

drove off with his _____BRAVE_____ wife.
                ADJECTIVE

MAD LIBS®

QUICK REVIEW

In case you have forgotten what adjectives, adverbs, nouns, and verbs are, here is a quick review:

An ADJECTIVE describes something or somebody. *Lumpy, soft, ugly, messy,* and *short* are adjectives.

An ADVERB tells how something is done. It modifies a verb and usually ends in "ly." *Modestly, stupidly, greedily,* and *carefully* are adverbs.

A NOUN is the name of a person, place, or thing. *Sidewalk, umbrella, bridle, bathtub,* and *nose* are nouns.

A VERB is an action word. *Run, pitch, jump,* and *swim* are verbs. Put the verbs in past tense if the directions say PAST TENSE. *Ran, pitched, jumped,* and *swam* are verbs in the past tense.

When we ask for A PLACE, we mean any sort of place: a country or city *(Spain, Cleveland)* or a room *(bathroom, kitchen).*

An EXCLAMATION or SILLY WORD is any sort of funny sound, gasp, grunt, or outcry, like *Wow!, Ouch!, Whomp!, Ick!,* and *Gadzooks!*

When we ask for specific words, like a NUMBER, a COLOR, an ANIMAL, or a PART OF THE BODY, we mean a word that is one of those things, like *seven, blue, horse,* or *head.*

When we ask for a PLURAL, it means more than one. For example, *cat* pluralized is *cats.*

MAD LIBS® is fun to play with friends, but you can also play it by yourself! To begin with, DO NOT look at the story on the page below. Fill in the blanks on this page with the words called for. Then, using the words you have selected, fill in the blank spaces in the story.

Now you've created your own hilarious MAD LIBS® game!

WHAT I'M THANKFUL FOR

ADJECTIVE _____

PERSON IN ROOM _____

NOUN _____

NOUN _____

NOUN _____

PART OF THE BODY _____

PLURAL NOUN _____

TYPE OF LIQUID _____

PART OF THE BODY _____

NOUN _____

ADJECTIVE _____

NOUN _____

NOUN _____

PLURAL NOUN _____

NUMBER _____

NOUN _____

MAD LIBS
WHAT I'M THANKFUL FOR

This Thanksgiving, I'm thankful for all the _____ things in my life.
ADJECTIVE

Even though I complain about how _____ is always
PERSON IN ROOM

getting on my nerves, or how my _____ homework is boring, or how I
NOUN

hate cleaning my _____, I know I am a very lucky _____. I have
NOUN _NOUN_

a roof over my _____. I always have enough _____ to eat
PART OF THE BODY _PLURAL NOUN_

and _____ to drink. I have a good _____ on my
TYPE OF LIQUID _PART OF THE BODY_

shoulders, and I am as healthy as a/an _____. My _____ family
NOUN _ADJECTIVE_

loves me, even when I act like a devil-_____. And my friends always
NOUN

have my best _____ at heart. Yep, I've got all the _____ I
NOUN _PLURAL NOUN_

need, and now I get to eat a/an _____-course Thanksgiving meal, too.
NUMBER

What more could a/an _____ ask for?
NOUN

MAD LIBS® is fun to play with friends, but you can also play it by yourself! To begin with, DO NOT look at the story on the page below. Fill in the blanks on this page with the words called for. Then, using the words you have selected, fill in the blank spaces in the story.

Now you've created your own hilarious MAD LIBS® game!

WHAT'S FOR DINNER?

NOUN _____

PERSON IN ROOM _____

VERB _____

PART OF THE BODY (PLURAL) _____

ADJECTIVE _____

NOUN _____

NOUN _____

PLURAL NOUN _____

TYPE OF LIQUID _____

ADJECTIVE _____

NOUN _____

NOUN _____

NOUN _____

PLURAL NOUN _____

PERSON IN ROOM (FEMALE) _____

NOUN _____

PART OF THE BODY (PLURAL) _____

MAD LIBS
WHAT'S FOR DINNER?

It was Thanksgiving, and the scent of succulent roast _____ wafted

NOUN

through my house. "_____, it's time to _____!" my

PERSON IN ROOM · VERB

mother called. I couldn't wait to get my _____ on that

PART OF THE BODY (PLURAL)

_____ Thanksgiving meal. My family sat around the dining-room

ADJECTIVE

_____ . The table was laid out with every kind of _____ imaginable.

NOUN · NOUN

There was a basket of hot buttered _____ and glasses of sparkling

PLURAL NOUN

_____ . The _____ turkey sat, steaming, next to a tureen

TYPE OF LIQUID · ADJECTIVE

of _____ gravy. A bowl of ruby-red _____ sauce, a

NOUN · NOUN

sweet-_____ casserole, and a dish of mashed _____ tempted my

NOUN · PLURAL NOUN

taste buds. But the dish I looked forward to most was Grandma

_____'s famous _____ pie. Thanksgiving is my favorite

PERSON IN ROOM (FEMALE) · NOUN

holiday, _____ down.

PART OF THE BODY (PLURAL)

MAD LIBS® is fun to play with friends, but you can also play it by yourself! To begin with, DO NOT look at the story on the page below. Fill in the blanks on this page with the words called for. Then, using the words you have selected, fill in the blank spaces in the story.

Now you've created your own hilarious MAD LIBS® game!

BALLOON GOES BUST

ADJECTIVE _____

A PLACE _____

NOUN _____

A PLACE _____

VERB ENDING IN "ING" _____

ADJECTIVE _____

EXCLAMATION _____

NOUN _____

PART OF THE BODY _____

ADJECTIVE _____

PART OF THE BODY (PLURAL) _____

PART OF THE BODY _____

PLURAL NOUN _____

PART OF THE BODY (PLURAL) _____

VERB ENDING IN "ING" _____

MAD LIBS®
BALLOON GOES BUST

This story is to be read aloud by two _____ narrators.
_____ADJECTIVE_____

TV Announcer #1: Welcome, viewers, to the thirty-third annual

_____ Thanksgiving parade.
____A PLACE____

TV Announcer #2: These floats are a/an _____ to behold.
_____NOUN_____

Look! The famous _____ turkey balloon is _____
_____A PLACE_____VERB ENDING IN "ING"_____

our way!

TV Anouncer #1: Oh no! The balloon is caught on a/an _____
_____ADJECTIVE_____

traffic light!

TV Announcer #2: _____! It appears a/an
_____EXCLAMATION_____

_____ has pierced the balloon's _____! The
____NOUN_____PART OF THE BODY____

turkey is losing air at a/an _____ rate!
_____ADJECTIVE_____

TV Announcer #1: Children along the parade route are crying their

_____ out. This is not a sight for the faint of
PART OF THE BODY (PLURAL)

_____, folks.
PART OF THE BODY

TV Announcer #2: TV viewers, if you have small _____ at home,
_____PLURAL NOUN_____

cover their _____! It's a Thanks-_____
____PART OF THE BODY (PLURAL)_____VERB ENDING IN "ING"____

disaster!

MAD LIBS® is fun to play with friends, but you can also play it by yourself! To begin with, DO NOT look at the story on the page below. Fill in the blanks on this page with the words called for. Then, using the words you have selected, fill in the blank spaces in the story.

Now you've created your own hilarious MAD LIBS® game!

HOW TO ROAST A TURKEY

PART OF THE BODY _____

NUMBER _____

TYPE OF LIQUID _____

PLURAL NOUN _____

PLURAL NOUN _____

PLURAL NOUN _____

NOUN _____

NOUN _____

ADVERB _____

PART OF THE BODY _____

NOUN _____

TYPE OF LIQUID _____

PART OF THE BODY _____

PART OF THE BODY _____

NUMBER _____

ADJECTIVE _____

ADVERB _____

MAD LIBS®
HOW TO ROAST A TURKEY

To roast a turkey, you first have to remove the turkey's neck, heart, gizzard, and

_____. Then preheat the oven to _____ degrees. Wash
   PART OF THE BODY   NUMBER

out the turkey with _____, then fill it with stuffing. Popular stuffing
                          TYPE OF LIQUID

ingredients include cubed _____, celery, raisins, onion,
                                PLURAL NOUN

and _____. Close up the turkey cavity using string or metal
          PLURAL NOUN

_____. Rub melted _____ or _____ oil all over the outside
 PLURAL NOUN   NOUN   NOUN

of the turkey, then sprinkle it _____ with salt and pepper. Place the whole
                           ADVERB

thing, _____ down, in a pan, and add several sprigs of fresh
           PART OF THE BODY

_____. Put it in the oven with a tray beneath it to catch any _____
 NOUN   TYPE OF LIQUID

that might drip from the turkey's _____. Every half hour,
                              PART OF THE BODY

stick a thermometer into the turkey's _____ to make sure it
                                 PART OF THE BODY

doesn't rise above _____ degrees. The turkey is done when its juices appear
              NUMBER

_____. Take the turkey out of the oven, carve _____, and enjoy!
 ADJECTIVE   ADVERB

MAD LIBS® is fun to play with friends, but you can also play it by yourself! To begin with, DO NOT look at the story on the page below. Fill in the blanks on this page with the words called for. Then, using the words you have selected, fill in the blank spaces in the story.

Now you've created your own hilarious MAD LIBS® game!

FOOTBALL FIASCO

PLURAL NOUN _____

A PLACE _____

PLURAL NOUN _____

NUMBER _____

SAME NUMBER _____

NOUN _____

ADJECTIVE _____

ADVERB _____

NUMBER _____

VERB (PAST TENSE) _____

ADJECTIVE _____

ADJECTIVE _____

VERB ENDING IN "ING" _____

PART OF THE BODY _____

ADVERB _____

VERB (PAST TENSE) _____

ADVERB _____

MAD LIBS®
FOOTBALL FIASCO

It was the fourth quarter in the big Thanksgiving Day matchup between the

Detroit _____ and (the) _____ _____. The score was
　　　　　 PLURAL NOUN　　　　　　　　 A PLACE　　　 PLURAL NOUN

tied _____–_____, and you could feel the tension throughout
　　　 NUMBER　　 SAME NUMBER

_____ Stadium. With five minutes left in the game, Detroit had just
　 NOUN

called a time-out when, suddenly, fans noticed a/an _____ commotion
　　　　　　　　　　　　　　　　　　　　　　　　 ADJECTIVE

down on the field. A turkey had somehow gotten loose and was running

_____ across the _____-yard line! The crowd _____ with
　 ADVERB　　　　　　　　 NUMBER　　　　　　　　　 VERB (PAST TENSE)

laughter as the referees chased the _____ bird. Members of both teams
　　　　　　　　　　　　　　　　　　 ADJECTIVE

joined the refs in chasing the _____ turkey, which tried to outrun the
　　　　　　　　　　　　　　　 ADJECTIVE

Detroit _____ back who eventually caught him by the
　　　　 VERB ENDING IN "ING"

_____. After that, the tension throughout the stadium _____
 PART OF THE BODY　　　　　　　　　　　　　　　　　　　　　　　　 ADVERB

broken, the fans hardly cared who won or _____. The runaway
　　　　　　　　　　　　　　　　　　　 VERB (PAST TENSE)

turkey had _____ stolen the show!
　　　　　 ADVERB

MAD LIBS® is fun to play with friends, but you can also play it by yourself! To begin with, DO NOT look at the story on the page below. Fill in the blanks on this page with the words called for. Then, using the words you have selected, fill in the blank spaces in the story.

Now you've created your own hilarious MAD LIBS® game!

THE FIRST THANKSGIVING

NUMBER _____

A PLACE _____

NOUN _____

ADJECTIVE _____

PLURAL NOUN _____

ADJECTIVE _____

PERSON IN ROOM _____

PLURAL NOUN _____

PLURAL NOUN _____

ADJECTIVE _____

ADJECTIVE _____

NUMBER _____

PLURAL NOUN _____

ADJECTIVE _____

NOUN _____

ADVERB _____

PLURAL NOUN _____

ADJECTIVE _____

MAD LIBS
THE FIRST THANKSGIVING

In late 1620, _____ Pilgrims arrived at Plymouth Rock. They had come all
                NUMBER

the way from (the) _____ to find religious freedom in America. But life
                  A PLACE

in the New _____ was not easy. Their first winter was _____, and
           NOUN   ADJECTIVE

many _____ fell ill. Luckily, the following year, a/an _____ Native
     PLURAL NOUN   ADJECTIVE

American named _____ taught the Pilgrims how to grow crops like
               PERSON IN ROOM

corn and _____. By that November, the Pilgrims had plenty of
         PLURAL NOUN

_____ to harvest, so they decided to have a/an _____ feast. They
PLURAL NOUN   ADJECTIVE

invited their _____ Native American friends to join them, and the festival
              ADJECTIVE

lasted for _____ days. They ate the _____ of their harvest as well as
           NUMBER   PLURAL NOUN

deer and several _____ birds. It was a/an _____ to remember,
                 ADJECTIVE   NOUN

and has since become known as the first Thanksgiving. While the menu has

changed _____ over the years, Thanksgiving is still a time to celebrate
        ADVERB

our _____ and our _____ fortune.
    PLURAL NOUN   ADJECTIVE

MAD LIBS® is fun to play with friends, but you can also play it by yourself! To begin with, DO NOT look at the story on the page below. Fill in the blanks on this page with the words called for. Then, using the words you have selected, fill in the blank spaces in the story.

Now you've created your own hilarious MAD LIBS® game!

TRAVEL DISASTER

ADJECTIVE _____

ADJECTIVE _____

A PLACE _____

PERSON IN ROOM (FEMALE) _____

PERSON IN ROOM (MALE) _____

NOUN _____

NOUN _____

VERB (PAST TENSE) _____

NUMBER _____

NOUN _____

NOUN _____

ADJECTIVE _____

ADJECTIVE _____

ADJECTIVE _____

ADVERB _____

PLURAL NOUN _____

NOUN _____

MAD LIBS
TRAVEL DISASTER

Flying for Thanksgiving is always a/an _____ nightmare, but this year

ADJECTIVE

was particularly _____. My family was supposed to go to (the) boring

ADJECTIVE

old _____ to visit my aunt _____ and uncle

A PLACE   PERSON IN ROOM (FEMALE)

_____. But when we got to the airport, a/an _____ storm

PERSON IN ROOM (MALE)   NOUN

delayed our flight. After we boarded the _____, we _____

NOUN   VERB (PAST TENSE)

on the runway for _____ hours because of a mechanical difficulty. They

NUMBER

eventually drove us back to the gate and rescheduled us on a new _____.

NOUN

When we finally took off, the pilot said, "Welcome aboard _____ Airlines.

NOUN

Enjoy your _____ flight to Hawaii." *Hawaii?!* We were on the wrong

ADJECTIVE

plane! But we embraced the _____ screwup. Hawaii was a far more

ADJECTIVE

_____ destination than our aunt and uncle's! We laughed _____

ADJECTIVE   ADVERB

the whole flight there and enjoyed frozen coconut _____ on the beach

PLURAL NOUN

for our Thanksgiving dinner. It was a/an _____ to remember!

NOUN

MAD LIBS® is fun to play with friends, but you can also play it by yourself! To begin with, DO NOT look at the story on the page below. Fill in the blanks on this page with the words called for. Then, using the words you have selected, fill in the blank spaces in the story.

Now you've created your own hilarious MAD LIBS® game!

HOW THANKSGIVING BECAME A HOLIDAY

ADJECTIVE _____

PLURAL NOUN _____

ADJECTIVE _____

A PLACE _____

VERB _____

ADJECTIVE _____

PLURAL NOUN _____

PLURAL NOUN _____

ADJECTIVE _____

ADJECTIVE _____

PERSON IN ROOM _____

ADJECTIVE _____

PLURAL NOUN _____

Even though the first Thanksgiving took place in 1621, Thanksgiving didn't

become a national holiday until a/an _____ woman named Sarah Josepha
ADJECTIVE

Hale came along. In the 1800s, Ms. Hale was one of the first female

_____ at a/an _____ magazine. She was famous throughout
PLURAL NOUN   ADJECTIVE

(the) _____ for her articles encouraging women to _____,
A PLACE   VERB

exercise, and get a/an _____ education. But one of Sarah's biggest ideas
ADJECTIVE

was to make Thanksgiving a national holiday, to be celebrated by _____
PLURAL NOUN

across America. At the time, Thanksgiving was only celebrated by a few

_____. Sarah wrote _____ letters to one president after another,
PLURAL NOUN   ADJECTIVE

trying to convince them of how _____ Thanksgiving was. No one
ADJECTIVE

listened—at least not until President _____. He/She declared
PERSON IN ROOM

Thanksgiving a/an _____ holiday in 1863, and _____ everywhere
ADJECTIVE   PLURAL NOUN

have been celebrating it ever since.

MAD LIBS® is fun to play with friends, but you can also play it by yourself! To begin with, DO NOT look at the story on the page below. Fill in the blanks on this page with the words called for. Then, using the words you have selected, fill in the blank spaces in the story.

Now you've created your own hilarious MAD LIBS® game!

LIFE'S A MAIZE

ADJECTIVE _____

NOUN _____

ADJECTIVE _____

NOUN _____

NOUN _____

VERB ENDING IN "ING" _____

NOUN _____

PLURAL NOUN _____

PLURAL NOUN _____

NOUN _____

PLURAL NOUN _____

PLURAL NOUN _____

ADJECTIVE _____

PLURAL NOUN _____

NOUN _____

NOUN _____

PLURAL NOUN _____

NOUN _____

MAD LIBS®
LIFE'S A MAIZE

Corn is a/an _____ staple of the autumn harvest, and it can be
                  ADJECTIVE

found on many a Thanksgiving _____. But corn has many other
                                      NOUN

_____ uses, too! Corn can be found in:
      ADJECTIVE

Food products: Aside from corn on the _____, you can find
                                                  NOUN

corn in _____ butter, _____ gum, and
              NOUN   VERB ENDING IN "ING"

_____ sodas.
      NOUN

Plastics: Plastics made from corn _____ are more popular than ever
                                         PLURAL NOUN

before. You can often recycle plastic _____ made from corn, too!
                                            PLURAL NOUN

Fuel: Ethanol is a popular corn _____ used to fuel cars,
                                         NOUN

_____, and even rocket _____.
   PLURAL NOUN   PLURAL NOUN

Household products: Manufacturers often use corn to help make

_____ soaps, scented _____, _____ polish,
   ADJECTIVE   PLURAL NOUN   NOUN

and even _____ batteries!
               NOUN

Everywhere you look, corn _____ can be found. It's not just a
                              PLURAL NOUN

super food, it's a super _____, too!
                               NOUN

MAD LIBS® is fun to play with friends, but you can also play it by yourself! To begin with, DO NOT look at the story on the page below. Fill in the blanks on this page with the words called for. Then, using the words you have selected, fill in the blank spaces in the story.

Now you've created your own hilarious MAD LIBS® game!

STUFFING YOURSELF SILLY

NOUN _____

NOUN _____

ADJECTIVE _____

PLURAL NOUN _____

PLURAL NOUN _____

PLURAL NOUN _____

NOUN _____

NOUN _____

ADJECTIVE _____

SILLY WORD _____

SAME SILLY WORD _____

PLURAL NOUN _____

PART OF THE BODY _____

PLURAL NOUN _____

NOUN _____

NOUN _____

MAD LIBS®
STUFFING YOURSELF SILLY

Thanksgiving is not a/an _____ to be taken lightly. In order to eat as
NOUN

much _____ as possible, you need to have a/an _____
NOUN   ADJECTIVE

strategy. Follow these handy dandy _____ , and you, too, can own
PLURAL NOUN

Thanksgiving.

Tip #1: Load up on the most popular _____ first. Mashed
PLURAL NOUN

_____ and gravy tend to be the first to go, and sweet potato
PLURAL NOUN

_____ and cranberry _____ go fast, too. Get 'em while
NOUN   NOUN

they're _____!
ADJECTIVE

Tip #2: Stick with light meat. Dark meat contains more _____
SILLY WORD

than light meat, and everyone knows that _____ makes you
SAME SILLY WORD

sleepy when you eat it. If you're sleeping, you won't be able to eat

_____!
PLURAL NOUN

Tip #3: Don't worry about saving room in your _____
PART OF THE BODY

for dessert. Studies by famous _____ show that no matter how
PLURAL NOUN

much _____ you've eaten, you always have room for dessert—
NOUN

especially if it's _____ pie!
NOUN

MAD LIBS® is fun to play with friends, but you can also play it by yourself! To begin with, DO NOT look at the story on the page below. Fill in the blanks on this page with the words called for. Then, using the words you have selected, fill in the blank spaces in the story.

Now you've created your own hilarious MAD LIBS® game!

CANADIAN THANKSGIVING

NUMBER _____

A PLACE _____

PERSON IN ROOM _____

ADJECTIVE _____

NOUN _____

ADJECTIVE _____

PLURAL NOUN _____

PLURAL NOUN _____

ADJECTIVE _____

MAD LIBS®
CANADIAN THANKSGIVING

Did you know that the first Thanksgiving in North America was actually in

Canada, _____ years before the Pilgrims arrived in (the) _____?
NUMBER   A PLACE

The first Canadian Thanksgiving took place in 1578, when explorer

_____ arrived in Newfoundland and wanted to give thanks for
PERSON IN ROOM

his/her _____ arrival in the New World. Beginning in 1957, Canadian
ADJECTIVE

Parliament declared that the second Monday in October would be a day to

celebrate "the bountiful _____ with which Canada has been blessed."
NOUN

Today, Canadians celebrate their own _____ Thanksgiving, which is
ADJECTIVE

similar to American Thanksgiving in many ways. Canadians eat turkey and

_____, and they watch Canadian football, too! Most importantly,
PLURAL NOUN

Canadians give thanks for all of their _____. And what's more
PLURAL NOUN

_____ than that, eh?
ADJECTIVE

MAD LIBS® is fun to play with friends, but you can also play it by yourself! To begin with, DO NOT look at the story on the page below. Fill in the blanks on this page with the words called for. Then, using the words you have selected, fill in the blank spaces in the story.

Now you've created your own hilarious MAD LIBS® game!

A THANKSGIVING SPECIAL

A PLACE _____

ADJECTIVE _____

VERB (PAST TENSE) _____

NOUN _____

EXCLAMATION _____

NOUN _____

NOUN _____

ADJECTIVE _____

PERSON IN ROOM (MALE) _____

NOUN _____

ADJECTIVE _____

ADJECTIVE _____

PLURAL NOUN _____

PLURAL NOUN _____

NOUN _____

NOUN _____

NOUN _____

PLURAL NOUN _____

PLURAL NOUN _____

NOUN _____

MAD LIBS
A THANKSGIVING SPECIAL

It was Thanksgiving, and all the people in (the) _____ were ready for
                                              A PLACE

their annual Thanksgiving celebration. There was just one problem: The

_____ turkey was missing! The townspeople _____ high and
ADJECTIVE   VERB (PAST TENSE)

low, but the _____ was nowhere to be found. "_____!" little Sally
             NOUN   EXCLAMATION

_____ said. "We can't have Thanksgiving without a/an _____!" Just
NOUN   NOUN

then, a/an _____ figure appeared. It was _____, the mean old
           ADJECTIVE   PERSON IN ROOM (MALE)

_____ who lived on top of a/an _____ hill and never came to visit.
NOUN   ADJECTIVE

"I took your _____ turkey!" he shouted. "You _____ are so
             ADJECTIVE   PLURAL NOUN

thankful, but what do you have to be thankful for?" "We have our friends, our

families, and our _____!" said little Sally _____. "Just because
                  PLURAL NOUN   NOUN

you don't have any doesn't mean you should ruin our Thanksgiving, you mean

old _____!" The townspeople cheered, and the grumpy _____ saw the
    NOUN   NOUN

error of his ways. He returned the town turkey and joined the _____
                                                              PLURAL NOUN

in celebration. "Happy Thanksgiving to _____ everywhere!" little Sally
                                       PLURAL NOUN

_____ cheered.
NOUN

MAD LIBS® is fun to play with friends, but you can also play it by yourself! To begin with, DO NOT look at the story on the page below. Fill in the blanks on this page with the words called for. Then, using the words you have selected, fill in the blank spaces in the story.

Now you've created your own hilarious MAD LIBS® game!

PILGRIM KID

ADJECTIVE _____

PLURAL NOUN _____

NOUN _____

PART OF THE BODY _____

PLURAL NOUN _____

NOUN _____

NOUN _____

PERSON IN ROOM (MALE) _____

PERSON IN ROOM (FEMALE) _____

ADJECTIVE _____

ADJECTIVE _____

ADVERB _____

PART OF THE BODY (PLURAL) _____

NOUN _____

VERB (PAST TENSE) _____

MAD LIBS®
PILGRIM KID

Dear Ye Olde Diary,

Life as a wee Pilgrim child is more _____ by the day. Today, Mother sent
                                    ADJECTIVE

me to the garden to pick some fresh _____ for supper. The sun was
                                     PLURAL NOUN

hot, and I was wearing my black-and-white _____, which did not keep
                                           NOUN

my _____ cool. Afterward, Father insisted I help him hunt for
   PART OF THE BODY

_____ using a bow and _____, but we only shot one small
PLURAL NOUN   NOUN

_____. Alas! While Mother and Father cooked dinner, I went to play
NOUN

with my brother _____ and sister _____, but
                PERSON IN ROOM (MALE)   PERSON IN ROOM (FEMALE)

we hath only one toy—a/an _____ rock. Our _____ game of Kick the
                          ADJECTIVE   ADJECTIVE

Rock soon became _____ tiresome. Nay, we were bored out of our
                 ADVERB

_____! Aye, life as a Pilgrim _____ is not all it's
PART OF THE BODY (PLURAL)   NOUN

_____ up to be!
VERB (PAST TENSE)

MAD LIBS® is fun to play with friends, but you can also play it by yourself! To begin with, DO NOT look at the story on the page below. Fill in the blanks on this page with the words called for. Then, using the words you have selected, fill in the blank spaces in the story.

Now you've created your own hilarious MAD LIBS® game!

THE LAST TURKEY

NOUN _____

A PLACE _____

ADJECTIVE _____

TYPE OF ANIMAL _____

ADJECTIVE _____

PERSON IN ROOM _____

NOUN _____

PART OF THE BODY (PLURAL) _____

PLURAL NOUN _____

PLURAL NOUN _____

VERB ENDING IN "ING" _____

VERB ENDING IN "ING" _____

SAME VERB ENDING IN "ING" _____

PERSON IN ROOM (FEMALE) _____

ADJECTIVE _____

ADJECTIVE _____

ADJECTIVE _____

MAD LIBS
THE LAST TURKEY

It was Thanksgiving, and our family didn't have a/an _____ to roast. We

_{NOUN}

hopped into the car and drove to (the) _____, but they were all out of

_{A PLACE}

_____ turkeys. "We have ham and duck and _____, though!"

_{ADJECTIVE}   _{TYPE OF ANIMAL}

said the man at the deli counter. "It's not Thanksgiving without a/an _____

_{ADJECTIVE}

turkey!" my dad replied. So we got back into the car and drove to

_____'s Grocery. They had one turkey left—but another _____

_{PERSON IN ROOM}   _{NOUN}

grabbed the turkey before we could get our _____ on it.

_{PART OF THE BODY (PLURAL)}

"Come on, _____," said my mom. "Let's just go out for Chinese

_{PLURAL NOUN}

_____ instead." But on the drive to the restaurant, we spotted a wild

_{PLURAL NOUN}

turkey _____ across the road. "Are you _____

_{VERB ENDING IN "ING"}   _{VERB ENDING IN "ING"}

what I'm _____?" my sister _____ said. We

_{SAME VERB ENDING IN "ING"}   _{PERSON IN ROOM (FEMALE)}

all got out of the car and chased the _____ bird down the road. But once

_{ADJECTIVE}

we got the _____ turkey home, we couldn't bear to eat him—so we made

_{ADJECTIVE}

him our _____ family pet instead!

_{ADJECTIVE}

MAD LIBS® is fun to play with friends, but you can also play it by yourself! To begin with, DO NOT look at the story on the page below. Fill in the blanks on this page with the words called for. Then, using the words you have selected, fill in the blank spaces in the story.

Now you've created your own hilarious MAD LIBS® game!

THANKS, SQUANTO

NOUN _____

A PLACE _____

VERB (PAST TENSE) _____

VERB (PAST TENSE) _____

ADJECTIVE _____

ADJECTIVE _____

VERB _____

PLURAL NOUN _____

PLURAL NOUN _____

PLURAL NOUN _____

ADJECTIVE _____

ADJECTIVE _____

MAD LIBS®
THANKS, SQUANTO

The first Thanksgiving would never have been possible without Squanto, a

Native American _____ . Squanto had learned to speak English in (the)
NOUN

_____ , England. When Squanto left England and _____
A PLACE   VERB (PAST TENSE)

back to America, he discovered that his tribe no longer _____
                                                          VERB (PAST TENSE)

there. In 1620, Squanto settled with the _____ Pilgrims, who had just
                                          ADJECTIVE

survived a/an _____ winter. The Pilgrims, it turned out, had no idea how
              ADJECTIVE

to _____ in the New World. Luckily, Squanto taught them how to plant
   VERB

_____ , fish for _____ , and hunt for wild _____ .
PLURAL NOUN   PLURAL NOUN   PLURAL NOUN

Without Squanto's help, the Pilgrims would never have survived, much less

had food to make a/an _____ feast for the first Thanksgiving. Maybe this
                       ADJECTIVE

Thanksgiving we should give thanks for Squanto. After all, if it weren't for him,

we wouldn't celebrate this _____ holiday!
                            ADJECTIVE

MAD LIBS® is fun to play with friends, but you can also play it by yourself! To begin with, DO NOT look at the story on the page below. Fill in the blanks on this page with the words called for. Then, using the words you have selected, fill in the blank spaces in the story.

Now you've created your own hilarious MAD LIBS® game!

THANKSGIVING FACTS

PLURAL NOUN _____

PLURAL NOUN _____

NUMBER _____

ADJECTIVE _____

NOUN _____

NOUN _____

NOUN _____

PLURAL NOUN _____

PLURAL NOUN _____

PLURAL NOUN _____

PLURAL NOUN _____

PLURAL NOUN _____

VERB (PAST TENSE) _____

PLURAL NOUN _____

PLURAL NOUN _____

- Each Thanksgiving, _____ in the United States consume
  PLURAL NOUN

  forty-six million _____. That's almost _____ pounds
  PLURAL NOUN   NUMBER

  of turkey per person!

- _____ inventor and politician Benjamin Franklin wanted the
  ADJECTIVE

  turkey to be the national _____ of the United States.
  NOUN

- TV dinners originated when a company called _____had
  NOUN

  too much leftover frozen _____ after Thanksgiving; they
  NOUN

  began packaging the turkey with potatoes, _____, and
  PLURAL NOUN

  other foods into the first frozen meals.

- The tradition of Thanksgiving football began when the owner of the

  Detroit _____ wanted to build up the team's loyal
  PLURAL NOUN

  _____. On Thanksgiving Day 1934, they played the
  PLURAL NOUN

  Chicago _____ and lost.
  PLURAL NOUN

- According to *Guinness World* _____, the largest
  PLURAL NOUN

  pumpkin pie ever _____ weighed two thousand
  VERB (PAST TENSE)

  _____ and was over twelve _____ long.
  PLURAL NOUN   PLURAL NOUN

MAD LIBS® is fun to play with friends, but you can also play it by yourself! To begin with, DO NOT look at the story on the page below. Fill in the blanks on this page with the words called for. Then, using the words you have selected, fill in the blank spaces in the story.

Now you've created your own hilarious MAD LIBS® game!

PARDON THAT TURKEY

PLURAL NOUN _____

ADJECTIVE _____

PLURAL NOUN _____

ADJECTIVE _____

NOUN _____

COLOR _____

PLURAL NOUN _____

A PLACE _____

ADJECTIVE _____

VERB _____

ADJECTIVE _____

PERSON IN ROOM _____

ADJECTIVE _____

ADJECTIVE _____

VERB (PAST TENSE) _____

MAD LIBS
PARDON THAT TURKEY

Each year, the president of the United _____ is presented with two

PLURAL NOUN

_____ turkeys to pardon. That means he spares them from being eaten by

ADJECTIVE

_____ on Thanksgiving. The president formally pardons the _____

PLURAL NOUN   ADJECTIVE

birds in the _____ Garden of the _____ House, while television

NOUN   COLOR

_____ and families from all over (the) _____ witness the

PLURAL NOUN   A PLACE

_____ spectacle. The pardoned turkeys get to _____ out the rest of

ADJECTIVE   VERB

their days on a/an _____ farm at President _____'s estate,

ADJECTIVE   PERSON IN ROOM

Mount Vernon. To this day, twenty-two _____ turkeys have been

ADJECTIVE

pardoned by the _____ president. To those turkeys, it must feel like

ADJECTIVE

they've _____ the lottery!

VERB (PAST TENSE)

MAD LIBS® is fun to play with friends, but you can also play it by yourself! To begin with, DO NOT look at the story on the page below. Fill in the blanks on this page with the words called for. Then, using the words you have selected, fill in the blank spaces in the story.

Now you've created your own hilarious MAD LIBS® game!

PICK YOUR PIE

VERB ENDING IN "ING" _____

NOUN _____

ADJECTIVE _____

ADJECTIVE _____

PLURAL NOUN _____

ADJECTIVE _____

ADJECTIVE _____

VERB _____

ADJECTIVE _____

ADJECTIVE _____

ADJECTIVE _____

NOUN _____

ADJECTIVE _____

NOUN _____

MAD LIBS®
PICK YOUR PIE

Do you love _____ pie on Thanksgiving? Who doesn't! The
          VERB ENDING IN "ING"

only problem is choosing which _____ to eat! Take this quiz to find
                                      NOUN

out your _____ preference!
           ADJECTIVE

1. Your favorite kind of pie involves (a) _____ slices of fruit,
                                               ADJECTIVE

   (b) nuts and _____, or (c) _____ vegetables.
                   PLURAL NOUN   ADJECTIVE

2. Of these three _____ options, your favorite color of food to
                      ADJECTIVE

   _____ is (a) yellow, (b) brown, or (c) orange.
       VERB

3. Do you prefer your food to be (a) gooey and sweet with a touch

   of _____ cinnamon, (b) sweet with a sprinkling of
          ADJECTIVE

   _____ salt, or (c) mushy and _____.
       ADJECTIVE   ADJECTIVE

If you picked mostly *a*'s, apple _____ is your favorite Thanksgiving
                                         NOUN

treat. If you picked mostly *b*'s, you are a fan of _____ pecan pie.
                                                        ADJECTIVE

If you picked mostly *c*'s, you can't say no to a heaping _____ of
                                                              NOUN

pumpkin or sweet potato pie!

MAD LIBS® is fun to play with friends, but you can also play it by yourself! To begin with, DO NOT look at the story on the page below. Fill in the blanks on this page with the words called for. Then, using the words you have selected, fill in the blank spaces in the story.

Now you've created your own hilarious MAD LIBS® game!

EXCERPT FROM A THANKSGIVING PAGEANT

ADJECTIVE _____

NOUN _____

ADJECTIVE _____

PLURAL NOUN _____

PLURAL NOUN _____

ADJECTIVE _____

PLURAL NOUN _____

NOUN _____

ADJECTIVE _____

ADJECTIVE _____

PLURAL NOUN _____

ADJECTIVE _____

EXCLAMATION _____

NOUN _____

ADJECTIVE _____

This is a/an _____ scene from a children's Thanksgiving _____
\
ADJECTIVE   NOUN

pageant. This scene can be read aloud by several _____
\
ADJECTIVE

_____.
\
PLURAL NOUN

Pilgrim #1: Welcome to the first Thanksgiving, our dear friends and

_____!
\
PLURAL NOUN

Pilgrim #2: We want to say a/an _____ thank-you to our Native
\
ADJECTIVE

American _____, without whom this _____ would
\
PLURAL NOUN   NOUN

not be possible!

Native American #1: Thank you, _____ Pilgrims! We appreciate
\
ADJECTIVE

your sharing this _____ harvest with us.
\
ADJECTIVE

Native American #2: Yes, we can't wait to eat these tasty _____!
\
PLURAL NOUN

We are thankful for your _____ friendship.
\
ADJECTIVE

Pilgrim #1: _____! Let's eat this _____ before it gets
\
EXCLAMATION   NOUN

_____!
\
ADJECTIVE

MAD LIBS® is fun to play with friends, but you can also play it by yourself! To begin with, DO NOT look at the story on the page below. Fill in the blanks on this page with the words called for. Then, using the words you have selected, fill in the blank spaces in the story.

Now you've created your own hilarious MAD LIBS® game!

WHAT IN THE GOURD?

PLURAL NOUN _____

PLURAL NOUN _____

ADJECTIVE _____

PLURAL NOUN _____

PLURAL NOUN _____

ADJECTIVE _____

ADJECTIVE _____

ADJECTIVE _____

PLURAL NOUN _____

TYPE OF LIQUID _____

PLURAL NOUN _____

PLURAL NOUN _____

PLURAL NOUN _____

VERB _____

NOUN _____

MAD LIBS

WHAT IN THE GOURD?

Gourds are funny little _____ often used to decorate holiday
PLURAL NOUN

_____ at Thanksgiving. But what *are* these _____ little
PLURAL NOUN   ADJECTIVE

_____? They may look like tiny pumpkins or miniature
PLURAL NOUN

_____, but you don't want to eat them. They smell _____ and
PLURAL NOUN   ADJECTIVE

they taste _____, too. Gourds are related to squash and pumpkins, and
ADJECTIVE

are considered a/an _____ fruit. But unlike those _____, they
ADJECTIVE   PLURAL NOUN

are used only for decoration or to store _____ or other _____.
TYPE OF LIQUID   PLURAL NOUN

They are also often used as musical _____. Gourds sure are adorable little
PLURAL NOUN

_____, but look, don't _____, when you see them on your
PLURAL NOUN   VERB

Thanksgiving _____!
NOUN

MAD LIBS® is fun to play with friends, but you can also play it by yourself! To begin with, DO NOT look at the story on the page below. Fill in the blanks on this page with the words called for. Then, using the words you have selected, fill in the blank spaces in the story.

Now you've created your own hilarious MAD LIBS® game!

TOM THE TURKEY

PLURAL NOUN _____

NOUN _____

PLURAL NOUN _____

NOUN _____

NOUN _____

PART OF THE BODY _____

NOUN _____

NOUN _____

PLURAL NOUN _____

NOUN _____

PLURAL NOUN _____

NOUN _____

PLURAL NOUN _____

ADJECTIVE _____

NOUN _____

NOUN _____

On Christmas, _____ get visited by Santa Claus. On Easter, the
                    PLURAL NOUN

Easter Bunny hops into your _____. But who comes to give you
                                NOUN

_____ on Thanksgiving? Tom the Turkey, that's who! If you have been
PLURAL NOUN

a thankful little girl or _____, Tom the Turkey just might come visit your
                             NOUN

_____ on Thanksgiving. While you rest your pretty little
    NOUN

_____ during your post-meal nap, this magical _____
    PART OF THE BODY   NOUN

flies through the _____ and leaves cornucopias filled with _____
                      NOUN   PLURAL NOUN

at your front _____. Your cornucopia might be filled with candy, presents,
                  NOUN

and _____, if you're lucky. But if you've been an ungrateful little
        PLURAL NOUN

_____, you'll get a cornucopia filled with _____! So be a/an
    NOUN   PLURAL NOUN

_____ little _____, and maybe this year Tom the Turkey
    ADJECTIVE   NOUN

will come to your _____!
                      NOUN

MAD LIBS®

HISTORY OF THE WORLD
MAD LIBS

Mad Libs
An Imprint of Penguin Random House

MAD LIBS

INSTRUCTIONS

MAD LIBS® is a game for people who don't like games!
It can be played by one, two, three, four, or forty.

• RIDICULOUSLY SIMPLE DIRECTIONS

In this tablet you will find stories containing blank spaces where words are left out.
One player, the READER, selects one of these stories. The READER does not tell anyone
what the story is about. Instead, he/she asks the other players, the WRITERS, to give
him/her words. These words are used to fill in the blank spaces in the story.

• TO PLAY

The READER asks each WRITER in turn to call out a word—an adjective or a noun or
whatever the space calls for—and uses them to fill in the blank spaces in the story. The
result is a MAD LIBS® game.

When the READER then reads the completed MAD LIBS® game to the other players,
they will discover that they have written a story that is fantastic, screamingly funny,
shocking, silly, crazy, or just plain dumb—depending upon which words each WRITER
called out.

• EXAMPLE (*Before* and *After*)

"_____!" he said _____
     EXCLAMATION   ADVERB

as he jumped into his convertible _____ and
                                        NOUN

drove off with his _____ wife.
                      ADJECTIVE

"_____OUCH_____!" he said _____STUPIDLY_____
     EXCLAMATION   ADVERB

as he jumped into his convertible _____CAT_____ and
                                        NOUN

drove off with his _____BRAVE_____ wife.
                      ADJECTIVE

QUICK REVIEW

In case you have forgotten what adjectives, adverbs, nouns, and verbs are, here is a quick review:

An ADJECTIVE describes something or somebody. *Lumpy, soft, ugly, messy,* and *short* are adjectives.

An ADVERB tells how something is done. It modifies a verb and usually ends in "ly." *Modestly, stupidly, greedily,* and *carefully* are adverbs.

A NOUN is the name of a person, place, or thing. *Sidewalk, umbrella, bridle, bathtub,* and *nose* are nouns.

A VERB is an action word. *Run, pitch, jump,* and *swim* are verbs. Put the verbs in past tense if the directions say PAST TENSE. *Ran, pitched, jumped,* and *swam* are verbs in the past tense.

When we ask for A PLACE, we mean any sort of place: a country or city *(Spain, Cleveland)* or a room *(bathroom, kitchen).*

An EXCLAMATION or SILLY WORD is any sort of funny sound, gasp, grunt, or outcry, like *Wow!, Ouch!, Whomp!, Ick!,* and *Gadzooks!*

When we ask for specific words, like a NUMBER, a COLOR, an ANIMAL, or a PART OF THE BODY, we mean a word that is one of those things, like *seven, blue, horse,* or *head.*

When we ask for a PLURAL, it means more than one. For example, *cat* pluralized is *cats.*

MAD LIBS® is fun to play with friends, but you can also play it by yourself! To begin with, DO NOT look at the story on the page below. Fill in the blanks on this page with the words called for. Then, using the words you have selected, fill in the blank spaces in the story.

Now you've created your own hilarious MAD LIBS® game!

LIGHT MY FIRE

PART OF THE BODY (PLURAL) _____

ADJECTIVE _____

ADJECTIVE _____

ADJECTIVE _____

A PLACE _____

ANIMAL _____

PART OF THE BODY _____

NOUN _____

ADJECTIVE _____

ADVERB _____

EXCLAMATION _____

ADJECTIVE _____

PERSON IN ROOM _____

NOUN _____

MAD LIBS®
LIGHT MY FIRE

At one time man walked on four _____, spoke in
PART OF THE BODY (PLURAL)

_____ grunts, and did not know how to make a/an _____ fire.
ADJECTIVE   ADJECTIVE

Here is the story of the day that changed mankind forever (translated from the

_____ cave-speak):
ADJECTIVE

Caveman #1: It's colder than (the) _____ in this cave. Even my
A PLACE

warmest _____ fur won't keep my _____ from
ANIMAL   PART OF THE BODY

shivering.

Caveman #2: If only there was a way to make the cold _____
NOUN

warmer.

Caveman #1: I'm bored. I think I'll play with these _____ sticks
ADJECTIVE

of wood.

Caveman #2: Why don't you rub them _____ together and see
ADVERB

what happens?

Caveman #1: _____! There's smoke coming off these
EXCLAMATION

_____ sticks!
ADJECTIVE

Caveman #2: Ouch! It's hot! In the name of _____—we made
PERSON IN ROOM

heat!

Caveman #1: We shall call this magical flaming _____ _fire_.
NOUN

MAD LIBS® is fun to play with friends, but you can also play it by yourself! To begin with, DO NOT look at the story on the page below. Fill in the blanks on this page with the words called for. Then, using the words you have selected, fill in the blank spaces in the story.

Now you've created your own hilarious MAD LIBS® game!

EUREKA!

PLURAL NOUN _____

OCCUPATION (PLURAL) _____

NOUN _____

PLURAL NOUN _____

PLURAL NOUN _____

NOUN _____

NOUN _____

PLURAL NOUN _____

PLURAL NOUN _____

ADJECTIVE _____

NOUN _____

NOUN _____

NOUN _____

MAD LIBS

EUREKA!

Throughout history, inventors have been responsible for everyday things like

computers, cars, and _____. These are some of the most famous

PLURAL NOUN

_____ known today:

OCCUPATION (PLURAL)

Benjamin Franklin was not only a founding _____ of the United

NOUN

States, he also invented many things, including bifocal glasses, which allow

people to see _____ near and far. He also invented the lightning rod,

PLURAL NOUN

which protects _____ from electric bolts of _____.

PLURAL NOUN   NOUN

Johannes Gutenberg was a German _____ who invented the printing

NOUN

press, a machine that could print words and _____ to make books,

PLURAL NOUN

newspapers, and _____.

PLURAL NOUN

Thomas Edison was a/an _____ inventor perhaps best known for

ADJECTIVE

making a lightbulb that the average _____ could use. He also invented

NOUN

the phonograph, which was the first _____ to be able to record the

NOUN

human _____ and then play it back.

NOUN

MAD LIBS® is fun to play with friends, but you can also play it by yourself! To begin with, DO NOT look at the story on the page below. Fill in the blanks on this page with the words called for. Then, using the words you have selected, fill in the blank spaces in the story.

Now you've created your own hilarious MAD LIBS® game!

NEWS FLASH!: WORLD NOT FLAT

ADJECTIVE _____

ADJECTIVE _____

NOUN _____

TYPE OF FOOD _____

PLURAL NOUN _____

VERB (PAST TENSE) _____

NOUN _____

PLURAL NOUN _____

ADJECTIVE _____

SILLY WORD _____

ADJECTIVE _____

PERSON IN ROOM (FEMALE) _____

ADJECTIVE _____

MAD LIBS®
NEWS FLASH!:
WORLD NOT FLAT

In _____ news for explorers everywhere, it has recently been discovered
    ADJECTIVE

that the Earth is round. That's right: Earth is shaped like a/an _____
                                                               ADJECTIVE

ball! For as long as any _____ can remember, it has been widely believed
                                NOUN

that the Earth is as flat as a/an _____. Many _____
                                      TYPE OF FOOD   PLURAL NOUN

believed that if you _____ too far, you would fall off the edge of
                        VERB (PAST TENSE)

the _____. Now, some _____ are trying to prove that the
       NOUN   PLURAL NOUN

_____ Earth rotates around the sun, though most people think this is a
ADJECTIVE

bunch of _____! We will keep you updated as this _____
            SILLY WORD   ADJECTIVE

story develops. In the meantime, back to you, _____, with
                                           PERSON IN ROOM (FEMALE)

the day's _____ stories.
         ADJECTIVE

MAD LIBS® is fun to play with friends, but you can also play it by yourself! To begin with, DO NOT look at the story on the page below. Fill in the blanks on this page with the words called for. Then, using the words you have selected, fill in the blank spaces in the story.

Now you've created your own hilarious MAD LIBS® game!

CAT FANCY

ADJECTIVE _____

PLURAL NOUN _____

ADJECTIVE _____

PLURAL NOUN _____

ADJECTIVE _____

ADJECTIVE _____

PLURAL NOUN _____

ADJECTIVE _____

NOUN _____

ADVERB _____

PART OF THE BODY (PLURAL) _____

NOUN _____

PLURAL NOUN _____

ADJECTIVE _____

MAD LIBS®
CAT FANCY

You might say the ancient Egyptians were _____ cat people. After
                                                  ADJECTIVE

all, they built an entire religion around worshipping their feline _____!
                         PLURAL NOUN

Cats were well-liked by Egyptians for their ability to kill _____ vermin
                    ADJECTIVE

like rodents and wild _____. Cats were thought to be graceful and
          PLURAL NOUN

_____ creatures. Some _____ cats were mummified and buried in
ADJECTIVE   ADJECTIVE

_____ along with their _____ owners. Harming a cat was
PLURAL NOUN   ADJECTIVE

a crime punishable by _____. And when a cat died, its family would
        NOUN

mourn _____, shaving their _____ as a symbol of
   ADVERB   PART OF THE BODY (PLURAL)

their _____. So maybe it's a little funny that ancient _____
   NOUN   PLURAL NOUN

worshipped cats. But, then again, so does the _____ Internet!
                   ADJECTIVE

MAD LIBS® is fun to play with friends, but you can also play it by yourself! To begin with, DO NOT look at the story on the page below. Fill in the blanks on this page with the words called for. Then, using the words you have selected, fill in the blank spaces in the story.

Now you've created your own hilarious MAD LIBS® game!

THE CODE
OF THE SAMURAI

ADJECTIVE _____

ADJECTIVE _____

PLURAL NOUN _____

ADJECTIVE _____

PLURAL NOUN _____

VERB _____

PLURAL NOUN _____

PLURAL NOUN _____

NOUN _____

PLURAL NOUN _____

VERB _____

PLURAL NOUN _____

NOUN _____

Samurai were ancient, _____ Japanese warriors who followed a/an
                        ADJECTIVE

_____ code of virtue, which contained these eight _____:
ADJECTIVE   PLURAL NOUN

1. Samurai believed **justice** was the most _____ virtue.
                                             ADJECTIVE

2. They always showed **courage** in the face of _____.
                                                  PLURAL NOUN

3. Samurai may have had the power to _____, but they also needed to
                                     VERB

   show **mercy** toward all _____.
                             PLURAL NOUN

4. It was important to be **polite** and considerate of other people's _____.
                                                                       PLURAL NOUN

5. Samurai also thought **honesty** was the best _____.
                                                 NOUN

6. _____ were not an option for the Samurai, who tried to _____
   PLURAL NOUN   VERB

   with **honor**.

7. Samurai were **loyal** to their fellow _____.
                                          PLURAL NOUN

8. And, finally, they had to show **character** and that they knew the difference

   between right and _____.
                     NOUN

MAD LIBS® is fun to play with friends, but you can also play it by yourself! To begin with, DO NOT look at the story on the page below. Fill in the blanks on this page with the words called for. Then, using the words you have selected, fill in the blank spaces in the story.

Now you've created your own hilarious MAD LIBS® game!

GOD SAVE THE QUEEN

PERSON IN ROOM (MALE) _____

PERSON IN ROOM (FEMALE) _____

NUMBER _____

NOUN _____

VERB ENDING IN "ING" _____

ADJECTIVE _____

FIRST NAME (MALE) _____

ADJECTIVE _____

PERSON IN ROOM _____

A PLACE _____

A PLACE _____

PLURAL NOUN _____

ADJECTIVE _____

PLURAL NOUN _____

NOUN _____

PART OF THE BODY _____

MAD LIBS®
GOD SAVE THE QUEEN

Elizabeth I of England was the daughter of King _____ VIII
                                           PERSON IN ROOM (MALE)

and his wife _____. At age _____, she was crowned
            PERSON IN ROOM (FEMALE)   NUMBER

_____ of England in a royal _____ ceremony. During
   NOUN   VERB ENDING IN "ING"

her reign, England was a very _____ place to live. Famous writer
                              ADJECTIVE

_____ Shakespeare wrote many _____ plays, and explorer
 FIRST NAME (MALE)   ADJECTIVE

_____ discovered (the) _____. In a war against
 PERSON IN ROOM   A PLACE

(the) _____, Queen Elizabeth I led her army of _____ to
      A PLACE   PLURAL NOUN

a/an _____ victory. Today, many _____ consider Queen
     ADJECTIVE   PLURAL NOUN

Elizabeth the most famous _____ in English history. Some even say she
                          NOUN

ruled England with an iron _____!
                           PART OF THE BODY

MAD LIBS® is fun to play with friends, but you can also play it by yourself! To begin with, DO NOT look at the story on the page below. Fill in the blanks on this page with the words called for. Then, using the words you have selected, fill in the blank spaces in the story.

Now you've created your own hilarious MAD LIBS® game!

WHAT A
WONDERFUL WORLD

NOUN _____

ADJECTIVE _____

NOUN _____

ADJECTIVE _____

PERSON IN ROOM (FEMALE) _____

NOUN _____

CELEBRITY (FEMALE) _____

COLOR _____

CELEBRITY (MALE) _____

PERSON IN ROOM _____

PERSON IN ROOM _____

A PLACE _____

CELEBRITY (MALE) _____

A PLACE _____

NOUN _____

MAD LIBS®
WHAT A
WONDERFUL WORLD

These are considered the Seven Wonders of the Ancient _____:
NOUN

1. **The Giza Necropolis** is a site in Egypt where you can see the Great Pyramids and the _____ Sphinx.
ADJECTIVE

2. **The Hanging Gardens** were in the ancient _____ of Babylon and
NOUN
were built as a gift from Nebuchadnezzar II to his _____ wife,
ADJECTIVE
_____.
PERSON IN ROOM (FEMALE)

3. **The Temple of Artemis at Ephesus** was a Greek _____ dedicated to
NOUN
the goddess _____.
CELEBRITY (FEMALE)

4. **The Statue of Zeus at Olympia** was a giant forty-three-foot ivory and
_____ statue of _____.
COLOR   CELEBRITY (MALE)

5. **The Mausoleum at Halicarnassus** was a tomb built by _____
PERSON IN ROOM
and _____ of (the) _____.
PERSON IN ROOM   A PLACE

6. **The Colossus of Rhodes** was a statue of Greek god _____, built
CELEBRITY (MALE)
to commemorate victory over (the) _____.
A PLACE

7. **The Lighthouse of Alexandria** was at one time the tallest _____ on
NOUN
Earth.

MAD LIBS® is fun to play with friends, but you can also play it by yourself! To begin with, DO NOT look at the story on the page below. Fill in the blanks on this page with the words called for. Then, using the words you have selected, fill in the blank spaces in the story.

Now you've created your own hilarious MAD LIBS® game!

FAMOUS FIRSTS

PERSON IN ROOM _____

NOUN _____

PERSON IN ROOM _____

NOUN _____

NOUN _____

PERSON IN ROOM _____

PERSON IN ROOM _____

PLURAL NOUN _____

PERSON IN ROOM _____

PART OF THE BODY _____

A PLACE _____

PERSON IN ROOM _____

VERB _____

PERSON IN ROOM _____

ANIMAL _____

MAD LIBS®
FAMOUS FIRSTS

- In 1901, _____ became the first person to go over Niagara
  <u>PERSON IN ROOM</u>

  Falls in a/an _____ and survive.
  <u>NOUN</u>

- In 1933, _____ became the first _____ to fly an
  <u>PERSON IN ROOM</u>   <u>NOUN</u>

  airplane around the _____.
  <u>NOUN</u>

- In 1953, _____ and _____ became the first
  <u>PERSON IN ROOM</u>   <u>PERSON IN ROOM</u>

  _____ to climb to the top of Mount Everest.
  <u>PLURAL NOUN</u>

- In 1963, _____ became the first person to receive a/an
  <u>PERSON IN ROOM</u>

  _____ transplant in (the) _____, South Africa.
  <u>PART OF THE BODY</u>   <u>A PLACE</u>

- In 1969, _____ became the first person to _____ on
  <u>PERSON IN ROOM</u>   <u>VERB</u>

  the moon.

- In 1996, in Scotland, _____became the world's first clone
  <u>PERSON IN ROOM</u>

  of a/an _____.
  <u>ANIMAL</u>

MAD LIBS® is fun to play with friends, but you can also play it by yourself! To begin with, DO NOT look at the story on the page below. Fill in the blanks on this page with the words called for. Then, using the words you have selected, fill in the blank spaces in the story.

Now you've created your own hilarious MAD LIBS® game!

LAND, HO!

PLURAL NOUN _____

PLURAL NOUN _____

ADJECTIVE _____

NOUN _____

VERB (PAST TENSE) _____

ADJECTIVE _____

NOUN _____

NOUN _____

NOUN _____

NOUN _____

PLURAL NOUN _____

NOUN _____

PERSON IN ROOM (FEMALE) _____

PLURAL NOUN _____

PART OF THE BODY _____

PLURAL NOUN _____

MAD LIBS®
LAND, HO!

Throughout history, _____ with a sense of adventure have traveled
                         PLURAL NOUN

the world in search of new lands and _____. Here are a few of the
                                        PLURAL NOUN

most _____ explorers:
        ADJECTIVE

Leif Ericson was a famous Viking _____ who _____ to
                                       NOUN   VERB (PAST TENSE)

the Americas five hundred years before _____ Christopher Columbus.
                                          ADJECTIVE

Ferdinand Magellan, a Portuguese _____, became the first _____
                                        NOUN   NOUN

to cross the Pacific Ocean while he tried to discover a route to the _____
                                                                        NOUN

Islands.

Marco Polo traveled in a/an _____ from Italy to China and helped many
                                   NOUN

Western _____ learn about the Eastern _____.
          PLURAL NOUN   NOUN

Lewis and Clark, led by _____, were the first _____
                             PERSON IN ROOM (FEMALE)   PLURAL NOUN

to travel by _____ across the continental United _____.
               PART OF THE BODY   PLURAL NOUN

MAD LIBS® is fun to play with friends, but you can also play it by yourself! To begin with, DO NOT look at the story on the page below. Fill in the blanks on this page with the words called for. Then, using the words you have selected, fill in the blank spaces in the story.

Now you've created your own hilarious MAD LIBS® game!

WALK LIKE AN EGYPTIAN

ADJECTIVE _____

NOUN _____

ADJECTIVE _____

ADJECTIVE _____

PLURAL NOUN _____

ADJECTIVE _____

PLURAL NOUN _____

ADVERB _____

NOUN _____

NOUN _____

VERB (PAST TENSE) _____

ADJECTIVE _____

OCCUPATION _____

NOUN _____

CELEBRITY (FEMALE) _____

MAD LIBS®
WALK LIKE AN EGYPTIAN

Cleopatra was a/an _____ Egyptian pharaoh. Well-educated and clever
                      ADJECTIVE

as a/an _____, Cleopatra spoke many _____ languages. She
         NOUN   ADJECTIVE

was also known for being particularly _____ . When she was eighteen,
                                        ADJECTIVE

Cleopatra took the throne, though she was chased out by a bunch of unruly

_____ . In response, Cleopatra put together an army of _____
PLURAL NOUN   ADJECTIVE

_____, marched _____ back into Egypt, and took back the
PLURAL NOUN   ADVERB

_____ for herself. Cleopatra fell in love with the Roman _____,
NOUN   NOUN

Julius Caesar. After Caesar _____, Cleopatra fell in love
                             VERB (PAST TENSE)

with another _____ Roman, Mark Antony. Cleopatra was the most
              ADJECTIVE

famous and powerful _____ to rule a/an _____. She was even
                     OCCUPATION   NOUN

played by the legendary actress _____ in a movie!
                                 CELEBRITY (FEMALE)

MAD LIBS® is fun to play with friends, but you can also play it by yourself! To begin with, DO NOT look at the story on the page below. Fill in the blanks on this page with the words called for. Then, using the words you have selected, fill in the blank spaces in the story.

Now you've created your own hilarious MAD LIBS® game!

CROOKS DOWN UNDER

NOUN _____

ADJECTIVE _____

PLURAL NOUN _____

ADJECTIVE _____

PERSON IN ROOM _____

ADJECTIVE _____

NUMBER _____

PLURAL NOUN _____

ADJECTIVE _____

VERB _____

PLURAL NOUN _____

PERSON IN ROOM (FEMALE) _____

ANIMAL _____

NUMBER _____

PART OF THE BODY _____

MAD LIBS
CROOKS DOWN UNDER

Australia—known as the _____ Down Under—has a/an
NOUN

_____ criminal past. In the late 1700s, Britain's prisons were overrun
ADJECTIVE

with _____, so they began transporting their _____ prisoners
PLURAL NOUN   ADJECTIVE

to Australia. Captain _____ was in charge of setting up the first
PERSON IN ROOM

_____ colony for prisoners. Over _____ years, fifty-five thousand
ADJECTIVE   NUMBER

criminal _____ came from England to live there! With _____
PLURAL NOUN   ADJECTIVE

behavior, these prisoners could _____ their way to freedom and gain
VERB

work as butchers, farmers, and professional _____. One resident in
PLURAL NOUN

the colony was a thirteen-year-old named _____, who had
PERSON IN ROOM (FEMALE)

come to the colony for stealing a/an _____. She eventually became one
ANIMAL

of Australia's first businesswomen, and today, Australia's _____-dollar bill
NUMBER

features her _____!
PART OF THE BODY

MAD LIBS® is fun to play with friends, but you can also play it by yourself! To begin with, DO NOT look at the story on the page below. Fill in the blanks on this page with the words called for. Then, using the words you have selected, fill in the blank spaces in the story.

Now you've created your own hilarious MAD LIBS® game!

WHEREFORE ART THOU SHAKESPEARE?

NOUN_____

PERSON IN ROOM (FEMALE)_____

NOUN_____

ADJECTIVE_____

ADJECTIVE_____

NOUN_____

ADJECTIVE_____

PLURAL NOUN_____

NOUN_____

NOUN_____

NOUN_____

PLURAL NOUN_____

PART OF THE BODY (PLURAL)_____

NOUN_____

William Shakespeare is the most famous writer in the history of the

_____ . He wrote many plays, including *Romeo and* _____

NOUN   PERSON IN ROOM (FEMALE)

and *A Midsummer Night's* _____ . He also wrote many _____

       NOUN   ADJECTIVE

poems. Here is a selection from one of his most _____ sonnets:

       ADJECTIVE

Shall I compare thee to a summer's _____ ?

       NOUN

Thou art more lovely and more _____ .

       ADJECTIVE

Rough winds do shake the darling _____ of May,

       PLURAL NOUN

And summer's _____ hath all too short a/an _____ . . .

       NOUN   NOUN

But thy eternal _____ shall not fade . . .

       NOUN

So long as _____ can breathe,

       PLURAL NOUN

or _____ can see,

       PART OF THE BODY (PLURAL)

So long lives this, and this gives _____ to thee.

       NOUN

MAD LIBS® is fun to play with friends, but you can also play it by yourself! To begin with, DO NOT look at the story on the page below. Fill in the blanks on this page with the words called for. Then, using the words you have selected, fill in the blank spaces in the story.

Now you've created your own hilarious MAD LIBS® game!

WANTED:
FOUNTAIN OF YOUTH

ADJECTIVE_____

VERB ENDING IN "S"_____

ANIMAL_____

PART OF THE BODY_____

ADJECTIVE_____

PLURAL NOUN_____

A PLACE_____

ADJECTIVE_____

SILLY WORD_____

NOUN_____

PLURAL NOUN_____

NOUN_____

Spanish explorer Ponce de Leon seeks a/an _____ Fountain of
ADJECTIVE

Youth. Anyone who drinks or _____ in its waters will
VERB ENDING IN "S"

have eternal youth. It can also cure illnesses from _____ pox to the
ANIMAL

_____ flu. It has been rumored for many _____
PART OF THE BODY ADJECTIVE

years that the Fountain of Youth exists. Some _____ believe
PLURAL NOUN

it is either in the New World or (the) _____. If you find this
A PLACE

_____ fountain, please contact Ponce de Leon at 555-_____ or
ADJECTIVE SILLY WORD

poncedeleon@_____-mail.com. You will be rewarded with gold and
NOUN

_____, as well as eternal _____.
PLURAL NOUN NOUN

MAD LIBS® is fun to play with friends, but you can also play it by yourself! To begin with, DO NOT look at the story on the page below. Fill in the blanks on this page with the words called for. Then, using the words you have selected, fill in the blank spaces in the story.

Now you've created your own hilarious MAD LIBS® game!

O.M.O. (OH MY ODIN)

PLURAL NOUN _____

A PLACE _____

ADJECTIVE _____

A PLACE _____

PLURAL NOUN _____

VERB _____

ADJECTIVE _____

COLOR _____

SAME COLOR _____

ADJECTIVE _____

ADJECTIVE _____

PLURAL NOUN _____

PLURAL NOUN _____

PLURAL NOUN _____

PLURAL NOUN _____

NOUN _____

MAD LIBS®
O.M.O. (OH MY ODIN)

Vikings were seafaring _____ from Scandinavia, which includes
                          PLURAL NOUN

modern-day countries like Denmark, Norway, and (the) _____. Vikings
                                                       A PLACE

traveled in their _____ boats from Europe to Russia and then to (the)
                    ADJECTIVE

_____, raiding _____ and establishing villages to _____
  A PLACE   PLURAL NOUN   VERB

in. The Vikings were known to be _____ fighters. One famous Viking
                                   ADJECTIVE

warrior was Erik the _____, who was nicknamed this because of his
                       COLOR

flowing _____ beard. There were also _____ Viking female
          SAME COLOR   ADJECTIVE

warriors who wore _____ shields when fighting _____. The
                    ADJECTIVE   PLURAL NOUN

Vikings even had their own gods and goddesses, like Odin, who was thought

to be the ruler of all _____, and who also represented war, battle, and
                        PLURAL NOUN

_____. The Vikings were a serious bunch of _____—you
 PLURAL NOUN   PLURAL NOUN

sure didn't want to get on their bad _____!
                                       NOUN

MAD LIBS® is fun to play with friends, but you can also play it by yourself! To begin with, DO NOT look at the story on the page below. Fill in the blanks on this page with the words called for. Then, using the words you have selected, fill in the blank spaces in the story.

Now you've created your own hilarious MAD LIBS® game!

PEACE, LOVE, AND

_____
PLURAL NOUN

PLURAL NOUN _____

ADJECTIVE _____

PLURAL NOUN _____

NOUN _____

PLURAL NOUN _____

A PLACE _____

VERB ENDING IN "ING" _____

PLURAL NOUN _____

NOUN _____

NOUN _____

A PLACE _____

ADJECTIVE _____

A PLACE _____

PLURAL NOUN _____

PLURAL NOUN _____

MAD LIBS®
PEACE, LOVE, AND

_____
PLURAL NOUN

Since the beginning of time, _____ have fought with one another
PLURAL NOUN

for many _____ reasons. But these brave people devoted their lives to
ADJECTIVE

helping their fellow _____:
PLURAL NOUN

Gandhi led India to freedom from the British _____, who had taken
NOUN

it over. He inspired people all over the world to be peaceful _____.
PLURAL NOUN

Martin Luther King Jr. led the Civil Rights Movement in (the) _____,
A PLACE

helping gain equal rights for African Americans by _____
VERB ENDING IN "ING"

peacefully.

Nelson Mandela helped end racist _____ in South Africa. For his
PLURAL NOUN

hard work, he won the Nobel Peace _____ and the US Presidential
NOUN

_____ of Freedom.
NOUN

Mother Teresa was a nun from (the) _____ who devoted her life to helping
A PLACE

sick and _____ people all over (the) _____.
ADJECTIVE   A PLACE

Clara Barton was a nurse who helped found the American Red Cross, which

educates _____ and gives assistance to _____ in need.
PLURAL NOUN   PLURAL NOUN

MAD LIBS® is fun to play with friends, but you can also play it by yourself! To begin with, DO NOT look at the story on the page below. Fill in the blanks on this page with the words called for. Then, using the words you have selected, fill in the blank spaces in the story.

Now you've created your own hilarious MAD LIBS® game!

DID I DO THAT?

PLURAL NOUN _____

PLURAL NOUN _____

PERSON IN ROOM _____

NOUN _____

PLURAL NOUN _____

VERB _____

NOUN _____

PERSON IN ROOM (MALE) _____

VERB _____

VERB _____

ADJECTIVE _____

A PLACE _____

ADJECTIVE _____

PERSON IN ROOM _____

NOUN _____

ADJECTIVE _____

Oops! We should thank our lucky _____ for these _____
                                    PLURAL NOUN   PLURAL NOUN

that were invented by accident!

The microwave: In 1945, _____ was experimenting with
                              PERSON IN ROOM

a/an _____ when he discovered it could melt _____ and make
        NOUN   PLURAL NOUN

popcorn _____. He then built the first microwave _____.
           VERB   NOUN

The Slinky: In 1943, naval engineer _____ attempted to
                                          PERSON IN ROOM (MALE)

create a spring to help ships _____, when he got the idea for a toy spring
                                 VERB

that could _____ down the stairs all by itself. It became the _____
              VERB   ADJECTIVE

Slinky!

Potato chips: At a restaurant in (the) _____ in 1853, a customer
                                            A PLACE

complained that his fried potatoes were too _____'. The chef,
                                               ADJECTIVE

_____, cut the potatoes as thin as possible and fried them
  PERSON IN ROOM

to a/an _____, accidentally inventing the _____ potato chip!
           NOUN   ADJECTIVE

MAD LIBS® is fun to play with friends, but you can also play it by yourself! To begin with, DO NOT look at the story on the page below. Fill in the blanks on this page with the words called for. Then, using the words you have selected, fill in the blank spaces in the story.

Now you've created your own hilarious MAD LIBS® game!

STATE OF WONDER

NOUN _____

PLURAL NOUN _____

ADJECTIVE _____

PLURAL NOUN _____

A PLACE _____

A PLACE _____

ADJECTIVE _____

PLURAL NOUN _____

PLURAL NOUN _____

ADJECTIVE _____

NOUN _____

ADJECTIVE _____

NOUN _____

ADJECTIVE _____

PERSON IN ROOM (MALE) _____

CELEBRITY _____

MAD LIBS®
STATE OF WONDER

The Seven Wonders of the Modern _____ were chosen by _____
                                                NOUN   PLURAL NOUN

like me and you!

1. **The Great Wall of China** is a/an _____ wall made of stones, bricks,
                                       ADJECTIVE

   and _____ that stretches all the way from (the) _____ to
               PLURAL NOUN   A PLACE

   (the) _____.
          A PLACE

2. **Petra** is a/an _____ city in Jordan, also known as the Rose City
                   ADJECTIVE

   for its pink-colored _____.
                  PLURAL NOUN

3. **The Colosseum** is an ancient Roman amphitheater built by _____.
                                                                     PLURAL NOUN

4. **Chichén Itzá** is a/an _____ city in Mexico built during the
                         ADJECTIVE

   _____ Empire.
      NOUN

5. **Machu Picchu** is a/an _____ estate built into a huge _____
                    ADJECTIVE   NOUN

   in Peru.

6. **Taj Mahal** is a/an _____ mausoleum in India, built by Emperor
                  ADJECTIVE

   _____.
   PERSON IN ROOM (MALE)

7. **Christ the Redeemer** in Brazil is a hundred-foot-tall statue of

   _____.
   CELEBRITY

MAD LIBS® is fun to play with friends, but you can also play it by yourself! To begin with, DO NOT look at the story on the page below. Fill in the blanks on this page with the words called for. Then, using the words you have selected, fill in the blank spaces in the story.

Now you've created your own hilarious MAD LIBS® game!

MONGOLIAN WARRIOR

ADJECTIVE _____

NUMBER _____

ADJECTIVE _____

PLURAL NOUN _____

ADJECTIVE _____

A PLACE _____

PLURAL NOUN _____

ADJECTIVE _____

PLURAL NOUN _____

PLURAL NOUN _____

ADJECTIVE _____

NOUN _____

ADJECTIVE _____

VERB (PAST TENSE) _____

ADJECTIVE _____

MAD LIBS®
MONGOLIAN WARRIOR

Genghis Khan was a/an _____ Mongolian leader. Starting at the
                          ADJECTIVE

young age of _____, Genghis Khan began to build a/an _____
              NUMBER   ADJECTIVE

army of _____. He wanted to destroy _____ tribes in (the)
         PLURAL NOUN   ADJECTIVE

Northeast _____ so he could rule over all the _____ in the
           A PLACE   PLURAL NOUN

land. He and his _____ armies marched into _____
                  ADJECTIVE   PLURAL NOUN

all around Asia. They brutally fought and killed many _____ and
                                                       PLURAL NOUN

eventually created the _____ Mongolian Empire, which was the largest
                       ADJECTIVE

_____ in the world. Today, Genghis Khan is considered one of the most
 NOUN

ruthless and _____ warriors that ever _____. You
              ADJECTIVE   VERB (PAST TENSE)

wouldn't have wanted to meet him alone in a/an _____ alley!
                                                ADJECTIVE

MAD LIBS® is fun to play with friends, but you can also play it by yourself! To begin with, DO NOT look at the story on the page below. Fill in the blanks on this page with the words called for. Then, using the words you have selected, fill in the blank spaces in the story.

Now you've created your own hilarious MAD LIBS® game!

NAPOLEON COMPLEX

OCCUPATION _____

PLURAL NOUN _____

PLURAL NOUN _____

ADJECTIVE _____

NOUN _____

NOUN _____

NOUN _____

ADJECTIVE _____

NOUN _____

PLURAL NOUN _____

PLURAL NOUN _____

ADJECTIVE _____

A PLACE _____

A PLACE _____

PLURAL NOUN _____

VERB (PAST TENSE) _____

ADJECTIVE _____

MAD LIBS
NAPOLEON COMPLEX

Napoleon Bonaparte was the first _____ of France. He made his way to
OCCUPATION

the top during the French Revolution, where regular old _____ rose
PLURAL NOUN

up to fight against royal _____. But Napoleon was known for having
PLURAL NOUN

a/an _____ temper. He would fly off the _____ at the drop
ADJECTIVE   NOUN

of a/an _____. Napoleon was also not a very tall _____. Some
NOUN   NOUN

say his small size made him feel _____. In order to feel like more of
ADJECTIVE

a/an _____, he would act out, invade _____, and fight wars
NOUN   PLURAL NOUN

with _____! This made him feel _____ and powerful, despite
PLURAL NOUN   ADJECTIVE

his small size. And, for a while, it worked, and Napoleon ruled over all of (the)

_____. But eventually, at the Battle of (the) _____, Napoleon was
A PLACE   A PLACE

captured by British _____, and he _____.
PLURAL NOUN   VERB (PAST TENSE)

One thing's for sure: What Napoleon lacked in size, he made up for with his

_____ personality!
ADJECTIVE

MAD LIBS® is fun to play with friends, but you can also play it by yourself! To begin with, DO NOT look at the story on the page below. Fill in the blanks on this page with the words called for. Then, using the words you have selected, fill in the blank spaces in the story.

Now you've created your own hilarious MAD LIBS® game!

WHEN IN ROME

ADJECTIVE _____

PLURAL NOUN _____

ADJECTIVE _____

ADJECTIVE _____

PLURAL NOUN _____

ADJECTIVE _____

PLURAL NOUN _____

VERB _____

ADJECTIVE _____

PART OF THE BODY (PLURAL) _____

PLURAL NOUN _____

NOUN _____

NOUN _____

NOUN _____

MAD LIBS®
WHEN IN ROME

The Roman Empire is one of the most _____ empires in world history.
ADJECTIVE

Two thousand years ago, one in four _____ lived under Roman rule.
PLURAL NOUN

The Roman Empire was led by _____ emperors—a bunch of
ADJECTIVE

powerful men who wore _____ robes and decided the fate of Rome's
ADJECTIVE

many _____. The most famous Roman emperor was Caesar
PLURAL NOUN

Augustus, a/an _____ leader who helped Rome become one of the most
ADJECTIVE

powerful _____ the world had ever seen. The Roman people, rich and
PLURAL NOUN

poor, loved to mingle, gossip, and _____ at the _____ Roman
VERB _ADJECTIVE_

baths, a place for bathing and exercising your _____.
PART OF THE BODY (PLURAL)

Romans also enjoyed watching gladiators fight wild _____ in coliseums
PLURAL NOUN

and racing chariots around a/an _____. For about five hundred years,
NOUN

Romans ruled the _____—which is why the Roman Empire is thought
NOUN

of by some people as the most powerful _____ to ever exist.
NOUN

MAD LIBS® is fun to play with friends, but you can also play it by yourself! To begin with, DO NOT look at the story on the page below. Fill in the blanks on this page with the words called for. Then, using the words you have selected, fill in the blank spaces in the story.

Now you've created your own hilarious MAD LIBS® game!

AN APPLE A DAY

ADJECTIVE _____

ADJECTIVE _____

ADJECTIVE _____

ADJECTIVE _____

PERSON IN ROOM (FEMALE) _____

SILLY WORD _____

A PLACE _____

VERB ENDING IN "ING" _____

NOUN _____

ADVERB _____

NOUN _____

ADJECTIVE _____

NOUN _____

ADJECTIVE _____

VERB _____

MAD LIBS®
AN APPLE A DAY

Here is the story of how a/an _____ scientist named Sir Isaac Newton
__ADJECTIVE__

came up with the _____ theory of gravity. One day, a/an _____
__ADJECTIVE__   __ADJECTIVE__

Isaac went to visit his _____ mother, _____ ,
__ADJECTIVE__   __PERSON IN ROOM (FEMALE)__

at _____ Manor, her country home in (the) _____. While
__SILLY WORD__   __A PLACE__

_____ in the garden, Isaac saw an apple fall from a/an
__VERB ENDING IN "ING"__

_____. *Why does that apple fall _____ to the ground?* thought
__NOUN__   __ADVERB__

Isaac. *Why doesn't the apple fall sideways, or go upward, toward the* _____
__NOUN__

in the sky? Before long, Isaac decided that the _____ apple must be
__ADJECTIVE__

drawn to the Earth's core, right in the middle of the _____. And thus,
__NOUN__

Sir Isaac Newton came up with the _____ concept of gravity—that
__ADJECTIVE__

whatever goes up must _____ down.
__VERB__

MAD LIBS®

MAD SCIENTIST MAD LIBS

Mad Libs
An Imprint of Penguin Random House

INSTRUCTIONS

MAD LIBS® is a game for people who don't like games! It can be played by one, two, three, four, or forty.

• RIDICULOUSLY SIMPLE DIRECTIONS

In this tablet you will find stories containing blank spaces where words are left out. One player, the READER, selects one of these stories. The READER does not tell anyone what the story is about. Instead, he/she asks the other players, the WRITERS, to give him/her words. These words are used to fill in the blank spaces in the story.

• TO PLAY

The READER asks each WRITER in turn to call out a word—an adjective or a noun or whatever the space calls for—and uses them to fill in the blank spaces in the story. The result is a MAD LIBS® game.

When the READER then reads the completed MAD LIBS® game to the other players, they will discover that they have written a story that is fantastic, screamingly funny, shocking, silly, crazy, or just plain dumb—depending upon which words each WRITER called out.

• EXAMPLE (*Before* and *After*)

"_____!" he said _____
    EXCLAMATION   ADVERB

as he jumped into his convertible _____ and
                                    NOUN

drove off with his _____ wife.
                      ADJECTIVE

"_____OUCH_____!" he said _____STUPIDLY_____
    EXCLAMATION   ADVERB

as he jumped into his convertible _____CAT_____ and
                                    NOUN

drove off with his _____BRAVE_____ wife.
                      ADJECTIVE

QUICK REVIEW

In case you have forgotten what adjectives, adverbs, nouns, and verbs are, here is a quick review:

An ADJECTIVE describes something or somebody. *Lumpy, soft, ugly, messy,* and *short* are adjectives.

An ADVERB tells how something is done. It modifies a verb and usually ends in "ly." *Modestly, stupidly, greedily,* and *carefully* are adverbs.

A NOUN is the name of a person, place, or thing. *Sidewalk, umbrella, bridle, bathtub,* and *nose* are nouns.

A VERB is an action word. *Run, pitch, jump,* and *swim* are verbs. Put the verbs in past tense if the directions say PAST TENSE. *Ran, pitched, jumped,* and *swam* are verbs in the past tense.

When we ask for A PLACE, we mean any sort of place: a country or city *(Spain, Cleveland)* or a room *(bathroom, kitchen).*

An EXCLAMATION or SILLY WORD is any sort of funny sound, gasp, grunt, or outcry, like *Wow!, Ouch!, Whomp!, Ick!,* and *Gadzooks!*

When we ask for specific words, like a NUMBER, a COLOR, an ANIMAL, or a PART OF THE BODY, we mean a word that is one of those things, like *seven, blue, horse,* or *head.*

When we ask for a PLURAL, it means more than one. For example, *cat* pluralized is *cats.*

MAD LIBS® is fun to play with friends, but you can also play it by yourself! To begin with, DO NOT look at the story on the page below. Fill in the blanks on this page with the words called for. Then, using the words you have selected, fill in the blank spaces in the story.

Now you've created your own hilarious MAD LIBS® game!

HOW TO GET MY LOOK
BY ALBERT EINSTEIN

OCCUPATION _____

ADVERB _____

ADJECTIVE _____

NOUN _____

ADJECTIVE _____

ADJECTIVE _____

COLOR _____

ADJECTIVE _____

PART OF THE BODY _____

NOUN _____

ARTICLE OF CLOTHING _____

OCCUPATION _____

MAD LIBS®
HOW TO GET MY LOOK
BY ALBERT EINSTEIN

Hallo. I am famous German _____ Albert Einstein. Some people
OCCUPATION

say I look _____ insane. And zey are right, I do! But I am not
ADVERB

actually _____. Zis is just how I like to look. If you would also like
ADJECTIVE

to look like zis, use ze makeover tips I have outlined below.

- Never comb your _____: It is supposed to look like zis! Ze
NOUN

  more _____, the better, as I always say. It also helps if your
  ADJECTIVE

  hair is a/an _____ shade of _____.
  ADJECTIVE   COLOR

- Make _____ faces as often as possible. For example, stick out
  ADJECTIVE

  your _____ in pictures. Why? Because life is fun! Do zis when
  PART OF THE BODY

  your eager _____ students photograph you. Zey will love it!
  NOUN

- Always wear a white lab _____. Zis way, you will
  ARTICLE OF CLOTHING

  look like a real _____.
  OCCUPATION

MAD LIBS® is fun to play with friends, but you can also play it by yourself! To begin with, DO NOT look at the story on the page below. Fill in the blanks on this page with the words called for. Then, using the words you have selected, fill in the blank spaces in the story.

Now you've created your own hilarious MAD LIBS® game!

THE BIOGRAPHY OF ALBERT EINSTEIN

A PLACE _____

NUMBER _____

OCCUPATION _____

ADJECTIVE _____

COLOR _____

ADJECTIVE _____

ADVERB _____

ADJECTIVE _____

PLURAL NOUN _____

PLURAL NOUN _____

VERB (PAST TENSE) _____

NOUN _____

NOUN _____

NOUN _____

PART OF THE BODY _____

A PLACE _____

Albert Einstein was born in (the) _____ in Germany in the year 18-

A PLACE

_____. He grew up to be a genius _____ with a/an _____

NUMBER   OCCUPATION   ADJECTIVE

_____ head of hair and a/an _____ sense of humor. Even

COLOR   ADJECTIVE

though he was _____ smart, the people who knew him thought he acted

ADVERB

pretty _____. He was notorious for losing _____ and forgetting

ADJECTIVE   PLURAL NOUN

the _____ in his equations. Einstein became famous for inventing

PLURAL NOUN

things like E equals MC _____, the theory of _____,

VERB (PAST TENSE)   NOUN

and the quantum _____ of light. In 1921, he won the Nobel _____

NOUN   NOUN

in Physics. After his death in 1955, Einstein's _____ was

PART OF THE BODY

donated to (the) _____ Medical Center.

A PLACE

MAD LIBS® is fun to play with friends, but you can also play it by yourself! To begin with, DO NOT look at the story on the page below. Fill in the blanks on this page with the words called for. Then, using the words you have selected, fill in the blank spaces in the story.

Now you've created your own hilarious MAD LIBS® game!

QUIZ: ARE YOU A MAD SCIENTIST?

ADJECTIVE _____

ADJECTIVE _____

EXCLAMATION _____

ADJECTIVE _____

ADJECTIVE _____

VERB (PAST TENSE) _____

TYPE OF LIQUID _____

ANIMAL (PLURAL) _____

COLOR _____

ADJECTIVE _____

NOUN _____

NOUN _____

ADJECTIVE _____

ARTICLE OF CLOTHING _____

ADJECTIVE _____

OCCUPATION _____

Are you crazy about science? Do you go nuts for _____ experiments?
ADJECTIVE

Take this _____ quiz to find out if you're a mad scientist.
ADJECTIVE

1. Your favorite saying is: a) "Oh, _____! What did I do?",
EXCLAMATION

   b) "It's _____!", c) "This _____ experiment went exactly as
   ADJECTIVE   ADJECTIVE

   _____."
   VERB (PAST TENSE)

2. Your lab always contains: a) test tubes filled with _____,
   TYPE OF LIQUID

   b) _____ floating in jars, c) a few _____ mice in cages.
   ANIMAL (PLURAL)   COLOR

3. Your favorite thing to do at night is: a) go to bed and have _____
   ADJECTIVE

   dreams, b) laugh maniacally while bringing to life an evil _____,
   NOUN

   c) plan tomorrow's _____-work.
   NOUN

If you answered mostly b's, guess what? You're a/an _____ scientist! Go
ADJECTIVE

put on your long white _____ and experiment in your
ARTICLE OF CLOTHING

_____ laboratory. If you answered mostly a's and c's, you're better off as
ADJECTIVE

a/an _____!
OCCUPATION

MAD LIBS® is fun to play with friends, but you can also play it by yourself! To begin with, DO NOT look at the story on the page below. Fill in the blanks on this page with the words called for. Then, using the words you have selected, fill in the blank spaces in the story.

Now you've created your own hilarious MAD LIBS® game!

LAB RAT ON THE LOOSE

SILLY WORD _____

ADJECTIVE _____

NUMBER _____

NOUN _____

VERB ENDING IN "ING" _____

NOUN _____

TYPE OF LIQUID _____

ADJECTIVE _____

PART OF THE BODY _____

ADJECTIVE _____

VERB ENDING IN "ING" _____

ADJECTIVE _____

ANIMAL _____

ADJECTIVE _____

MAD LIBS
LAB RAT ON THE LOOSE

Uh-oh! Last night, _____ the lab rat escaped from his cage and ran amok
_____SILLY WORD_____

in the science lab. He was out to get revenge on the _____ scientists
_____ADJECTIVE___

who'd held him captive for _____ weeks. First, he ran straight to the
_____NUMBER___

_____ tubes and knocked them over, _____ glass all
___NOUN___   VERB ENDING IN "ING"

over the _____. Then he jumped into a vat of _____ and
_____NOUN___   TYPE OF LIQUID

left _____ _____-prints all over the floor. Later on,
____ADJECTIVE___   PART OF THE BODY

the _____ rat finally got tired of _____ around and went
___ADJECTIVE___   VERB ENDING IN "ING"

to sleep under a/an _____-scope. Looks like that silly _____ is
_____ADJECTIVE___   ANIMAL

finally done with all his _____ hijinks. For now, at least . . .
_____ADJECTIVE___

MAD LIBS® is fun to play with friends, but you can also play it by yourself! To begin with, DO NOT look at the story on the page below. Fill in the blanks on this page with the words called for. Then, using the words you have selected, fill in the blank spaces in the story.

Now you've created your own hilarious MAD LIBS® game!

THE STORY OF FRANKENSTEIN

PERSON IN ROOM (MALE) _____

ADJECTIVE _____

NOUN _____

NOUN _____

A PLACE _____

PART OF THE BODY (PLURAL) _____

NUMBER _____

PLURAL NOUN _____

NOUN _____

ADJECTIVE _____

NOUN _____

ADJECTIVE _____

A PLACE _____

NOUN _____

NOUN _____

ADVERB _____

VERB (PAST TENSE) _____

MAD●LIBS®
THE STORY OF FRANKENSTEIN

Mary Shelley wrote a science-fiction book about a villainous mad scientist

called _____ Frankenstein. Frankenstein was a/an
　　　　　　　PERSON IN ROOM (MALE)

_____ scientist from the nineteenth _____. His greatest wish was to
ADJECTIVE　　　　　　　　　　　　　　　　　　NOUN

one day become a real _____. So he went to (the) _____ and took
　　　　　　　　　　　　　NOUN　　　　　　　　　　　　　A PLACE

a brain, some _____, and _____ legs from several dead
　　　　　　　PART OF THE BODY (PLURAL)　　　NUMBER

_____. Once he had sewn the body parts together, Frankenstein used
PLURAL NOUN

electricity to make the hideous _____ come to life. Soon, in the middle
　　　　　　　　　　　　　　　　　NOUN

of a/an _____ and stormy _____, the creature awoke! It was
　　　　ADJECTIVE　　　　　　　　NOUN

Frankenstein's greatest creation, and one of the most _____ beings to
　　　　　　　　　　　　　　　　　　　　　　　　　ADJECTIVE

ever live—until it started terrorizing the citizens of (the) _____.
　　　　　　　　　　　　　　　　　　　　　　　　　　　A PLACE

Frankenstein had to take action. He armed himself with a/an _____
　　　　　　　　　　　　　　　　　　　　　　　　　　　　　NOUN

and went on a hunt for the _____ he'd created. After searching
　　　　　　　　　　　　　　NOUN

_____ for months, Frankenstein finally had to give up his search because
ADVERB

he _____ .
　　VERB (PAST TENSE)

MAD LIBS® is fun to play with friends, but you can also play it by yourself! To begin with, DO NOT look at the story on the page below. Fill in the blanks on this page with the words called for. Then, using the words you have selected, fill in the blank spaces in the story.

Now you've created your own hilarious MAD LIBS® game!

ANNOUNCEMENT: THE SCIENCE FAIR WINNERS

CITY _____

ADVERB _____

ADJECTIVE _____

PERSON IN ROOM (FEMALE) _____

NOUN _____

SILLY WORD _____

PERSON IN ROOM (MALE) _____

ADJECTIVE _____

VERB (PAST TENSE) _____

PERSON IN ROOM _____

VERB ENDING IN "ING" _____

NUMBER _____

COLOR _____

ADJECTIVE _____

NOUN _____

ADJECTIVE _____

MAD⊙LIBS®
ANNOUNCEMENT: THE
SCIENCE FAIR WINNERS

Thank you all for participating in the _____ Middle School Science Fair.
CITY

Everyone worked very _____ on their projects, and it shows. We will
ADVERB

now announce the first-, second-, and _____-place winners.
ADJECTIVE

_____ won first prize for her miniature erupting
PERSON IN ROOM (FEMALE)

_____, which was a model of the largest volcano in history, Mount
NOUN

_____.
SILLY WORD

_____ got second place for his super _____ miniature
PERSON IN ROOM (MALE)   ADJECTIVE

solar system, in which all the planets _____ in circles.
VERB (PAST TENSE)

_____ was given a third-place ribbon for _____ an
PERSON IN ROOM   VERB ENDING IN "ING"

ant farm using sand and _____ tiny _____ ants.
NUMBER   COLOR

That's it for the _____ annual science fair. We'll see you next _____
ADJECTIVE   NOUN

for another round of _____ science experiments.
ADJECTIVE

MAD LIBS® is fun to play with friends, but you can also play it by yourself! To begin with, DO NOT look at the story on the page below. Fill in the blanks on this page with the words called for. Then, using the words you have selected, fill in the blank spaces in the story.

Now you've created your own hilarious MAD LIBS® game!

THE PERIODIC TABLE

PLURAL NOUN _____

NOUN _____

NOUN _____

ADJECTIVE _____

A PLACE _____

LAST NAME _____

PLURAL NOUN _____

NUMBER _____

NOUN _____

PLURAL NOUN _____

NOUN _____

LETTER OF THE ALPHABET _____

LETTER OF THE ALPHABET _____

PLURAL NOUN _____

VERB _____

MAD LIBS

THE PERIODIC TABLE

The periodic table of _____ hangs in classrooms and _____
                        PLURAL NOUN   NOUN

laboratories all around the _____. So what's this _____ chart
                             NOUN   ADJECTIVE

all about? Well, in the eighteenth century, a chemist from (the) _____
                                                                 A PLACE

named Dmitri _____ created the very first periodic table of
                  LAST NAME

_____. There are more than _____ elements on the periodic table,
PLURAL NOUN   NUMBER

organized by atomic _____. The elements all have a certain number of
                     NOUN

protons, neutrons, and _____. Each element on the periodic
                        PLURAL NOUN

_____ has a symbol that is often the first two letters of the element's
NOUN

name. For example, helium's symbol is _____
                                        LETTER OF THE ALPHABET

_____. Some scientists say more _____ should be
LETTER OF THE ALPHABET   PLURAL NOUN

added to the table. Maybe someday you'll _____ one yourself!
                                          VERB

MAD LIBS® is fun to play with friends, but you can also play it by yourself! To begin with, DO NOT look at the story on the page below. Fill in the blanks on this page with the words called for. Then, using the words you have selected, fill in the blank spaces in the story.

Now you've created your own hilarious MAD LIBS® game!

DR. JEKYLL AND MR. HYDE

OCCUPATION _____

CITY _____

NOUN _____

ADJECTIVE _____

PLURAL NOUN _____

VERB (PAST TENSE) _____

ADJECTIVE _____

ADVERB _____

VERB _____

PLURAL NOUN _____

ADJECTIVE _____

OCCUPATION _____

NOUN _____

NOUN _____

ADJECTIVE _____

NOUN _____

ADJECTIVE _____

TYPE OF LIQUID _____

PART OF THE BODY _____

MAD LIBS®
DR. JEKYLL AND MR. HYDE

Dr. Jekyll was a friendly old _____ living in _____, England. Mr.
                      OCCUPATION   CITY

Hyde was an evil young _____ who did _____ things to every
                             NOUN   ADJECTIVE

person he met. But these two _____ were also a lot alike. They even
                           PLURAL NOUN

kind of _____ the same! But Hyde had a/an _____
         VERB (PAST TENSE)   ADJECTIVE

power over the doctor, and became _____ evil as time went on. He was
                                 ADVERB

willing to _____ anyone who got in his way, and even took _____
         VERB   PLURAL NOUN

from the _____ townspeople. Then Hyde murdered a well-known
        ADJECTIVE

_____! But, what a surprise—it wasn't Hyde after all. It was Jekyll! They
OCCUPATION

were the same exact _____. Turns out, Jekyll had split-_____
                      NOUN   NOUN

disorder. To fix this, Jekyll did _____ experiments on himself so that
                            ADJECTIVE

Hyde would leave his _____ once and for all. But the experiments were
                     NOUN

too _____. The chemicals and _____ didn't work. In the
     ADJECTIVE   TYPE OF LIQUID

end, Hyde took over Jekyll's _____, and Jekyll was never
                            PART OF THE BODY

seen again.

MAD LIBS® is fun to play with friends, but you can also play it by yourself! To begin with, DO NOT look at the story on the page below. Fill in the blanks on this page with the words called for. Then, using the words you have selected, fill in the blank spaces in the story.

Now you've created your own hilarious MAD LIBS® game!

LABORATORY SAFETY DOS AND DON'TS

PART OF THE BODY (PLURAL) _____

NOUN _____

ADVERB _____

VERB ENDING IN "ING" _____

NOUN _____

VERB _____

ADJECTIVE _____

PART OF THE BODY (PLURAL) _____

TYPE OF FOOD _____

ADJECTIVE _____

TYPE OF CONTAINER _____

ANIMAL (PLURAL) _____

MAD LIBS®
LABORATORY SAFETY
DOS AND DON'TS

Do wear safety goggles. They will protect your _____ .
PART OF THE BODY (PLURAL)

Don't light anything on fire. Always keep a/an _____ extinguisher handy
NOUN

in case you _____ set your laboratory aflame.
ADVERB

Do clean the lens of the microscope before _____ it. You
VERB ENDING IN "ING"

might think you're looking at a cell when really you're just looking at a piece of

_____ .
NOUN

Don't get too close to the test tubes after combining their contents. They might

_____ all over you!
VERB

Do clean up after yourself. Experiments can leave you with _____ hands
ADJECTIVE

and stinky _____ .
PART OF THE BODY (PLURAL)

Don't leave any experiments unattended. If you get hungry and want to grab

a/an _____ sandwich, stop! You need to stay put until the _____
TYPE OF FOOD   _ADJECTIVE_

chemicals in your beakers are done boiling and you've put them safely away in

a/an _____ .
TYPE OF CONTAINER

Do remember to feed your lab _____ . They're not only
ANIMAL (PLURAL)

your test subjects, they're your friends.

MAD LIBS® is fun to play with friends, but you can also play it by yourself! To begin with, DO NOT look at the story on the page below. Fill in the blanks on this page with the words called for. Then, using the words you have selected, fill in the blank spaces in the story.

Now you've created your own hilarious MAD LIBS® game!

I NEED A NEW LAB PARTNER!

PERSON IN ROOM (MALE) _____

ADJECTIVE _____

LAST NAME _____

PERSON IN ROOM (FEMALE) _____

ADJECTIVE _____

VERB (PAST TENSE) _____

NOUN _____

ADJECTIVE _____

NOUN _____

ADJECTIVE _____

ADJECTIVE _____

PLURAL NOUN _____

ADJECTIVE _____

To Whom It May Concern:

Hi. My name is _____, and I am looking for a new,
        PERSON IN ROOM (MALE)

_____ lab partner for Mrs. _____ 's biology class. My
  ADJECTIVE   LAST NAME

last lab partner, _____, was really _____ and
        PERSON IN ROOM (FEMALE)   ADJECTIVE

never _____ our experiments on time. So I asked to
    VERB (PAST TENSE)

switch, and the teacher said if I wanted another _____ partner,
                            NOUN

I had to find one all by myself. If you are smart, _____ in school,
                                ADJECTIVE

and always turn your _____-work in on time, you'd be a/an
                   NOUN

_____ lab partner for me. Please only contact me if you're
   ADJECTIVE

_____ about science and love doing scientific
   ADJECTIVE

_____. If this describes you, contact me at
    PLURAL NOUN

scienceluvr1@-_____-mail.com, or just find me by my locker
            ADJECTIVE

after lunch.

MAD LIBS® is fun to play with friends, but you can also play it by yourself! To begin with, DO NOT look at the story on the page below. Fill in the blanks on this page with the words called for. Then, using the words you have selected, fill in the blank spaces in the story.

Now you've created your own hilarious MAD LIBS® game!

MY WACKY CHEMISTRY TEACHER

LAST NAME _____

PART OF THE BODY (PLURAL) _____

NOUN _____

EXCLAMATION _____

PERSON IN ROOM (FEMALE) _____

ADJECTIVE _____

NOUN _____

ADJECTIVE _____

NOUN _____

EXCLAMATION _____

VERB (PAST TENSE) _____

NOUN _____

ADJECTIVE _____

MAD LIBS®
MY WACKY
CHEMISTRY TEACHER

There are a lot of rumors going around about Mr. _____ , our chemistry
LAST NAME

teacher. He always has a crazy look in his _____ . Sometimes,
PART OF THE BODY (PLURAL)

in the middle of a/an _____ lesson, he'll shout "_____!" for
NOUN EXCLAMATION

no reason at all. My friend _____ told me that he acts
PERSON IN ROOM (FEMALE)

_____ because one time during a/an _____-storm he was struck
ADJECTIVE NOUN

by lightning in his classroom. Ouch! That would probably explain why he is

so _____ all the time and shakes whenever he writes on the
ADJECTIVE

_____-board. Last week, while doing an experiment in class, he yelled,
NOUN

"_____! It's alive!" and then _____ around the
EXCLAMATION VERB (PAST TENSE)

room holding a/an _____ full of mysterious bubbling liquid. Maybe the
NOUN

rumors are true; maybe my teacher really is _____!
ADJECTIVE

MAD LIBS® is fun to play with friends, but you can also play it by yourself! To begin with, DO NOT look at the story on the page below. Fill in the blanks on this page with the words called for. Then, using the words you have selected, fill in the blank spaces in the story.

Now you've created your own hilarious MAD LIBS® game!

AT-HOME EXPERIMENT #1: FLOATING PAPER CLIPS!

NUMBER _____

ADJECTIVE _____

ADJECTIVE _____

TYPE OF LIQUID _____

ADJECTIVE _____

ADVERB _____

NOUN _____

VERB ENDING IN "S" _____

VERB _____

PART OF THE BODY (PLURAL) _____

MAD LIBS
AT-HOME EXPERIMENT #1:
FLOATING PAPER CLIPS!

Materials:

_____ paper clips
_{NUMBER}

A piece of _____ paper
_{ADJECTIVE}

A see-through _____-size bowl
_{ADJECTIVE}

A pencil

Instructions:

1. Fill the bowl with _____ .
   _{TYPE OF LIQUID}

2. Rip a/an _____ piece of tissue paper and _____ drop it
   _{ADJECTIVE}   _{ADVERB}

   onto the water.

3. Drop one of the _____ clips onto the tissue paper.
   _{NOUN}

4. Use the pencil to gently nudge the tissue paper until the paper clip

   _____ .
   _{VERB ENDING IN "S"}

5. If you do this just right, the paper clip will start to _____ in
   _{VERB}

   front of your very _____ !
   _{PART OF THE BODY (PLURAL)}

MAD LIBS® is fun to play with friends, but you can also play it by yourself! To begin with, DO NOT look at the story on the page below. Fill in the blanks on this page with the words called for. Then, using the words you have selected, fill in the blank spaces in the story.

Now you've created your own hilarious MAD LIBS® game!

FAMOUS SCIENTISTS

PLURAL NOUN _____

ADJECTIVE _____

NOUN _____

ADJECTIVE _____

VERB _____

NOUN _____

ADJECTIVE _____

SILLY WORD _____

PLURAL NOUN _____

ADJECTIVE _____

VERB (PAST TENSE) _____

ADVERB _____

ANIMAL _____

PLURAL NOUN _____

MAD LIBS
FAMOUS SCIENTISTS

Over the years, many famous _____ have developed _____

PLURAL NOUN   ADJECTIVE

theories, inventions, and ideas that have contributed to the evolution of

_____-kind. Below are some of the most _____ scientists to ever

NOUN   ADJECTIVE

_____.

VERB

Galileo Galilei was an Italian _____ who invented telescopes and found

NOUN

out a lot of information about the _____ Way Galaxy, the solar system,

ADJECTIVE

and planets like Jupiter and _____.

SILLY WORD

Sir Isaac Newton discovered most of what we now know about gravity. He

also wrote scientific _____ called the First Law of Motion, the Second

PLURAL NOUN

Law of Motion, and the _____ Law of Motion.

ADJECTIVE

Charles Darwin invented theories about natural selection, which proved how

different species _____ over hundreds of years on Earth.

VERB (PAST TENSE)

He _____ studied several species of _____ on the Galapagos

ADVERB   ANIMAL

_____.

PLURAL NOUN

MAD LIBS® is fun to play with friends, but you can also play it by yourself! To begin with, DO NOT look at the story on the page below. Fill in the blanks on this page with the words called for. Then, using the words you have selected, fill in the blank spaces in the story.

Now you've created your own hilarious MAD LIBS® game!

TURN YOUR BEDROOM INTO A SECRET LAB

ADJECTIVE _____

ADJECTIVE _____

VERB ENDING IN "ING" _____

NOUN _____

VERB _____

PLURAL NOUN _____

NOUN _____

ADJECTIVE _____

TYPE OF CONTAINER (PLURAL) _____

TYPE OF LIQUID _____

ADVERB _____

ADJECTIVE _____

VERB ENDING IN "ING" _____

MAD LIBS
TURN YOUR BEDROOM
INTO A SECRET LAB

Follow these _____ steps to turn your boring, _____ bedroom into
             ADJECTIVE   ADJECTIVE

a fully _____ science lab! First, put a big _____ on your
       VERB ENDING IN "ING"   NOUN

bedroom door that reads KEEP OUT! Scientists need to _____ in silence
                                                   VERB

without any annoying _____ interrupting them. Then clear off your
                         PLURAL NOUN

_____. You'll need it to hold all your oozy, _____ chemicals. Gather
  NOUN   ADJECTIVE

a bunch of _____ and put them all over your desk. Connect
       TYPE OF CONTAINER (PLURAL)

them with tubing so you can watch all the _____ run through
                                         TYPE OF LIQUID

them—_____ cool! Finally, pull your curtains shut—you don't want
      ADVERB

anyone to see what kind of _____ concoctions you're
                                 ADJECTIVE

_____!
VERB ENDING IN "ING"

MAD LIBS® is fun to play with friends, but you can also play it by yourself! To begin with, DO NOT look at the story on the page below. Fill in the blanks on this page with the words called for. Then, using the words you have selected, fill in the blank spaces in the story.

Now you've created your own hilarious MAD LIBS® game!

THE MAD SCIENTIST'S SHOPPING LIST

PLURAL NOUN _____

PART OF THE BODY _____

ARTICLE OF CLOTHING _____

VERB ENDING IN "ING" _____

ANIMAL (PLURAL) _____

PLURAL NOUN _____

NOUN _____

ADJECTIVE _____

VERB _____

NOUN _____

- Long, rubbery black _____ to wear on your hands
  PLURAL NOUN

- Giant round _____-glasses with black frames
  PART OF THE BODY

- Long white lab _____
  ARTICLE OF CLOTHING

- Two beakers—one to hold in each hand while _____
  VERB ENDING IN "ING"

  maniacally

- Several cages for all your lab _____
  ANIMAL (PLURAL)

- Assorted _____ floating in formaldehyde to add to your
  PLURAL NOUN

  collection

- A chalkboard and a piece of _____ to write down your
  NOUN

  _____ hypotheses and equations
  ADJECTIVE

- A giant electrical power switch to turn on when you need to

  _____ something to life
  VERB

- A Bunsen burner to light every _____ on fire!
  NOUN

MAD LIBS® is fun to play with friends, but you can also play it by yourself! To begin with, DO NOT look at the story on the page below. Fill in the blanks on this page with the words called for. Then, using the words you have selected, fill in the blank spaces in the story.

Now you've created your own hilarious MAD LIBS® game!

MORE FAMOUS SCIENTISTS

ADJECTIVE _____

ADJECTIVE _____

NOUN _____

PLURAL NOUN _____

PERSON IN ROOM (MALE) _____

OCCUPATION _____

NOUN _____

VERB _____

NOUN _____

PLURAL NOUN _____

COLOR _____

NOUN _____

Here are a few more _____ scientists!
ADJECTIVE

Nikola Tesla was born in Croatia. Later, he moved to the _____ States
ADJECTIVE
of America and became an inventor. He helped create fluorescent
_____-bulbs so that people wouldn't have to use _____ to light
NOUN   PLURAL NOUN
their homes. Tesla also invented radio and worked with _____
                                                         PERSON IN ROOM (MALE)
Edison to invent things that helped electricity work.

Alexander Graham Bell was a/an _____ from the nineteenth
OCCUPATION
century. His mother was deaf, as was his _____. Because of this, Bell was
NOUN
interested in speech and hearing. He decided to create something that would
help people _____ each other, no matter where they were. He invented
VERB
the tele-_____ so that people could talk to one another.
NOUN

Stephen Hawking is a British physicist who studies galaxies and solar
_____. He has discovered a lot about _____ holes. His most
PLURAL NOUN   COLOR
famous book is called *A Brief History of* _____.
NOUN

MAD LIBS® is fun to play with friends, but you can also play it by yourself! To begin with, DO NOT look at the story on the page below. Fill in the blanks on this page with the words called for. Then, using the words you have selected, fill in the blank spaces in the story.

Now you've created your own hilarious MAD LIBS® game!

FRANKENSTEIN'S MONSTER

NUMBER _____

NOUN _____

ADJECTIVE _____

COLOR _____

NOUN _____

PLURAL NOUN _____

PART OF THE BODY _____

PART OF THE BODY _____

ADJECTIVE _____

VERB (PAST TENSE) _____

ARTICLE OF CLOTHING _____

ADJECTIVE _____

ADJECTIVE _____

NOUN _____

MAD LIBS®
FRANKENSTEIN'S MONSTER

Frankenstein's monster was a hideous, _____-foot-tall _____.
NUMBER   NOUN

His skin was a/an _____ shade of _____, his head was shaped like
ADJECTIVE   COLOR

a/an _____, and he had _____ sticking out of both sides of his
NOUN   PLURAL NOUN

neck. Frankenstein's monster also had black lips and spiky black hair on his

_____, and his _____ was filled with big
PART OF THE BODY   PART OF THE BODY

white teeth. His _____ arms stuck straight out whenever he
ADJECTIVE

_____ down the street, because the black shirt and
VERB (PAST TENSE)

_____ he always wore were too small on his grotesque,
ARTICLE OF CLOTHING

_____ body. What a/an _____-looking _____ he was!
ADJECTIVE   ADJECTIVE   NOUN

MAD LIBS® is fun to play with friends, but you can also play it by yourself! To begin with, DO NOT look at the story on the page below. Fill in the blanks on this page with the words called for. Then, using the words you have selected, fill in the blank spaces in the story.

Now you've created your own hilarious MAD LIBS® game!

AT-HOME EXPERIMENT #2: ERUPTING VOLCANO!

NOUN _____

ADJECTIVE _____

COLOR _____

VERB ENDING IN "ING" _____

TYPE OF LIQUID _____

ADJECTIVE _____

NOUN _____

PLURAL NOUN _____

ADJECTIVE _____

NUMBER _____

VERB _____

MAD LIBS®
AT-HOME EXPERIMENT #2:
ERUPTING VOLCANO!

Materials:

A homemade volcano made out of plaster or _____-mâché
                                                    NOUN

A small _____ container
           ADJECTIVE

_____ or yellow food coloring
    COLOR

_____ soda
  VERB ENDING IN "ING"

_____
    TYPE OF LIQUID
Dish soap

Instructions:

1. Put the _____ container at the top of your volcano.
              ADJECTIVE

2. Pour in a little bit of baking soda and some dish _____.
                                                         NOUN

3. Add a few _____ of _____ food coloring.
               PLURAL NOUN   ADJECTIVE

4. Pour in _____ ounces of vinegar.
             NUMBER

5. Watch your volcano _____ with lava!
                         VERB

MAD LIBS® is fun to play with friends, but you can also play it by yourself! To begin with, DO NOT look at the story on the page below. Fill in the blanks on this page with the words called for. Then, using the words you have selected, fill in the blank spaces in the story.

Now you've created your own hilarious MAD LIBS® game!

THE WORST SCI-FI NIGHTMARE I EVER HAD

OCCUPATION _____

PART OF THE BODY _____

ADJECTIVE _____

PLURAL NOUN _____

VERB _____

ADJECTIVE _____

NOUN _____

PART OF THE BODY (PLURAL) _____

VERB _____

COLOR _____

TYPE OF LIQUID _____

NOUN _____

ADJECTIVE _____

I had a dream last night that a crazy _____ was trying to perform
                                        OCCUPATION

experiments on me. He took a strand of my _____ and looked
                                              PART OF THE BODY

at it under a microscope. Then he told me to sit in his _____
                                                          ADJECTIVE

chair. But I was scared—there were a bunch of electrical _____
                                                            PLURAL NOUN

tied to it, and I was afraid he was going to _____ me in it! I said,
                                                VERB

"No, thanks, you _____ scientist—I'm getting the
                   ADJECTIVE

_____ out of here." He looked me right in the
          NOUN

_____ and said, "Don't you dare try to leave my dungeon!
PART OF THE BODY (PLURAL)

You can't _____ —the door's locked!" Suddenly, he pounced on
            VERB

me, and everything turned to _____. I woke up with
                                COLOR

_____ running down my temples. Thank _____ that
TYPE OF LIQUID   NOUN

nightmare is over. I hope I never see that _____ scientist again!
                                              ADJECTIVE

MAD LIBS® is fun to play with friends, but you can also play it by yourself! To begin with, DO NOT look at the story on the page below. Fill in the blanks on this page with the words called for. Then, using the words you have selected, fill in the blank spaces in the story.

Now you've created your own hilarious MAD LIBS® game!

AT-HOME EXPERIMENT #3: TORNADO IN A BOTTLE!

NOUN _____

VERB ENDING IN "ING" _____

VERB _____

ADJECTIVE _____

ADJECTIVE _____

VERB _____

NOUN _____

ADJECTIVE _____

NOUN _____

ADJECTIVE _____

NOUN _____

ADJECTIVE _____

VERB (PAST TENSE) _____

MAD LIBS®
AT-HOME EXPERIMENT #3:
TORNADO IN A BOTTLE!

Materials:

Water

A see-through plastic soda _____ with a cap
                            NOUN

Glitter, to see debris _____ in the bottle
                       VERB ENDING IN "ING"

Dish soap to make your tornado _____
                               VERB

Instructions:

1. Fill the entire _____ bottle with water until it is almost all the
                   ADJECTIVE

   way _____.
       ADJECTIVE

2 _____ a few drops of dish _____ into the bottle. Add the
   VERB   NOUN

   _____ glitter.
   ADJECTIVE

3. Screw the _____ onto the top of the bottle.
             NOUN

4. Turn the bottle upside_____ and hold it near the cap.
                         ADJECTIVE

5. Spin the bottle in a/an _____-wise rotation.
                           NOUN

6. Stop spinning the bottle and admire the _____ tornado you
                                            ADJECTIVE

   _____!
   VERB (PAST TENSE)

MAD LIBS® is fun to play with friends, but you can also play it by yourself! To begin with, DO NOT look at the story on the page below. Fill in the blanks on this page with the words called for. Then, using the words you have selected, fill in the blank spaces in the story.

Now you've created your own hilarious MAD LIBS® game!

THE FIRST WEEK OF SCIENCE CLASS

ADJECTIVE _____

LAST NAME _____

PLURAL NOUN _____

PLURAL NOUN _____

NOUN _____

NOUN _____

ANIMAL (PLURAL) _____

PERSON IN ROOM _____

ADJECTIVE _____

VERB _____

MAD LIBS®
THE FIRST WEEK OF
SCIENCE CLASS

My first few days of science class were so _____! Our teacher, Miss
___ADJECTIVE___

_____, taught us all about matter and energy, atoms and
___LAST NAME___

_____, and the difference between solids, _____, and gases. We
___PLURAL NOUN___   ___PLURAL NOUN___

even got to watch a video about gravity and why things in outer _____
___NOUN___

float but things on Earth fall to the _____! Our teacher says that next
___NOUN___

week we're going to do our first experiment and that, if we want, some day this

year we can even dissect _____! My friend _____
___ANIMAL (PLURAL)___   ___PERSON IN ROOM___

thought dissecting sounded gross, but I think it sounds really _____!
___ADJECTIVE___

I can't wait to _____ more about science next week.
___VERB___

MAD LIBS®

SPY MAD LIBS

Mad Libs
An Imprint of Penguin Random House

INSTRUCTIONS

MAD LIBS® is a game for people who don't like games!
It can be played by one, two, three, four, or forty.

• RIDICULOUSLY SIMPLE DIRECTIONS

In this tablet you will find stories containing blank spaces where words are left out.
One player, the READER, selects one of these stories. The READER does not tell anyone
what the story is about. Instead, he/she asks the other players, the WRITERS, to give
him/her words. These words are used to fill in the blank spaces in the story.

• TO PLAY

The READER asks each WRITER in turn to call out a word—an adjective or a noun or
whatever the space calls for—and uses them to fill in the blank spaces in the story. The
result is a MAD LIBS® game.

When the READER then reads the completed MAD LIBS® game to the other players,
they will discover that they have written a story that is fantastic, screamingly funny,
shocking, silly, crazy, or just plain dumb—depending upon which words each WRITER
called out.

• EXAMPLE (*Before* and *After*)

"_____!" he said _____
　　　　EXCLAMATION　　　　　　　　　　　ADVERB

as he jumped into his convertible _____ and
　　　　　　　　　　　　　　　　　　　　　NOUN

drove off with his _____ wife.
　　　　　　　　ADJECTIVE

"_____OUCH_____!" he said _____STUPIDLY_____
　　　　EXCLAMATION　　　　　　　　　　　ADVERB

as he jumped into his convertible _____CAT_____ and
　　　　　　　　　　　　　　　　　　　NOUN

drove off with his _____BRAVE_____ wife.
　　　　　　　　ADJECTIVE

MAD LIBS®

QUICK REVIEW

In case you have forgotten what adjectives, adverbs, nouns, and verbs are, here is a quick review:

An ADJECTIVE describes something or somebody. *Lumpy, soft, ugly, messy,* and *short* are adjectives.

An ADVERB tells how something is done. It modifies a verb and usually ends in "ly." *Modestly, stupidly, greedily,* and *carefully* are adverbs.

A NOUN is the name of a person, place, or thing. *Sidewalk, umbrella, bridle, bathtub,* and *nose* are nouns.

A VERB is an action word. *Run, pitch, jump,* and *swim* are verbs. Put the verbs in past tense if the directions say PAST TENSE. *Ran, pitched, jumped,* and *swam* are verbs in the past tense.

When we ask for A PLACE, we mean any sort of place: a country or city *(Spain, Cleveland)* or a room *(bathroom, kitchen).*

An EXCLAMATION or SILLY WORD is any sort of funny sound, gasp, grunt, or outcry, like *Wow!, Ouch!, Whomp!, Ick!,* and *Gadzooks!*

When we ask for specific words, like a NUMBER, a COLOR, an ANIMAL, or a PART OF THE BODY, we mean a word that is one of those things, like *seven, blue, horse,* or *head.*

When we ask for a PLURAL, it means more than one. For example, *cat* pluralized is *cats.*

MAD LIBS® is fun to play with friends, but you can also play it by yourself! To begin with, DO NOT look at the story on the page below. Fill in the blanks on this page with the words called for. Then, using the words you have selected, fill in the blank spaces in the story.

Now you've created your own hilarious MAD LIBS® game!

THE ART OF ESPIONAGE

VERB ENDING IN "ING" _____

ADJECTIVE _____

ADJECTIVE _____

PLURAL NOUN _____

ADJECTIVE _____

PERSON IN ROOM _____

PLURAL NOUN _____

A PLACE _____

ADJECTIVE _____

CELEBRITY _____

NOUN _____

PLURAL NOUN _____

ADJECTIVE _____

PLURAL NOUN _____

PLURAL NOUN _____

NOUN _____

PLURAL NOUN _____

Espionage is the formal word for _____. In the shadowy
                                    VERB ENDING IN "ING"

world of spies, a/an _____ organization like the US government uses
                          ADJECTIVE

spies to infiltrate _____ groups for the purpose of obtaining top secret
                        ADJECTIVE

_____. For example, spies might have to crack the code for accessing
  PLURAL NOUN

confidential, _____ files, or their mission could be far more
                    ADJECTIVE

dangerous—like stealing the key ingredient for making _____'s
                                                        PERSON IN ROOM

award-winning Explosive Fudgy _____. Spies are found all over (the)
                                 PLURAL NOUN

_____—but they are not allowed to reveal their _____ identities.
  A PLACE   ADJECTIVE

A teacher, _____, or even the little old _____ with the cane and
             CELEBRITY   NOUN

fifteen pet _____ who lives next door to you could be a spy. The world
              PLURAL NOUN

of spying might seem glamorous and _____—but it's filled with risks
                                      ADJECTIVE

and _____! Sure, spies have a never-ending supply of supercool
        PLURAL NOUN

electronic _____, but they can't trust any _____—which is why
             PLURAL NOUN   NOUN

the number one rule of spies is to keep friends close—and _____ closer!
                                                            PLURAL NOUN

MAD LIBS® is fun to play with friends, but you can also play it by yourself! To begin with, DO NOT look at the story on the page below. Fill in the blanks on this page with the words called for. Then, using the words you have selected, fill in the blank spaces in the story.

Now you've created your own hilarious MAD LIBS® game!

SPY HALL OF FAME

PLURAL NOUN _____

ADJECTIVE _____

PERSON IN ROOM (MALE) _____

NUMBER _____

ADJECTIVE _____

NOUN _____

PART OF THE BODY _____

ADJECTIVE _____

PART OF THE BODY _____

ADJECTIVE _____

PLURAL NOUN _____

NOUN _____

PART OF THE BODY _____

NOUN _____

NOUN _____

VERB _____

CELEBRITY _____

NOUN _____

MAD LIBS®
SPY HALL OF FAME

The Spy Hall of Fame honors the brave _____ of that
PLURAL NOUN

_____ profession known as spying. Inductees include:
ADJECTIVE

- _____ **Bond**—Famously known as Agent Double
  PERSON IN ROOM (MALE)

  "O" _____, this spy was as handsome as he was _____. Not
  NUMBER   ADJECTIVE

  only did Bond nab the bad _____every time, he always won the
  NOUN

  _____ of the _____ woman, as well.
  PART OF THE BODY   ADJECTIVE

- **Chuck "Eagle _____" Spyglass**—Whether it was
  PART OF THE BODY

  designing a/an _____ pair of night-vision _____ or hiding a
  ADJECTIVE   PLURAL NOUN

  tiny camera inside a gold _____ that a spy could wear around
  NOUN

  his _____, Chuck was the go-to _____ for his
  PART OF THE BODY   NOUN

  wizardry in surveillance.

- **Joe the Spy**—Joe was your typical _____ next door. His high
  NOUN

  school yearbook denoted him as "Most Likely to _____." Who
  VERB

  would have thought this Average Joe would be the _____ of the spy
  CELEBRITY

  world when he single-handedly took down an international ring of

  _____ robbers?!
  NOUN

MAD LIBS® is fun to play with friends, but you can also play it by yourself! To begin with, DO NOT look at the story on the page below. Fill in the blanks on this page with the words called for. Then, using the words you have selected, fill in the blank spaces in the story.

Now you've created your own hilarious MAD LIBS® game!

HOW TO SPEAK LIKE A SPY

ADJECTIVE _____

NOUN _____

VERB _____

NOUN _____

VERB ENDING IN "ING" _____

PLURAL NOUN _____

ADJECTIVE _____

NOUN _____

ADJECTIVE _____

CELEBRITY _____

PERSON IN ROOM _____

NOUN _____

NOUN _____

PLURAL NOUN _____

ADJECTIVE _____

PLURAL NOUN _____

MAD LIBS

HOW TO SPEAK LIKE A SPY

Spies speak their own _____ language. Common terms include:
ADJECTIVE

- **Target**—a person or a/an _____ of interest whom a spy watches
  NOUN

  come and _____
  VERB

- **Surveillance**—to monitor or observe a/an _____ with visual,
  NOUN

  listening, or _____ equipment like cameras, satellites, or
  VERB ENDING IN "ING"

  long-distance _____
  PLURAL NOUN

- **Bug**—a/an _____ device that can be planted on an object such
  ADJECTIVE

  as a car, remote control, or _____ phone to listen in on a target's
  NOUN

  _____ conversations
  ADJECTIVE

- **Alias**—the name a spy uses, like _____ or _____, while
  CELEBRITY   PERSON IN ROOM

  undercover

- **Mole**—a/an _____ from one spy organization who gets a job
  NOUN

  within a rival _____ organization in order to obtain inside
  NOUN

  information or other secret _____
  PLURAL NOUN

- **Classified**—sensitive and _____ information that only certain
  ADJECTIVE

  levels of _____ have authorized clearance to access
  PLURAL NOUN

MAD LIBS® is fun to play with friends, but you can also play it by yourself! To begin with, DO NOT look at the story on the page below. Fill in the blanks on this page with the words called for. Then, using the words you have selected, fill in the blank spaces in the story.

Now you've created your own hilarious MAD LIBS® game!

A SPY BIRTHDAY PARTY

NUMBER _____

NOUN _____

ADJECTIVE _____

PLURAL NOUN _____

ADJECTIVE _____

PART OF THE BODY (PLURAL) _____

ADJECTIVE _____

VERB _____

ADJECTIVE _____

PLURAL NOUN _____

NOUN _____

NOUN _____

PLURAL NOUN _____

PART OF THE BODY (PLURAL) _____

PLURAL NOUN _____

ADJECTIVE _____

ADJECTIVE _____

NOUN _____

PLURAL NOUN _____

MAD LIBS
A SPY BIRTHDAY PARTY

When I turned _____ years old, my mom and _____ threw a/an
              NUMBER   NOUN

_____ spy-themed birthday party for me. I invited ten of my closest
ADJECTIVE

_____, and we spent a/an _____ afternoon doing cool spy stuff.
PLURAL NOUN   ADJECTIVE

We slipped black sunglasses over our _____, grabbed
                                     PART OF THE BODY (PLURAL)

_____ toy cell phones, and practiced our surveillance techniques with a
ADJECTIVE

game of hide-and-_____ around my backyard. We decoded _____
                  VERB   ADJECTIVE

messages that my parents had written on colorful _____. We pounded on
                                                 PLURAL NOUN

a/an _____-shaped piñata with a wooden _____, and we put spy
     NOUN   NOUN

tattoos like binoculars, computers, and micro-_____ all over our
                                              PLURAL NOUN

_____. Later my mom served cake and _____, and
PART OF THE BODY (PLURAL)   PLURAL NOUN

everyone sang "_____ Birthday" to me. I got a ton of _____ gifts,
               ADJECTIVE   ADJECTIVE

but my favorite was the motion-activated _____ that would alert me to
                                         NOUN

any _____ about to sneak into my room. Every good spy needs one of
    PLURAL NOUN

these!

MAD LIBS® is fun to play with friends, but you can also play it by yourself! To begin with, DO NOT look at the story on the page below. Fill in the blanks on this page with the words called for. Then, using the words you have selected, fill in the blank spaces in the story.

Now you've created your own hilarious MAD LIBS® game!

FROM THE SPY FILE

PERSON IN ROOM _____

ADJECTIVE _____

CELEBRITY _____

VERB ENDING IN "ING" _____

NOUN _____

ADJECTIVE _____

ADJECTIVE _____

NOUN _____

ADJECTIVE _____

ADJECTIVE _____

A PLACE _____

ADJECTIVE _____

NOUN _____

PART OF THE BODY _____

PLURAL NOUN _____

ADJECTIVE _____

PART OF THE BODY _____

ADJECTIVE _____

MAD LIBS
FROM THE SPY FILE

To Agent _____ : At this morning's _____ management
     PERSON IN ROOM   ADJECTIVE

meeting, it was decided by Agency Chief _____ that you are being
                                  CELEBRITY

assigned to the case known internally as Operation _____
                                           VERB ENDING IN "ING"

_____. This memo will provide the _____ details of the case, and
  NOUN   ADJECTIVE

you will be briefed further in the coming week. As you may know, this case

involves a band of _____ thieves who stole the blueprints to a top secret
                ADJECTIVE

robot _____ that threatens the security of our _____ country. They
     NOUN   ADJECTIVE

have hidden the prints somewhere in a/an _____ location on the
                                ADJECTIVE

outskirts of (the) _____. Their leader's name is Uno Ojo, which translates
           A PLACE

to _____ _____. You will know him by the black eye patch he
 ADJECTIVE   NOUN

wears over his _____. Be advised that he and his group of
         PART OF THE BODY

evil _____ are armed and _____, so use extreme caution if you
  PLURAL NOUN   ADJECTIVE

come face-to-_____ with any of them. As any good spy
       PART OF THE BODY

knows, you're of no use to the agency if you're _____.
                                 ADJECTIVE

MAD LIBS® is fun to play with friends, but you can also play it by yourself! To begin with, DO NOT look at the story on the page below. Fill in the blanks on this page with the words called for. Then, using the words you have selected, fill in the blank spaces in the story.

Now you've created your own hilarious MAD LIBS® game!

WELCOME TO HEADQUARTERS

NOUN _____

VERB _____

ADJECTIVE _____

ADJECTIVE _____

NOUN _____

PERSON IN ROOM _____

ADJECTIVE _____

PLURAL NOUN _____

PART OF THE BODY _____

CELEBRITY _____

ADJECTIVE _____

PLURAL NOUN _____

VERB ENDING IN "ING" _____

PART OF THE BODY _____

The new spy headquarters that just opened on the corner of Fifth Avenue and

_____ Street really makes people stop and _____. The building
NOUN   VERB

itself features _____, modern architecture on the outside and _____,
ADJECTIVE   ADJECTIVE

state-of-the-art technology on the inside. To gain entrance, you must step

through an electronic _____ while a security guard named
NOUN

_____ pats you down with a/an _____ wand to make sure
PERSON IN ROOM   ADJECTIVE

you aren't carrying any dangerous _____. Then you have to wear a
PLURAL NOUN

name badge around your _____ that says, "Hi! My name is
PART OF THE BODY

_____." There's a/an _____ elevator to take you anywhere
CELEBRITY   ADJECTIVE

you need to go. There are closed-circuit _____ everywhere, so if anyone
PLURAL NOUN

in the building starts _____ inappropriately, security will
VERB ENDING IN "ING"

instantly remove them. Certain areas are completely off-limits—unless, of

course, you place your _____ on the scanner and it gives
PART OF THE BODY

you authorized clearance.

MAD LIBS® is fun to play with friends, but you can also play it by yourself! To begin with, DO NOT look at the story on the page below. Fill in the blanks on this page with the words called for. Then, using the words you have selected, fill in the blank spaces in the story.

Now you've created your own hilarious MAD LIBS® game!

GEAR & GADGETS, PART 1

ADJECTIVE _____

ADJECTIVE _____

PART OF THE BODY _____

NOUN _____

PLURAL NOUN _____

PLURAL NOUN _____

ADJECTIVE _____

COLOR _____

VERB ENDING IN "ING" _____

TYPE OF LIQUID _____

ADJECTIVE _____

ADJECTIVE _____

CELEBRITY _____

PART OF THE BODY (PLURAL) _____

VERB ENDING IN "ING" _____

MAD LIBS
GEAR & GADGETS, PART 1

One of the most _____ parts about being a spy are the gadgets you get to
                        ADJECTIVE

use! Here are some examples:

- **Spy phones**—These do much more than make _____ calls. They
                                              ADJECTIVE

  can scan _____-prints on a drinking _____
              PART OF THE BODY   NOUN

  or shoot laser _____ if a spy is being chased.
                  PLURAL NOUN

- **X-ray vision** _____—These _____ glasses are so powerful
                    PLURAL NOUN   ADJECTIVE

  that they can help spies determine if an enemy is wearing _____
                                                             COLOR

  underwear.

- _____ **beans**—A must-have defense weapon for any
  VERB ENDING IN "ING"

  spy, the beans are dropped in a glass of _____ to render
                                            TYPE OF LIQUID

  an enemy _____.
            ADJECTIVE

- **Mini flashlight**—This clever and _____ little tool projects a
                                       ADJECTIVE

  holographic image of _____ to distract bad guys.
                        CELEBRITY

- **Eavesdropping ears**—Spies affix long-range earpieces to their

  _____ to detect where their targets are
  PART OF THE BODY (PLURAL)

  _____.
  VERB ENDING IN "ING"

MAD LIBS® is fun to play with friends, but you can also play it by yourself! To begin with, DO NOT look at the story on the page below. Fill in the blanks on this page with the words called for. Then, using the words you have selected, fill in the blank spaces in the story.

Now you've created your own hilarious MAD LIBS® game!

I, SPY

PERSON IN ROOM _____

NUMBER _____

ADJECTIVE _____

ADJECTIVE _____

A PLACE _____

NOUN _____

ADJECTIVE _____

PLURAL NOUN _____

SILLY WORD _____

PART OF THE BODY _____

ADJECTIVE _____

CELEBRITY _____

VERB ENDING IN "ING" _____

PLURAL NOUN _____

NOUN _____

PLURAL NOUN _____

ADJECTIVE _____

PLURAL NOUN _____

ADJECTIVE _____

PART OF THE BODY (PLURAL) _____

MAD LIBS

I, SPY

My name is _____, and I became a spy when I was only
PERSON IN ROOM

_____ years old. It certainly was an exciting, _____ time in my life!
NUMBER   ADJECTIVE

I was sent to _____ locations all over the world, including London, Paris,
ADJECTIVE

and (the) _____. Depending on the assignment, there could be
A PLACE

_____ chases, _____ explosions, or _____ collapsing around
NOUN   ADJECTIVE   PLURAL NOUN

me. _____, I'm lucky I didn't lose a/an _____
SILLY WORD   PART OF THE BODY

during some of my _____ spy adventures! One time my partner
ADJECTIVE

_____ and I were _____ in an alley in pursuit of a target
CELEBRITY   VERB ENDING IN "ING"

when a shower of flaming _____ shot out of the darkness. Another
PLURAL NOUN

time I was piloting a/an _____ when a flock of _____ flew right
NOUN   PLURAL NOUN

into the engines. Fortunately, I crash-landed in a/an _____ lake, so I
ADJECTIVE

managed to walk away with only a few scrapes and _____. Now that
PLURAL NOUN

I'm retired, my life isn't nearly as _____, but on the other hand, it's nice
ADJECTIVE

just to be able to put my _____ up and relax.
PART OF THE BODY (PLURAL)

MAD LIBS® is fun to play with friends, but you can also play it by yourself! To begin with, DO NOT look at the story on the page below. Fill in the blanks on this page with the words called for. Then, using the words you have selected, fill in the blank spaces in the story.

Now you've created your own hilarious MAD LIBS® game!

DRESSING IN DISGUISE

ADJECTIVE _____

ARTICLE OF CLOTHING (PLURAL) _____

ADJECTIVE _____

CELEBRITY _____

PERSON IN ROOM (MALE) _____

ADJECTIVE _____

PART OF THE BODY _____

NOUN _____

PLURAL NOUN _____

VERB _____

PLURAL NOUN _____

ADJECTIVE _____

PLURAL NOUN _____

COLOR _____

ADJECTIVE _____

PART OF THE BODY (PLURAL) _____

MAD LIBS
DRESSING IN DISGUISE

A superspy must excel in the _____ art of disguise. He needs to be
                      ADJECTIVE

able to use _____, makeup, and _____ acting
      ARTICLE OF CLOTHING (PLURAL)   ADJECTIVE

skills to morph into other characters, such as a superstar like _____
                                                    CELEBRITY

or just a regular guy like _____. Disguises can range from
                        PERSON IN ROOM (MALE)

simple to outrageously _____. One of the easiest disguises is a pair of
                      ADJECTIVE

eyeglasses with a large _____ and mustache attached.
                      PART OF THE BODY

Other disguises are more complicated, like a full-body _____ costume.
                                            NOUN

Sometimes spies even have to dress as _____—a particularly challenging
                               PLURAL NOUN

disguise as it's difficult to _____ while wearing _____! Once a
                      VERB   PLURAL NOUN

person advances to the level of spy, he's given a/an _____ Spy Disguise
                                        ADJECTIVE

Kit containing everything he needs to become anyone he wants. The kits

contain helpful disguise tools like _____ to color your hair
                              PLURAL NOUN

_____, _____ wigs, and—best of all—fake
    COLOR   ADJECTIVE

_____.
   PART OF THE BODY (PLURAL)

MAD LIBS® is fun to play with friends, but you can also play it by yourself! To begin with, DO NOT look at the story on the page below. Fill in the blanks on this page with the words called for. Then, using the words you have selected, fill in the blank spaces in the story.

Now you've created your own hilarious MAD LIBS® game!

ULTIMATE SPY MOBILE

NOUN _____

ADJECTIVE _____

PLURAL NOUN _____

NOUN _____

SILLY WORD _____

PLURAL NOUN _____

VERB _____

ADJECTIVE _____

NOUN _____

PART OF THE BODY _____

PLURAL NOUN _____

PLURAL NOUN _____

ADJECTIVE _____

NOUN _____

NOUN _____

ADJECTIVE _____

CELEBRITY _____

A top-notch spy deserves to drive a world-class _____ with all these
<u>NOUN</u>

_____ features:
<u>ADJECTIVE</u>

- Computers and TV monitors to communicate with _____ back
<u>PLURAL NOUN</u>

  at headquarters

- _____-activated doors that slide open when the password
<u>NOUN</u>

  "_____" is spoken
<u>SILLY WORD</u>

- Jet sprays that shoot _____ so that any enemy in pursuit will
<u>PLURAL NOUN</u>

  crash and _____
<u>VERB</u>

- A/an _____ punching _____ that will bonk an enemy on
<u>ADJECTIVE</u> <u>NOUN</u>

  the _____ if he gets inside the vehicle
<u>PART OF THE BODY</u>

- Razor-sharp _____ along the outside edges of the car to slice the
<u>PLURAL NOUN</u>

  tires of other passing _____
<u>PLURAL NOUN</u>

- A/an _____ battering ram on the front end to bash into a/an
<u>ADJECTIVE</u>

  _____ barricade
<u>NOUN</u>

- _____-boosters that will propel the vehicle into the air
<u>NOUN</u>

- Best of all, a/an _____ sound system that fills the vehicle with
<u>ADJECTIVE</u>

  the sweet melodies of _____
<u>CELEBRITY</u>

MAD LIBS® is fun to play with friends, but you can also play it by yourself! To begin with, DO NOT look at the story on the page below. Fill in the blanks on this page with the words called for. Then, using the words you have selected, fill in the blank spaces in the story.

Now you've created your own hilarious MAD LIBS® game!

A TRIP TO THE SPY MUSEUM

A PLACE _____

ADJECTIVE _____

VERB ENDING IN "ING" _____

PLURAL NOUN _____

PLURAL NOUN _____

ADJECTIVE _____

NOUN _____

PLURAL NOUN _____

ADJECTIVE _____

VERB ENDING IN "ING" _____

PLURAL NOUN _____

NOUN _____

ADJECTIVE _____

VERB ENDING IN "ING" _____

NOUN _____

ADJECTIVE _____

NOUN _____

PLURAL NOUN _____

ADJECTIVE _____

MAD LIBS
A TRIP TO THE SPY MUSEUM

Located in (the) _____, the International Spy Museum is the only
　　　　　　　　 A PLACE

_____ museum in the United States dedicated to the covert profession of
ADJECTIVE

_____. The museum features the largest collection of spy-
VERB ENDING IN "ING"

themed _____ ever placed on public display. These items bring to life the
　　　　 PLURAL NOUN

work of famous _____ as well as history-making _____ espionage
　　　　　　　 PLURAL NOUN　　　　　　　　　　　　ADJECTIVE

missions. The stories of spies are told through films, an interactive _____,
　　　　　　　　　　　　　　　　　　　　　　　　　　　　　　　　NOUN

and state-of-the-art _____. The museum contains a/an _____
　　　　　　　　　 PLURAL NOUN　　　　　　　　　　　　　　　ADJECTIVE

gift shop and a restaurant called _____ Spy Café. Young
　　　　　　　　　　　　　　　　　　VERB ENDING IN "ING"

_____ love to visit the spy museum for _____ parties, field
PLURAL NOUN　　　　　　　　　　　　　　　　　NOUN

trips, and _____ scavenger hunts. The exhibits teach up-
　　　　　　 ADJECTIVE

and-_____ spies about _____ surveillance, threat analysis,
　　 VERB ENDING IN "ING"　　　　　　 NOUN

and maintaining one's _____ cover. The goal of the International
　　　　　　　　　　　 ADJECTIVE

_____ Museum is to teach _____ about espionage in a fun,
NOUN　　　　　　　　　　　 PLURAL NOUN

_____ way. Who knows? It might even make them want to join
ADJECTIVE

the team someday!

MAD LIBS® is fun to play with friends, but you can also play it by yourself! To begin with, DO NOT look at the story on the page below. Fill in the blanks on this page with the words called for. Then, using the words you have selected, fill in the blank spaces in the story.

Now you've created your own hilarious MAD LIBS® game!

THE BEST SPY MOVIES

NOUN _____

ADVERB _____

PLURAL NOUN _____

NOUN _____

PERSON IN ROOM (MALE) _____

ADJECTIVE _____

CELEBRITY _____

NOUN _____

ADJECTIVE _____

PERSON IN ROOM (FEMALE) _____

NOUN _____

NOUN _____

NOUN _____

PART OF THE BODY _____

ADJECTIVE _____

COLOR _____

PART OF THE BODY _____

TYPE OF FOOD _____

MAD LIBS
THE BEST SPY MOVIES

Here are the best spy movies to curl up on the _____ and watch:
NOUN

- *Spy Story:* In this _____ colorful tale, toy _____ come to life!
  ADVERB   PLURAL NOUN

  The main character is a space-_____ named _____
                                  NOUN   PERSON IN ROOM (MALE)

  Lightyear who thinks he is an intergalactic spy, and a/an _____
                                                              ADJECTIVE

  cowboy action figure named _____ must convince him he's just
                              CELEBRITY

  a/an _____.
        NOUN

- *Beauty and the Spy:* A beautiful, _____ young girl named
                                      ADJECTIVE

  _____ wanders into a castle in the middle of a/an
  PERSON IN ROOM (FEMALE)

  _____ and meets a spy who's under the spell of a wicked old
  NOUN

  _____. He has been turned into a hideous _____
  NOUN   NOUN

  with hair all over his _____, and only she can break the
                          PART OF THE BODY

  enchantment.

- *Spy Wars:* A space tale in which spies from the _____ Rebel Forces
                                                    ADJECTIVE

  go up against a scary, robotic man in flowing _____ robes who
                                                 COLOR

  wears a large helmet on his _____ and calls himself Lord
                               PART OF THE BODY

  _____.
  TYPE OF FOOD

MAD LIBS® is fun to play with friends, but you can also play it by yourself! To begin with, DO NOT look at the story on the page below. Fill in the blanks on this page with the words called for. Then, using the words you have selected, fill in the blank spaces in the story.

Now you've created your own hilarious MAD LIBS® game!

TALES FROM SPY CAMP

ADJECTIVE _____

NOUN _____

VERB _____

ADJECTIVE _____

CELEBRITY _____

PLURAL NOUN _____

PLURAL NOUN _____

ADJECTIVE _____

VERB _____

PLURAL NOUN _____

ADVERB _____

EXCLAMATION _____

NOUN _____

PART OF THE BODY _____

VERB _____

NOUN _____

PLURAL NOUN _____

PLURAL NOUN _____

PERSON IN ROOM _____

MAD LIBS
TALES FROM SPY CAMP

Dear Mom and Dad,

Spy Camp is totally _____! Being a real _____-in-training is
         ADJECTIVE   NOUN

the coolest thing ever! We start each day with a/an _____ around
                                                        VERB

the campground for exercise. Next we do different _____ activities that
                                                     ADJECTIVE

Counselor _____ assigns. Sometimes we get buckets full of screws,
            CELEBRITY

magnets, and other _____ to build surveillance gadgets. Or we use leaves,
                      PLURAL NOUN

twigs, and _____ to make camouflage disguises. My favorite is when we
             PLURAL NOUN

play _____ games like Spy Paintball. We team up and _____
      ADJECTIVE   VERB

behind trees, boulders, and other large _____. We need to be _____
                                          PLURAL NOUN   ADVERB

stealthy to avoid detection; otherwise, we'll get nailed—and, _____, a
                                                                EXCLAMATION

paintball _____ to the _____ really hurts! Sometimes
            NOUN   PART OF THE BODY

we just _____ by a roaring _____ and roast _____—like
           VERB   NOUN   PLURAL NOUN

regular campers do. See you in a few weeks!

Hugs and _____, _____
            PLURAL NOUN   PERSON IN ROOM

MAD LIBS® is fun to play with friends, but you can also play it by yourself! To begin with, DO NOT look at the story on the page below. Fill in the blanks on this page with the words called for. Then, using the words you have selected, fill in the blank spaces in the story.

Now you've created your own hilarious MAD LIBS® game!

WANTED: A FEW GOOD SPIES

ADJECTIVE _____

PART OF THE BODY (PLURAL) _____

NOUN _____

TYPE OF FOOD _____

ADJECTIVE _____

A PLACE _____

ADJECTIVE _____

ADJECTIVE _____

PART OF THE BODY (PLURAL) _____

ADJECTIVE _____

ADJECTIVE _____

ARTICLE OF CLOTHING (PLURAL) _____

NUMBER _____

PLURAL NOUN _____

NOUN _____

VERB _____

MAD LIBS
WANTED: A FEW GOOD SPIES

Are you sneaky and _____? Do you keep your eyes and
_____ (ADJECTIVE)

_____ open at all times to things going on around you?
(PART OF THE BODY (PLURAL))

Can you take items like a piece of string, a cell phone, a/an _____, and
(NOUN)

some day-old _____ and build a makeshift homing device to track
(TYPE OF FOOD)

a/an _____ target? If so, then we want you to join our exclusive spy
(ADJECTIVE)

agency. We are hired out by the military, private corporations, and occasionally

the mayor of (the) _____ to infiltrate a/an _____ enemy and
(A PLACE)   (ADJECTIVE)

steal plans, crack codes, or perform other _____ duties as assigned.
(ADJECTIVE)

Although previous experience is not required, candidates who are fast on their

_____ when it comes to solving _____ problems
(PART OF THE BODY (PLURAL))   (ADJECTIVE)

will be given top consideration. Spy gear—including a backpack of

_____ gadgets and black _____—is provided.
(ADJECTIVE)   (ARTICLE OF CLOTHING (PLURAL))

Starting salary is _____ _____ a week. If you can move with the
(NUMBER)   (PLURAL NOUN)

stealth of a two-ton _____, then the job of a spy could be right for you.
(NOUN)

_____ today for an application!
(VERB)

MAD LIBS® is fun to play with friends, but you can also play it by yourself! To begin with, DO NOT look at the story on the page below. Fill in the blanks on this page with the words called for. Then, using the words you have selected, fill in the blank spaces in the story.

Now you've created your own hilarious MAD LIBS® game!

ODE TO SPIES

VERB ENDING IN "ING" _____

NOUN _____

ADJECTIVE _____

PLURAL NOUN _____

PLURAL NOUN _____

VERB _____

PART OF THE BODY (PLURAL) _____

ADJECTIVE _____

NOUN _____

NOUN _____

VERB _____

ADJECTIVE _____

PLURAL NOUN _____

PLURAL NOUN _____

PERSON IN ROOM _____

ADJECTIVE _____

NOUN _____

They're pros at _____ stealthily and the art of surprise.

VERB ENDING IN "ING"

Is that a/an _____ that I see—or a/an _____ spy in disguise?

NOUN   ADJECTIVE

They're sneaky as _____ so their covers don't get blown.

PLURAL NOUN

They hang with their best _____, but they *always* _____

PLURAL NOUN   VERB

alone.

Spies think with their _____, and they're fast on their feet.

PART OF THE BODY (PLURAL)

The high-tech gadgets they use are _____ and neat,

ADJECTIVE

Like _____-shaped bugs to plant on a moving car

NOUN

Or telescopic _____-glasses to help them _____ far.

NOUN   VERB

They crack _____ codes with _____ and speed.

ADJECTIVE   PLURAL NOUN

Steal _____? Learn secrets? They'll get what you need!

PLURAL NOUN

So don't you fear, _____! Don't make a/an _____ fuss!

PERSON IN ROOM   ADJECTIVE

Just pick up the _____ and dial 1-800-SPIES-R-US.

NOUN

MAD LIBS® is fun to play with friends, but you can also play it by yourself! To begin with, DO NOT look at the story on the page below. Fill in the blanks on this page with the words called for. Then, using the words you have selected, fill in the blank spaces in the story.

Now you've created your own hilarious MAD LIBS® game!

MOST WANTED LIST

PLURAL NOUN _____

ADJECTIVE _____

PLURAL NOUN _____

NOUN _____

ADVERB _____

NOUN _____

ADJECTIVE _____

PERSON IN ROOM _____

COLOR _____

NOUN _____

PART OF THE BODY (PLURAL) _____

PLURAL NOUN _____

NOUN _____

A PLACE _____

CELEBRITY _____

NOUN _____

ADJECTIVE _____

PLURAL NOUN _____

PART OF THE BODY (PLURAL) _____

PLURAL NOUN _____

MAD LIBS
MOST WANTED LIST

The Global Spy Organization's list of most wanted _____ is a long
<u>PLURAL NOUN</u>

one. Here are _____ profiles of the most notorious criminals:
<u>ADJECTIVE</u>

- **Max Von** _____ **III** is wanted for the kidnapping of Sir
<u>PLURAL NOUN</u>

 Puffy-_____, the _____ overweight pet _____ of His
 <u>NOUN</u> <u>ADVERB</u> <u>NOUN</u>

 _____ Majesty, King _____.
 <u>ADJECTIVE</u> <u>PERSON IN ROOM</u>

- **The** _____ **Shadow** is the head of an international ring of
 <u>COLOR</u>

 _____ thieves whose sticky _____ have lifted
 <u>NOUN</u> <u>PART OF THE BODY (PLURAL)</u>

 valuable _____ from museums around the world, including the
 <u>PLURAL NOUN</u>

 famous Le _____ located in (the) _____.
 <u>NOUN</u> <u>A PLACE</u>

- _____, a world-famous super-_____, is actually
 <u>CELEBRITY</u> <u>NOUN</u>

 the mastermind behind a/an _____ group of computer
 <u>ADJECTIVE</u>

 geeks and techno-_____ whose ultra-intelligent
 <u>PLURAL NOUN</u>

 _____ enable them to breach the highest levels of
 <u>PART OF THE BODY (PLURAL)</u>

 security and steal US military _____.
 <u>PLURAL NOUN</u>

MAD LIBS® is fun to play with friends, but you can also play it by yourself! To begin with, DO NOT look at the story on the page below. Fill in the blanks on this page with the words called for. Then, using the words you have selected, fill in the blank spaces in the story.

Now you've created your own hilarious MAD LIBS® game!

SPY VIDEO GAMES

PART OF THE BODY (PLURAL) _____

ADJECTIVE _____

COLOR _____

PLURAL NOUN _____

ADJECTIVE _____

A PLACE _____

PLURAL NOUN _____

NOUN _____

PERSON IN ROOM _____

ADJECTIVE _____

PLURAL NOUN _____

NOUN _____

PLURAL NOUN _____

PLURAL NOUN _____

VERB ENDING IN "ING" _____

ADJECTIVE _____

NOUN _____

NUMBER _____

PLURAL NOUN _____

PLURAL NOUN _____

NOUN _____

MAD LIBS®
SPY VIDEO GAMES

Grab your favorite controller, flex your _____, and get
                                        PART OF THE BODY (PLURAL)

ready to play spy in these _____ video games:
                           ADJECTIVE

- *Operation* _____ _____: You are a spy in the hot,
              COLOR   PLURAL NOUN

  _____ jungles of (the) _____. Your mission?
  ADJECTIVE   A PLACE

  Vaporize poisonous _____ as you search for the missing and
                     PLURAL NOUN

  priceless _____ Diamond, stolen by the rogue operative,
            NOUN

  _____.
  PERSON IN ROOM

- *Spies in Space*: The _____, evil scientist, Dr. Smarty
                        ADJECTIVE

  _____, has launched a/an _____ into space
  PLURAL NOUN   NOUN

  containing deadly _____ that, if sprinkled into the Earth's
                    PLURAL NOUN

  atmosphere, will destroy all living _____.
                                      PLURAL NOUN

- *Speedway Spies*: It's spy-on-spy _____ action on the
                                    VERB ENDING IN "ING"

  racetrack! You and your _____ opponent burn up the race
                          ADJECTIVE

  _____ at speeds topping _____ mph as you swerve to
  NOUN   NUMBER

  avoid toppling _____, slippery spills of _____, and,
                 PLURAL NOUN   PLURAL NOUN

  occasionally, a/an _____ trying to cross the road.
                     NOUN

MAD LIBS® is fun to play with friends, but you can also play it by yourself! To begin with, DO NOT look at the story on the page below. Fill in the blanks on this page with the words called for. Then, using the words you have selected, fill in the blank spaces in the story.

Now you've created your own hilarious MAD LIBS® game!

GEAR & GADGETS, PART 2

ADJECTIVE _____

PLURAL NOUN _____

PLURAL NOUN _____

PLURAL NOUN _____

ADJECTIVE _____

PART OF THE BODY (PLURAL) _____

VERB _____

TYPE OF LIQUID _____

ADJECTIVE _____

PLURAL NOUN _____

VERB _____

PART OF THE BODY (PLURAL) _____

NOUN _____

NOUN _____

PLURAL NOUN _____

PART OF THE BODY (PLURAL) _____

MAD LIBS
GEAR & GADGETS, PART 2

Whether it's to locate a/an _____ target or protect themselves from
                            ADJECTIVE

enemy _____, spies are always armed with the coolest gear and
        PLURAL NOUN

_____ imaginable.
PLURAL NOUN

- **Smoke** _____—When thrown at enemies, these explode
           PLURAL NOUN

  and send _____ smoke billowing into the bad guys'
              ADJECTIVE

  _____, making them unable to _____
  PART OF THE BODY (PLURAL)   VERB

  any longer.

- **Laser Pen**—This tool functions as a pen that writes with invisible

  _____, a telescope so spies can track _____
      TYPE OF LIQUID   ADJECTIVE

  enemies from a safe distance, and a flashlight that contains different

  color _____—yellow means "_____ with caution," blue
         PLURAL NOUN   VERB

  means "put up your _____ or else," and red means
                     PART OF THE BODY (PLURAL)

  "abort the _____."
              NOUN

- **Laser Trip Wire** _____—This gadget has invisible beams
                       NOUN

  that alert spies to intruding _____ whenever their
                                   PLURAL NOUN

  _____ hit the beam.
  PART OF THE BODY (PLURAL)

MAD LIBS® is fun to play with friends, but you can also play it by yourself! To begin with, DO NOT look at the story on the page below. Fill in the blanks on this page with the words called for. Then, using the words you have selected, fill in the blank spaces in the story.

Now you've created your own hilarious MAD LIBS® game!

SPY ROLES

ADJECTIVE _____

NOUN _____

NUMBER _____

PLURAL NOUN _____

PLURAL NOUN _____

NOUN _____

ADJECTIVE _____

NOUN _____

ADJECTIVE _____

PLURAL NOUN _____

ADJECTIVE _____

PLURAL NOUN _____

NOUN _____

PLURAL NOUN _____

ADJECTIVE _____

MAD LIBS®
SPY ROLES

There are lots of ways that spies can use their _____ training, including
<u>ADJECTIVE</u>

these:

- A *double agent* is a/an _____ who works for at least _____
  <u>NOUN</u>   <u>NUMBER</u>

  intelligence agencies and whose job is to secure classified _____
  <u>PLURAL NOUN</u>

  at one agency and deliver them to the _____ in charge at the
  <u>PLURAL NOUN</u>

  other agency.

- A *sleeper agent* lives as a regular _____ in a foreign country and
  <u>NOUN</u>

  is only called upon when a hostile or otherwise _____ situation
  <u>ADJECTIVE</u>

  develops.

- A *cobbler* is a/an _____ who creates false passports, diplomas,
  <u>NOUN</u>

  and other _____ documents to help create identities for
  <u>ADJECTIVE</u>

  _____ going undercover.
  <u>PLURAL NOUN</u>

- A *ghoul* is an agent who searches _____ death notices and
  <u>ADJECTIVE</u>

  graveyards for names of dead _____ and gives them to cobblers
  <u>PLURAL NOUN</u>

  for their documents.

- A *handler* is a/an _____ who handles _____ as they
  <u>NOUN</u>   <u>PLURAL NOUN</u>

  undergo _____ missions.
  <u>ADJECTIVE</u>

MAD LIBS® is fun to play with friends, but you can also play it by yourself! To begin with, DO NOT look at the story on the page below. Fill in the blanks on this page with the words called for. Then, using the words you have selected, fill in the blank spaces in the story.

Now you've created your own hilarious MAD LIBS® game!

SPY U

NOUN _____

ADJECTIVE _____

PLURAL NOUN _____

VERB ENDING IN "ING" _____

PLURAL NOUN _____

CELEBRITY _____

ADJECTIVE _____

ADJECTIVE _____

ADJECTIVE _____

PLURAL NOUN _____

VERB ENDING IN "ING" _____

PERSON IN ROOM _____

A PLACE _____

ADJECTIVE _____

PART OF THE BODY (PLURAL) _____

PLURAL NOUN _____

PART OF THE BODY _____

VERB _____

MAD LIBS
SPY U

Grab a pen and a/an _____ and get ready to take notes! Spy University
          NOUN

offers _____ classes for aspiring _____ who wish to enter
         ADJECTIVE   PLURAL NOUN

the covert world of espionage:

- **Introduction to** _____ : Do you have the patience,
                      VERB ENDING IN "ING"

  street smarts, and _____ to be a spy? Taught by world-renowned
                       PLURAL NOUN

  instructor _____, this class offers a/an _____ overview on
              CELEBRITY   ADJECTIVE

  what it takes to be a/an _____ spy.
                            ADJECTIVE

- **Stealth Mode:** A great spy has the _____ ability to sneak up on
                                          ADJECTIVE

  unsuspecting _____ without detection. This course provides
                 PLURAL NOUN

  field experience in _____ within different environments,
                       VERB ENDING IN "ING"

  such as _____'s room or even (the) _____.
           PERSON IN ROOM   A PLACE

- **Wise Spies:** Spies have many gadgets and _____ tools they use to
                                                ADJECTIVE

  pull the wool over their opponents' _____. But it's
                                       PART OF THE BODY (PLURAL)

  their wits and clever _____ that give them an advantage. Learn
                          PLURAL NOUN

  how to use your _____ to get your opponent to
                   PART OF THE BODY

  _____ exactly the way you want him to.
   VERB

MAD LIBS® is fun to play with friends, but you can also play it by yourself! To begin with, DO NOT look at the story on the page below. Fill in the blanks on this page with the words called for. Then, using the words you have selected, fill in the blank spaces in the story.

Now you've created your own hilarious MAD LIBS® game!

CRACK THE CODE

ADJECTIVE _____

A PLACE _____

ADJECTIVE _____

COLOR _____

VERB ENDING IN "ING" _____

NOUN _____

PART OF THE BODY _____

PLURAL NOUN _____

PLURAL NOUN _____

SAME PLURAL NOUN _____

NOUN _____

ADJECTIVE _____

ADJECTIVE _____

PERSON IN ROOM _____

PLURAL NOUN _____

NOUN _____

A PLACE _____

ADJECTIVE _____

CELEBRITY _____

Cracking _____ codes is a prized spy skill, like in this example:
　　　　　　ADJECTIVE

Coded message: The circus has come to (the) _____, and
　　　　　　　　　　　　　　　　　　　　　　　　　　A PLACE

there are _____ clowns with big _____ noses _____
　　　　　ADJECTIVE　　　　　　　　　COLOR　　　　VERB ENDING IN "ING"

in the streets. If you try to run away, they will stick out their _____ and trip
　　　　　　　　　　　　　　　　　　　　　　　　　　　　　　　　　NOUN

you so you fall _____-first into a puddle of _____.
　　　　　　　　　PART OF THE BODY　　　　　　　　　　　　PLURAL NOUN

Beware those _____—I repeat, beware those _____!
　　　　　　　PLURAL NOUN　　　　　　　　　　　　　　SAME PLURAL NOUN

Decoded message: To the brave _____ who deciphers this _____
　　　　　　　　　　　　　　　　　　NOUN　　　　　　　　　　　ADJECTIVE

note—be forewarned! Our agency has experienced a breach of security involving

_____ double agents. Agency Chief _____ desperately
ADJECTIVE　　　　　　　　　　　　　PERSON IN ROOM

needs _____ who have not been corrupted to be trained as new agents.
　　　PLURAL NOUN

Report promptly to _____ Headquarters located near (the) _____
　　　　　　　　　　NOUN　　　　　　　　　　　　　　　　　　A PLACE

and await further instructions. Keep this _____ message confidential.
　　　　　　　　　　　　　　　　　　　ADJECTIVE

Apply in person using the code phrase "I am president of the _____ Fan
　　　　　　　　　　　　　　　　　　　　　　　　　　　　CELEBRITY

Club."

MAD LIBS®

WE WISH YOU A MERRY MAD LIBS

Mad Libs
An Imprint of Penguin Random House

MAD  LIBS®

INSTRUCTIONS

MAD LIBS® is a game for people who don't like games!
It can be played by one, two, three, four, or forty.

• RIDICULOUSLY SIMPLE DIRECTIONS

In this tablet you will find stories containing blank spaces where words are left out. One player, the READER, selects one of these stories. The READER does not tell anyone what the story is about. Instead, he/she asks the other players, the WRITERS, to give him/her words. These words are used to fill in the blank spaces in the story.

• TO PLAY

The READER asks each WRITER in turn to call out a word—an adjective or a noun or whatever the space calls for—and uses them to fill in the blank spaces in the story. The result is a MAD LIBS® game.

When the READER then reads the completed MAD LIBS® game to the other players, they will discover that they have written a story that is fantastic, screamingly funny, shocking, silly, crazy, or just plain dumb—depending upon which words each WRITER called out.

• EXAMPLE (*Before* and *After*)

"_____!" he said _____
           EXCLAMATION   ADVERB

as he jumped into his convertible _____ and
                                           NOUN

drove off with his _____ wife.
                          ADJECTIVE

"_____OUCH_____!" he said ____STUPIDLY____
           EXCLAMATION   ADVERB

as he jumped into his convertible ____CAT____ and
                                           NOUN

drove off with his ____BRAVE____ wife.
                          ADJECTIVE

QUICK REVIEW

In case you have forgotten what adjectives, adverbs, nouns, and verbs are, here is a quick review:

An ADJECTIVE describes something or somebody. *Lumpy, soft, ugly, messy,* and *short* are adjectives.

An ADVERB tells how something is done. It modifies a verb and usually ends in "ly." *Modestly, stupidly, greedily,* and *carefully* are adverbs.

A NOUN is the name of a person, place, or thing. *Sidewalk, umbrella, bridle, bathtub,* and *nose* are nouns.

A VERB is an action word. *Run, pitch, jump,* and *swim* are verbs. Put the verbs in past tense if the directions say PAST TENSE. *Ran, pitched, jumped,* and *swam* are verbs in the past tense.

When we ask for A PLACE, we mean any sort of place: a country or city *(Spain, Cleveland)* or a room *(bathroom, kitchen).*

An EXCLAMATION or SILLY WORD is any sort of funny sound, gasp, grunt, or outcry, like *Wow!, Ouch!, Whomp!, Ick!,* and *Gadzooks!*

When we ask for specific words, like a NUMBER, a COLOR, an ANIMAL, or a PART OF THE BODY, we mean a word that is one of those things, like *seven, blue, horse,* or *head.*

When we ask for a PLURAL, it means more than one. For example, *cat* pluralized is *cats.*

MAD LIBS® is fun to play with friends, but you can also play it by yourself! To begin with, DO NOT look at the story on the page below. Fill in the blanks on this page with the words called for. Then, using the words you have selected, fill in the blank spaces in the story.

Now you've created your own hilarious MAD LIBS® game!

VISIT THE NORTH POLE!

ADJECTIVE _____

ADJECTIVE _____

NOUN _____

ADVERB _____

ADJECTIVE _____

PART OF THE BODY (PLURAL) _____

NOUN _____

PLURAL NOUN _____

NOUN _____

ADJECTIVE _____

ADJECTIVE _____

ADJECTIVE _____

PLURAL NOUN _____

ADJECTIVE _____

PART OF THE BODY _____

PLURAL NOUN _____

MAD LIBS

VISIT THE NORTH POLE!

Looking for a/an _____ destination for your next vacation? How about
              ADJECTIVE

the _____ North Pole? Located in the middle of the Arctic
        ADJECTIVE

_____ , it is made up of _____ shifting ice,
      NOUN   ADVERB

which makes it perfect for snowshoeing through the _____ tundra. As
                                                      ADJECTIVE

you trek across the ice, keep your _____ peeled for the
                                    PART OF THE BODY (PLURAL)

incredible wildlife that inhabits the North _____ —like furry white
                                              NOUN

polar _____ , _____ seals, and _____ arctic
        PLURAL NOUN   NOUN   ADJECTIVE

foxes. And when night falls you are in for a/an _____ treat.
                                                  ADJECTIVE

You'll be able to see the _____ aurora borealis, otherwise
                            ADJECTIVE

known as the northern _____ . This incredible display of
                        PLURAL NOUN

_____ lights will blow your _____ . So
  ADJECTIVE   PART OF THE BODY

call 1-800-555-3939 and make your travel _____ today!
                                            PLURAL NOUN

MAD LIBS® is fun to play with friends, but you can also play it by yourself! To begin with, DO NOT look at the story on the page below. Fill in the blanks on this page with the words called for. Then, using the words you have selected, fill in the blank spaces in the story.

Now you've created your own hilarious MAD LIBS® game!

SANTA BLOG

ADJECTIVE _____

ADJECTIVE _____

NOUN _____

ADJECTIVE _____

A PLACE _____

NOUN _____

PLURAL NOUN _____

PLURAL NOUN _____

ADVERB _____

NOUN _____

ADJECTIVE _____

VERB _____

VERB _____

ADJECTIVE _____

ADJECTIVE _____

PLURAL NOUN _____

NOUN _____

MAD LIBS®
SANTA BLOG

Ho, ho, ho, _____ blog fans! Santa here. It's crunch time at my
_____ADJECTIVE_____

_____ workshop, and everyone is as busy as a/an
_____ADJECTIVE_____

_____. I've received tons of _____ letters from
_____NOUN_____ _____ADJECTIVE_____

girls and boys around (the) _____, and the elves have been
_____A PLACE_____

working around the _____ to make all of their _____.
_____NOUN_____ _____PLURAL NOUN_____

Plus, I've finally finished putting together the list of naughty

_____, which I'm _____ happy to say is
_____PLURAL NOUN_____ _____ADVERB_____

much shorter than last year's! As I look out the _____, I can
_____NOUN_____

see the reindeer are groomed and look really _____, and my
_____ADJECTIVE_____

sleigh is polished and ready to _____. I will be able to
_____VERB_____

_____ through the _____ night sky as soon as
_____VERB_____ _____ADJECTIVE_____

Mrs. Claus finishes letting out my _____ red suit. I'm sorry
_____ADJECTIVE_____

to say, I ate a few too many _____ this past year!
_____PLURAL NOUN_____

See you soon! Your _____ , Santa
_____NOUN_____

MAD LIBS® is fun to play with friends, but you can also play it by yourself! To begin with, DO NOT look at the story on the page below. Fill in the blanks on this page with the words called for. Then, using the words you have selected, fill in the blank spaces in the story.

Now you've created your own hilarious MAD LIBS® game!

HOLIDAY WEATHER REPORT

ADJECTIVE _____

PERSON IN ROOM _____

NOUN _____

ADJECTIVE _____

ADJECTIVE _____

NUMBER _____

NOUN _____

NOUN _____

PLURAL NOUN _____

PLURAL NOUN _____

VERB ENDING IN "ING" _____

NUMBER _____

ADJECTIVE _____

PLURAL NOUN _____

VERB _____

NOUN _____

NOUN _____

ADJECTIVE _____

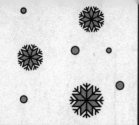

MAD LIBS®
HOLIDAY WEATHER REPORT

Good evening, and _____ holidays. I'm _____ with
　　　　　　　　　　　ADJECTIVE　　　　　　　　　　　　　　PERSON IN ROOM

your local weather _____ . First the good news: We're going
　　　　　　　　　　　　NOUN

to have a traditional _____ Christmas. A/An _____
　　　　　　　　　　　ADJECTIVE　　　　　　　　　　　　　　ADJECTIVE

snowstorm is heading our way. You can expect three to _____
　　　　　　　　　　　　　　　　　　　　　　　　　　　　　　NUMBER

feet of _____ to accumulate before the end of this
　　　　　　NOUN

_____ , plus several more _____ of snow by
　　　　NOUN　　　　　　　　　　　　　　　　PLURAL NOUN

midnight. And you may want to put on your warm _____ :
　　　　　　　　　　　　　　　　　　　　　　　　　　　PLURAL NOUN

Overnight, the temperature is going to drop below _____
　　　　　　　　　　　　　　　　　　　　　　　　　　VERB ENDING IN "ING"

level, with a windchill of negative _____ degrees. Now the
　　　　　　　　　　　　　　　　　　　NUMBER

bad news: Driving conditions will be extremely _____ . I strongly
　　　　　　　　　　　　　　　　　　　　　　　ADJECTIVE

suggest you stay off the _____ and _____ at home.
　　　　　　　　　　　　PLURAL NOUN　　　　　　　　VERB

Hunker down, light a/an _____ in the fireplace, and watch
　　　　　　　　　　　　　NOUN

the _____-flakes fall. And, most importantly, have a/an
　　　　NOUN

_____ Christmas!
　ADJECTIVE

MAD LIBS® is fun to play with friends, but you can also play it by yourself! To begin with, DO NOT look at the story on the page below. Fill in the blanks on this page with the words called for. Then, using the words you have selected, fill in the blank spaces in the story.

Now you've created your own hilarious MAD LIBS® game!

MOST POPULAR GIFTS

ADJECTIVE _____

PLURAL NOUN _____

NOUN _____

ADJECTIVE _____

PLURAL NOUN _____

NOUN _____

NOUN _____

NOUN _____

NOUN _____

NOUN _____

ADJECTIVE _____

NOUN _____

PLURAL NOUN _____

ADJECTIVE _____

NOUN _____

ADJECTIVE _____

NOUN _____

NOUN _____

ADJECTIVE _____

NOUN _____

MAD LIBS®
MOST POPULAR GIFTS

Here is a list of the most _____ gifts for your dear _____ :
                              ADJECTIVE   PLURAL NOUN

5. An i-_____ . This _____ device can store and play up
        NOUN   ADJECTIVE

to thirty thousand _____ .
                        PLURAL NOUN

4. A/An _____-cam. Shoot movies or film yourself acting like a/an
         NOUN

_____ . Then, upload your videos to You-_____ ,
     NOUN   NOUN

where everyone can see them!

3. Rock _____ . Ever wanted to be a famous _____? You
         NOUN   NOUN

can act like one with this _____ video game.
                               ADJECTIVE

2. A flat-screen _____. Watch your favorite movies and TV
                     NOUN

_____ in _____-definition on an LCD
   PLURAL NOUN   ADJECTIVE

_____ .
     NOUN

1. If you have _____ friends who are in short supply of self-esteem,
                  ADJECTIVE

buy them a talking _____ . With the push of a/an _____ ,
                       NOUN   NOUN

it will say things like, "You're so _____ !" and "You're the best
                                        ADJECTIVE

_____ ever!"
    NOUN

MAD LIBS® is fun to play with friends, but you can also play it by yourself! To begin with, DO NOT look at the story on the page below. Fill in the blanks on this page with the words called for. Then, using the words you have selected, fill in the blank spaces in the story.

Now you've created your own hilarious MAD LIBS® game!

TAKING CARE OF YOUR REINDEER

ADJECTIVE _____

ADJECTIVE _____

NOUN _____

ADJECTIVE _____

NUMBER _____

ADJECTIVE _____

PLURAL NOUN _____

ADJECTIVE _____

NOUN _____

ADJECTIVE _____

NUMBER _____

ADVERB _____

ADJECTIVE _____

NOUN _____

NOUN _____

ADVERB _____

ADJECTIVE _____

TAKING CARE OF
YOUR REINDEER

Congratulations! We hear you've adopted a/an _____ reindeer.
ADJECTIVE

They make _____ pets—but they require a lot of care and
ADJECTIVE

_____ . Here are some tips for keeping your reindeer happy
NOUN

and _____ :
ADJECTIVE

• Feed it _____ times a day. Not difficult to do, as reindeer
NUMBER

  have a very _____ diet. They eat grasses, moss, and
  ADJECTIVE

  _____ .
  PLURAL NOUN

• Make sure your reindeer gets _____ exercise. In the wild,
  ADJECTIVE

  they travel farther than any other land _____ . They go on
  NOUN

  _____ migrations, sometimes covering _____ miles.
  ADJECTIVE NUMBER

• Groom your reindeer _____ . Its _____ antlers
  ADVERB ADJECTIVE

  are covered in delicate _____ , which you can clean with a
  NOUN

  soft _____ . You should also brush its coat _____
  NOUN ADVERB

  once a month.

• Take your reindeer to the vet often to make sure it stays healthy and

  _____ .
  ADJECTIVE

MAD LIBS® is fun to play with friends, but you can also play it by yourself! To begin with, DO NOT look at the story on the page below. Fill in the blanks on this page with the words called for. Then, using the words you have selected, fill in the blank spaces in the story.

Now you've created your own hilarious MAD LIBS® game!

GET TO KNOW MRS. CLAUS

ADJECTIVE _____

NOUN _____

FIRST NAME (FEMALE) _____

NOUN _____

LAST NAME _____

ADJECTIVE _____

PLURAL NOUN _____

PLURAL NOUN _____

NOUN _____

NOUN _____

NOUN _____

NOUN _____

PART OF THE BODY (PLURAL) _____

ADJECTIVE _____

ADJECTIVE _____

ADJECTIVE _____

Here are some _____ facts you may not know about me, Santa
                          ADJECTIVE

Claus's dear _____ :
                    NOUN

Full name: Mrs. _____ Claus
                    FIRST NAME (FEMALE)

Hometown: The North _____
                              NOUN

Activities: Helping my husband, Santa _____ , get ready
                                              LAST NAME

for Christmas and taking care of the _____ elves
                                          ADJECTIVE

Interests: Baking Christmas _____ and knitting _____
                                  PLURAL NOUN   PLURAL NOUN

Favorite movies: *It's a Wonderful* _____ , *Rudolph the Red-Nosed*
                                              NOUN

_____
     NOUN

Favorite books: *The* _____ *Before Christmas, How the*
                              NOUN

_____ *Stole Christmas*
     NOUN

Favorite quotation: "All I want for Christmas is my two front

_____ ."
PART OF THE BODY (PLURAL)

About me: Have you ever wondered who brings _____ Santa
                                                    ADJECTIVE

his _____ gifts on Christmas Eve? Well, surprise! It's
          ADJECTIVE

little, _____ me!
            ADJECTIVE

MAD LIBS® is fun to play with friends, but you can also play it by yourself! To begin with, DO NOT look at the story on the page below. Fill in the blanks on this page with the words called for. Then, using the words you have selected, fill in the blank spaces in the story.

Now you've created your own hilarious MAD LIBS® game!

CHRISTMAS FUNNIES

ADJECTIVE _____

ADJECTIVE _____

ADJECTIVE _____

NOUN _____

NOUN _____

ADJECTIVE _____

NOUN _____

PLURAL NOUN _____

ADJECTIVE _____

FIRST NAME _____

MAD LIBS®
CHRISTMAS FUNNIES

Q: What do you get when you cross a/an _____ vampire
ADJECTIVE

with a/an _____ snowman?
ADJECTIVE

A: Frostbite!

Q: Why did the _____ reindeer cross the
ADJECTIVE

_____ ?
NOUN

A: To get to the other _____ !
NOUN

Q: What do _____ elves sing to Santa?
ADJECTIVE

A: "*Freeze* a Jolly Good _____ ."
NOUN

Q: What do polar _____ eat for lunch?
PLURAL NOUN

A: *Iceberg*-ers!

Q: What do you call a/an _____ person who is afraid of
ADJECTIVE

_____ Claus?
FIRST NAME

A: *Claus*trophobic.

MAD LIBS® is fun to play with friends, but you can also play it by yourself! To begin with, DO NOT look at the story on the page below. Fill in the blanks on this page with the words called for. Then, using the words you have selected, fill in the blank spaces in the story.

Now you've created your own hilarious MAD LIBS® game!

CHRISTMAS AROUND THE WORLD, PART 1

ADJECTIVE _____

PLURAL NOUN _____

NOUN _____

ADJECTIVE _____

PLURAL NOUN _____

ADVERB _____

NOUN _____

NOUN _____

NOUN _____

PLURAL NOUN _____

PLURAL NOUN _____

ADJECTIVE _____

ADJECTIVE _____

ADJECTIVE _____

PLURAL NOUN _____

PLURAL NOUN _____

PLURAL NOUN _____

Americans have many _____ Christmas traditions. They
                              ADJECTIVE

decorate Christmas _____, sing _____
                        PLURAL NOUN   NOUN

carols, and have _____ Christmas dinners with their families. But
                    ADJECTIVE

how do _____ around the world celebrate?
            PLURAL NOUN

- In **Sweden**, they_____celebrate St. Lucia's Day before Christmas.
                        ADVERB

  The youngest _____ in the family wears a white _____,
                  NOUN   NOUN

  a red _____, and a crown of _____with candles in it. She
            NOUN   PLURAL NOUN

  then serves coffee and _____to everyone in her _____
                            PLURAL NOUN   ADJECTIVE

  family.

- In **Australia**, it is hot and _____at Christmastime, because this
                                    ADJECTIVE

  _____holiday falls in the middle of their summer. _____
  ADJECTIVE   PLURAL NOUN

  gather outside at night to light _____ and sing Christmas
                                      PLURAL NOUN

  _____.
  PLURAL NOUN

MAD LIBS® is fun to play with friends, but you can also play it by yourself! To begin with, DO NOT look at the story on the page below. Fill in the blanks on this page with the words called for. Then, using the words you have selected, fill in the blank spaces in the story.

Now you've created your own hilarious MAD LIBS® game!

CHRISTMAS AROUND THE WORLD, PART 2

ADJECTIVE _____

PLURAL NOUN _____

ADJECTIVE _____

ADJECTIVE _____

PLURAL NOUN _____

PLURAL NOUN _____

ADJECTIVE _____

PLURAL NOUN _____

ADJECTIVE _____

NOUN _____

PLURAL NOUN _____

NOUN _____

NOUN _____

NOUN _____

PLURAL NOUN _____

- In **China**, people decorate their _____ homes with paper
  ADJECTIVE

  _____. They also put up _____ trees decorated with
  PLURAL NOUN   ADJECTIVE

  _____ lanterns, _____, and red _____.
  ADJECTIVE   PLURAL NOUN   PLURAL NOUN

- In **Mexico**, children look forward to a/an _____ party where
  ADJECTIVE

  young _____ take turns hitting a/an _____ piñata with
       PLURAL NOUN   ADJECTIVE

  a/an _____, until all the _____ and other treats fall out.
       NOUN   PLURAL NOUN

- In **Germany**, families celebrate the weeks leading up to Christmas with an

  Advent _____. Each Sunday, they light another _____
         NOUN   NOUN

  in the wreath. Before Christmas, Germans celebrate St. Nicholas Day,

  where kids put a/an _____ outside their door at night, and in
                      NOUN

  the morning it is filled with candy and _____.
                                          PLURAL NOUN

MAD LIBS® is fun to play with friends, but you can also play it by yourself! To begin with, DO NOT look at the story on the page below. Fill in the blanks on this page with the words called for. Then, using the words you have selected, fill in the blank spaces in the story.

Now you've created your own hilarious MAD LIBS® game!

A TROPICAL CHRISTMAS

PLURAL NOUN _____

NOUN _____

A PLACE _____

PLURAL NOUN _____

ADJECTIVE _____

NOUN _____

NOUN _____

PLURAL NOUN _____

ADJECTIVE _____

ADJECTIVE _____

PLURAL NOUN _____

ADJECTIVE _____

NOUN _____

ADJECTIVE _____

NOUN _____

NOUN _____

ADJECTIVE _____

MAD LIBS®
A TROPICAL CHRISTMAS

Some _____ can't imagine celebrating Christmas where there's no
  PLURAL NOUN

snow falling from the _____. But it's not all bad! Here in (the)
                          NOUN

_____, where it's always sunny, we decorate palm
  A PLACE

_____ with _____ lights instead of decorating
  PLURAL NOUN   ADJECTIVE

a pine _____. Instead of making a snow-_____, we
         NOUN   NOUN

make _____ out of sand. Best of all, we don't have to bundle up
       PLURAL NOUN

against the _____ wind and the _____ cold and freeze
              ADJECTIVE   ADJECTIVE

our _____ off. At Christmas, we happily splash around in the
      PLURAL NOUN

_____ ocean and bask in the _____-shine. Or we go
  ADJECTIVE   NOUN

surfing and catch _____ waves. As you can see, I no longer dream
                     ADJECTIVE

of a white _____. I'm happy celebrating Christmas on a sandy
              NOUN

_____ in the _____ sun!
  NOUN   ADJECTIVE

MAD LIBS® is fun to play with friends, but you can also play it by yourself! To begin with, DO NOT look at the story on the page below. Fill in the blanks on this page with the words called for. Then, using the words you have selected, fill in the blank spaces in the story.

Now you've created your own hilarious MAD LIBS® game!

CHRISTMAS IN JULY

LAST NAME _____

ADJECTIVE _____

A PLACE _____

NOUN _____

PLURAL NOUN _____

ADVERB _____

NUMBER _____

ADJECTIVE _____

NOUN _____

NOUN _____

PLURAL NOUN _____

ADJECTIVE _____

VERB _____

NOUN _____

MAD LIBS®
CHRISTMAS IN JULY

Hurry on down to _____ Furniture for our
                     LAST NAME

_____ Christmas-in-July sale! Yes, folks, Christmas has
   ADJECTIVE

come early here in (the) _____, and we're celebrating with
                        A PLACE

_____-wide savings on couches, tables, and
   NOUN

_____ ! With prices _____ reduced up to
PLURAL NOUN   ADVERB

_____ percent off, you can't afford to miss this
   NUMBER

_____ event! Purchase any _____ in the store
   ADJECTIVE   NOUN

with no down _____ and no _____ for
                 NOUN   PLURAL NOUN

twelve months. But our _____ sale only lasts through
                          ADJECTIVE

Thursday. So don't delay! _____ on down today, and have
                              VERB

a merry _____ in July!
           NOUN

MAD LIBS® is fun to play with friends, but you can also play it by yourself! To begin with, DO NOT look at the story on the page below. Fill in the blanks on this page with the words called for. Then, using the words you have selected, fill in the blank spaces in the story.

Now you've created your own hilarious MAD LIBS® game!

ELVES WANTED

PLURAL NOUN _____

NUMBER _____

ADJECTIVE _____

VERB _____

NOUN _____

PLURAL NOUN _____

NOUN _____

ADJECTIVE _____

NOUN _____

ADJECTIVE _____

ADJECTIVE _____

VERB _____

PLURAL NOUN _____

A PLACE _____

PART OF THE BODY (PLURAL) _____

MAD LIBS
ELVES WANTED

Attention, all _____! Santa Claus is looking for

PLURAL NOUN

_____ _____ elves to _____

NUMBER   ADJECTIVE   VERB

in his workshop at the North _____ . Job responsibilities

NOUN

include making toy _____ faster than the speed of

PLURAL NOUN

_____ ; taking care of eight _____

NOUN   ADJECTIVE

reindeer when it is necessary; repairing Santa's shiny, red _____;

NOUN

and, of course, sorting letters from _____ girls and boys. Some

ADJECTIVE

very _____ elves might get the chance to _____

ADJECTIVE   VERB

in Santa's sleigh on Christmas Eve and help him deliver

_____ all over (the) _____ . Most

PLURAL NOUN   A PLACE

importantly, candidates' _____ must be full of

PART OF THE BODY (PLURAL)

Christmas cheer!

MAD LIBS® is fun to play with friends, but you can also play it by yourself! To begin with, DO NOT look at the story on the page below. Fill in the blanks on this page with the words called for. Then, using the words you have selected, fill in the blank spaces in the story.

Now you've created your own hilarious MAD LIBS® game!

SNOW DAY!

NOUN _____

ADJECTIVE _____

NOUN _____

ADJECTIVE _____

NOUN _____

ADJECTIVE _____

NOUN _____

NOUN _____

NOUN _____

NOUN _____

NOUN _____

VERB _____

ADJECTIVE _____

PLURAL NOUN _____

NOUN _____

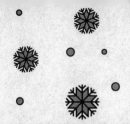

MAD LIBS
SNOW DAY!

This is your lucky _____. Because of the _____
                NOUN   ADJECTIVE

blizzard, school's been canceled. So how will you spend this unexpected

_____ ? Here are some _____ suggestions:
     NOUN   ADJECTIVE

- Stay inside and drink hot _____ while watching
                                      NOUN

  _____ cartoons on television.
  ADJECTIVE

- Grab your _____ and go sledding down a steep
                   NOUN

  _____.
  NOUN

- Find a frozen _____ and go ice-skating on it.
                   NOUN

- Build a/an _____ fort. Construct walls out of hard-packed
                NOUN

  _____, then _____ for hours on end.
  NOUN   VERB

- Break up into _____ teams and have a snowball fight with
               ADJECTIVE

  your neighborhood _____.
                   PLURAL NOUN

- Sleep the _____ away.
           NOUN

MAD LIBS® is fun to play with friends, but you can also play it by yourself! To begin with, DO NOT look at the story on the page below. Fill in the blanks on this page with the words called for. Then, using the words you have selected, fill in the blank spaces in the story.

Now you've created your own hilarious MAD LIBS® game!

THE NUTCRACKER

ADJECTIVE _____

NOUN _____

NOUN _____

ADJECTIVE _____

ADJECTIVE _____

NOUN _____

ADJECTIVE _____

PLURAL NOUN _____

ADJECTIVE _____

PLURAL NOUN _____

TYPE OF FOOD _____

TYPE OF LIQUID _____

VERB ENDING IN "ING" _____

ADJECTIVE _____

ADJECTIVE _____

The Nutcracker is a famous ballet that tells the _____ story

ADJECTIVE

of a little _____ named Clara whose godfather gives her a/an

NOUN

_____-cracker for Christmas. Amazingly, the nutcracker

NOUN

comes to life as a/an _____ prince who rescues Clara from some

ADJECTIVE

very _____ mice. Then Clara and her prince travel to a

ADJECTIVE

magical _____, where they are greeted by

NOUN

_____ snowflakes and dancing _____.

ADJECTIVE   PLURAL NOUN

They continue their enchanted journey and enter the _____

ADJECTIVE

land of the Sugar Plum _____, where people dressed like

PLURAL NOUN

_____ and _____ dance for them. When the

TYPE OF FOOD   TYPE OF LIQUID

festivities are over, Clara finds herself at home, _____

VERB ENDING IN "ING"

under the Christmas tree and holding her _____ nutcracker.

ADJECTIVE

It was all just a/an _____ dream!

ADJECTIVE

MAD LIBS® is fun to play with friends, but you can also play it by yourself! To begin with, DO NOT look at the story on the page below. Fill in the blanks on this page with the words called for. Then, using the words you have selected, fill in the blank spaces in the story.

Now you've created your own hilarious MAD LIBS® game!

SANTA TALKS

NOUN _____

ADJECTIVE _____

NOUN _____

NOUN _____

NOUN _____

PLURAL NOUN _____

NUMBER _____

PLURAL NOUN _____

PART OF THE BODY _____

NOUN _____

ADJECTIVE _____

PLURAL NOUN _____

ADJECTIVE _____

ADJECTIVE _____

ADJECTIVE _____

MAD LIBS®
SANTA TALKS

The following is an exclusive interview at the North _____ with
                                                            NOUN

the rotund man in the _____ suit:
                            ADJECTIVE

Q: You are described as a jolly _____ . Are you that way 24/7?
                                        NOUN

Santa: Ho, ho, ho. Does that answer your _____?
                                                  NOUN

Q: My next _____ may be somewhat embarrassing. Have you
                  NOUN

put on some extra _____ recently?
                        PLURAL NOUN

Santa: I'm actually at my average weight of _____ pounds.
                                                    NUMBER

Q: Doesn't that make it difficult for you to get down chimneys, especially

carrying a sack full of children's _____?
                                          PLURAL NOUN

Santa: No, I just suck in my _____ and squeeze down the
                                    PART OF THE BODY

_____ . I'm sorry, we're going to have to cut this _____
       NOUN   ADJECTIVE

interview short. I've got to get all the kids' _____ delivered.
                                                      PLURAL NOUN

Q: Wait—how do you get around the _____ world in one night?
                                              ADJECTIVE

Santa: I have a/an _____ sleigh and a/an _____ team
                          ADJECTIVE   ADJECTIVE

of reindeer—and most of the world is downhill these days. Ho, ho, ho!

MAD LIBS® is fun to play with friends, but you can also play it by yourself! To begin with, DO NOT look at the story on the page below. Fill in the blanks on this page with the words called for. Then, using the words you have selected, fill in the blank spaces in the story.

Now you've created your own hilarious MAD LIBS® game!

CHRISTMAS COOKIES

NOUN _____

NOUN _____

PLURAL NOUN _____

PLURAL NOUN _____

PLURAL NOUN _____

PLURAL NOUN _____

PLURAL NOUN _____

PLURAL NOUN _____

NOUN _____

PLURAL NOUN _____

NOUN _____

ADJECTIVE _____

ADJECTIVE _____

ADVERB _____

ADJECTIVE _____

ADJECTIVE _____

ADJECTIVE _____

MAD LIBS
CHRISTMAS COOKIES

Whether red or green, covered with sprinkles or just plain, old

_____ , Christmas cookies are the _____ 's
     NOUN   NOUN

meow! Some of the tastiest of these _____ include:
                                        PLURAL NOUN

- Sugar _____: These rank as one of the most popular
                PLURAL NOUN

  Christmas _____. They are often shaped like Christmas
                PLURAL NOUN

  _____ and _____, with frosting and
       PLURAL NOUN   PLURAL NOUN

  _____ sprinkled on top.
     PLURAL NOUN

- _____ macaroons: These coconut _____ delight
       NOUN   PLURAL NOUN

  the _____-buds, especially when they've been dipped in rich
         NOUN

  and _____ chocolate.
      ADJECTIVE

- Gingerbread cookies: Who can resist the _____ aroma of
                                  ADJECTIVE

  these _____ baked spicy classics? At Christmastime they are
         ADVERB

  usually cut into the shape of _____ girls and _____
                         ADJECTIVE   ADJECTIVE

  boys, and many families also build _____ gingerbread houses.
                                ADJECTIVE

MAD LIBS® is fun to play with friends, but you can also play it by yourself! To begin with, DO NOT look at the story on the page below. Fill in the blanks on this page with the words called for. Then, using the words you have selected, fill in the blank spaces in the story.

Now you've created your own hilarious MAD LIBS® game!

HOLIDAY ADVICE COLUMN

PERSON IN ROOM (FEMALE) _____

ADVERB _____

PERSON IN ROOM _____

NOUN _____

NOUN _____

ADJECTIVE _____

NOUN _____

NOUN _____

ADVERB _____

ADJECTIVE _____

A PLACE _____

SAME ADJECTIVE _____

ADJECTIVE _____

A PLACE _____

PART OF THE BODY _____

NOUN _____

A PLACE _____

ADJECTIVE _____

MAD LIBS®
HOLIDAY ADVICE COLUMN

Dear Miss _____ ,
                PERSON IN ROOM (FEMALE)

I _____ need your advice. I have to buy a Christmas present for my
        ADVERB

friend, _____ . We've known each other since the first day of
            PERSON IN ROOM

_____ school, and he/she means the _____ to
        NOUN   NOUN

me. So here's my _____ problem—my friend already owns every
                    ADJECTIVE

_____ known to man. What do I get for the
        NOUN

_____ who has everything?
        NOUN

_____ yours, _____ in (the) _____ .
        ADVERB   ADJECTIVE   A PLACE

Dear _____ ,
        SAME ADJECTIVE

The solution to your _____ dilemma is easy! We're talking about
                        ADJECTIVE

your best friend in all of (the) _____ . It doesn't matter what you
                                    A PLACE

give—so long as it comes from the _____ . Try making your
                                        PART OF THE BODY

friend a homemade _____ , or give him/her a gift certificate
                        NOUN

to (the) _____ . No matter what you decide, your friend will
            A PLACE

appreciate the _____ thought.
                    ADJECTIVE

MAD LIBS® is fun to play with friends, but you can also play it by yourself! To begin with, DO NOT look at the story on the page below. Fill in the blanks on this page with the words called for. Then, using the words you have selected, fill in the blank spaces in the story.

Now you've created your own hilarious MAD LIBS® game!

A SPECIAL RECIPE FOR HOT CHOCOLATE

ADJECTIVE _____

PART OF THE BODY (PLURAL) _____

PLURAL NOUN _____

ADJECTIVE _____

TYPE OF LIQUID _____

NOUN _____

NOUN _____

ADJECTIVE _____

NUMBER _____

NUMBER _____

ADVERB _____

ADJECTIVE _____

NOUN _____

NOUN _____

ADJECTIVE _____

NOUN _____

MAD LIBS®
A SPECIAL RECIPE FOR
HOT CHOCOLATE

There is nothing more comforting than a/an _____, frothy hot
                                          ADJECTIVE

chocolate to warm up your _____ on the coldest
                          PART OF THE BODY (PLURAL)

_____ of winter. Here is a recipe that has been passed down
PLURAL NOUN

from generation to generation in my _____ family. Pour one
                                     ADJECTIVE

cup of _____ , one _____ of half-and-half,
       TYPE OF LIQUID   NOUN

one tablespoon of vanilla, and two ounces of semisweet _____
                                                        NOUN

into a/an _____ pan. Place it on the stove and heat at
          ADJECTIVE

_____ degrees for _____ minutes.
        NUMBER   NUMBER

Stir _____ until the chocolate melts. Pour the liquid into two
     ADVERB

_____ mugs and serve with a dollop of whipped
ADJECTIVE

_____ on top. If you add some atmosphere, your
NOUN

_____ will taste even better: Enjoy your drink in front of
NOUN

a/an _____ fireplace or while watching the
     ADJECTIVE

_____ -flakes fall outside your window.
NOUN

MAD LIBS® is fun to play with friends, but you can also play it by yourself! To begin with, DO NOT look at the story on the page below. Fill in the blanks on this page with the words called for. Then, using the words you have selected, fill in the blank spaces in the story.

Now you've created your own hilarious MAD LIBS® game!

HOW TO MAKE A SNOWMAN

ADJECTIVE _____

PLURAL NOUN _____

ADJECTIVE _____

ADJECTIVE _____

PART OF THE BODY _____

NOUN _____

ADJECTIVE _____

PLURAL NOUN _____

PART OF THE BODY (PLURAL) _____

NOUN _____

PART OF THE BODY _____

NOUN _____

NOUN _____

PLURAL NOUN _____

NOUN _____

ADJECTIVE _____

NOUN _____

MAD LIBS®
HOW TO MAKE A SNOWMAN

Want to make a/an _____ snowman? All you need is some snow
                          ADJECTIVE

and a few household _____. Then just follow this
                          PLURAL NOUN

_____ step-by-step guide:
          ADJECTIVE

• Roll three _____ balls out of snow: one for the base, one
                    ADJECTIVE

for the torso, and one for the _____. Then pile them on
                                   PART OF THE BODY

top of one another so they resemble a/an _____.
                                                NOUN

• To complete your snowman's _____ body, use some long, thin
                                    ADJECTIVE

_____ for arms and give him a pair of _____
PLURAL NOUN   PART OF THE BODY (PLURAL)

made of coal. Then add a button _____ and a carrot
                                       NOUN

_____.
PART OF THE BODY

• You can accessorize your snowy creation with a corncob

_____, a stovepipe _____, and some
      NOUN   NOUN

buttons made of _____. If it's really cold outside, you
                      PLURAL NOUN

can give him a knitted _____.
                            NOUN

• And don't forget to give your snowman a name! _____
                                                      ADJECTIVE

the _____-man is always a popular choice.
        NOUN

MAD LIBS® is fun to play with friends, but you can also play it by yourself! To begin with, DO NOT look at the story on the page below. Fill in the blanks on this page with the words called for. Then, using the words you have selected, fill in the blank spaces in the story.

Now you've created your own hilarious MAD LIBS® game!

ELF-MAIL

PERSON IN ROOM_____

PERSON IN ROOM_____

ADJECTIVE_____

ADJECTIVE_____

ADJECTIVE_____

PLURAL NOUN_____

ADJECTIVE_____

PERSON IN ROOM_____

NOUN_____

ADJECTIVE_____

ADJECTIVE_____

PERSON IN ROOM_____

NOUN_____

VERB_____

PLURAL NOUN_____

MAD LIBS®
ELF-MAIL

To: _____-elf@santasworkshop.elf
　　　　　　PERSON IN ROOM

From: _____ slittlehelper@santasworkshop.elf
　　　　　　PERSON IN ROOM

Hi there, _____ buddy! Just wanted to drop you a/an
　　　　　　　ADJECTIVE

_____ note to see how you are doing. It's been a/an
　　　ADJECTIVE

_____ Christmas season here. I've made so many toys—especially
　　ADJECTIVE

jack-in-the-_____—that I've lost count! On another _____
　　　　　　PLURAL NOUN　　　　　　　　　　　　　　　　　　　ADJECTIVE

note, are you getting excited about _____'s Christmas Eve elf
　　　　　　　　　　　　　　　PERSON IN ROOM

party? I hear DJ _____ Elf will be spinning some really
　　　　　　　　NOUN

_____ Christmas tunes! I've also got some _____ gossip: I
　ADJECTIVE　　　　　　　　　　　　　　　　　　　ADJECTIVE

hear _____ is a shoo-in for Elf of the Year! He/She totally deserves
　　PERSON IN ROOM

it for being such a hardworking _____. Well, I've gotta
　　　　　　　　　　　　　　NOUN

_____—it's back to the _____ at the workshop.
　　VERB　　　　　　　　　　　　PLURAL NOUN

See you soon!

MAD LIBS® is fun to play with friends, but you can also play it by yourself! To begin with, DO NOT look at the story on the page below. Fill in the blanks on this page with the words called for. Then, using the words you have selected, fill in the blank spaces in the story.

Now you've created your own hilarious MAD LIBS® game!

A CHRISTMAS CARD

ADJECTIVE _____

ADJECTIVE _____

NOUN _____

NOUN _____

ADJECTIVE _____

PLURAL NOUN _____

PLURAL NOUN _____

ADJECTIVE _____

NOUN _____

ADJECTIVE _____

VERB _____

ADJECTIVE _____

NOUN _____

PLURAL NOUN _____

NOUN _____

NOUN _____

PERSON IN ROOM _____

MAD LIBS®
A CHRISTMAS CARD

Dear Grandma and Grandpa,

Merry Christmas to my wonderful, _____ grandparents. Our house is
                                    ADJECTIVE

filled with _____ Christmas spirit. Yesterday, we went to the
              ADJECTIVE

_____ farm and bought a ten-foot-tall _____. We put it in our
  NOUN   NOUN

_____ living room and covered it with lights and _____.
  ADJECTIVE   PLURAL NOUN

Dad decorated the front of the house with strings of _____ and
                                                      PLURAL NOUN

_____ decorations. And Mom baked a lot of _____
  ADJECTIVE   NOUN

cookies that smell absolutely _____! I hope you're excited about
                                ADJECTIVE

coming to _____ with us! I can't wait to see you at our
              VERB

_____ Christmas dinner. We're having your favorite—roast
  ADJECTIVE

_____ and mashed _____! And, of course,
  NOUN   PLURAL NOUN

_____ pie for dessert!
  NOUN

Love from your grand-_____,
                          NOUN

_____
PERSON IN ROOM

MAD LIBS®

WINTER GAMES MAD LIBS

Mad Libs
An Imprint of Penguin Random House

INSTRUCTIONS

MAD LIBS® is a game for people who don't like games!
It can be played by one, two, three, four, or forty.

• RIDICULOUSLY SIMPLE DIRECTIONS

In this tablet you will find stories containing blank spaces where words are left out. One player, the READER, selects one of these stories. The READER does not tell anyone what the story is about. Instead, he/she asks the other players, the WRITERS, to give him/her words. These words are used to fill in the blank spaces in the story.

• TO PLAY

The READER asks each WRITER in turn to call out a word—an adjective or a noun or whatever the space calls for—and uses them to fill in the blank spaces in the story. The result is a MAD LIBS® game.

When the READER then reads the completed MAD LIBS® game to the other players, they will discover that they have written a story that is fantastic, screamingly funny, shocking, silly, crazy, or just plain dumb—depending upon which words each WRITER called out.

• EXAMPLE (*Before* and *After*)

"_____!" he said _____
        EXCLAMATION   ADVERB

as he jumped into his convertible _____ and
                                              NOUN

drove off with his _____ wife.
                        ADJECTIVE

"_____OUCH_____!" he said _____STUPIDLY_____
        EXCLAMATION   ADVERB

as he jumped into his convertible _____CAT_____ and
                                              NOUN

drove off with his _____BRAVE_____ wife.
                        ADJECTIVE

QUICK REVIEW

In case you have forgotten what adjectives, adverbs, nouns, and verbs are, here is a quick review:

An ADJECTIVE describes something or somebody. *Lumpy, soft, ugly, messy,* and *short* are adjectives.

An ADVERB tells how something is done. It modifies a verb and usually ends in "ly." *Modestly, stupidly, greedily,* and *carefully* are adverbs.

A NOUN is the name of a person, place, or thing. *Sidewalk, umbrella, bridle, bathtub,* and *nose* are nouns.

A VERB is an action word. *Run, pitch, jump,* and *swim* are verbs. Put the verbs in past tense if the directions say PAST TENSE. *Ran, pitched, jumped,* and *swam* are verbs in the past tense.

When we ask for A PLACE, we mean any sort of place: a country or city *(Spain, Cleveland)* or a room *(bathroom, kitchen).*

An EXCLAMATION or SILLY WORD is any sort of funny sound, gasp, grunt, or outcry, like *Wow!, Ouch!, Whomp!, Ick!,* and *Gadzooks!*

When we ask for specific words, like a NUMBER, a COLOR, an ANIMAL, or a PART OF THE BODY, we mean a word that is one of those things, like *seven, blue, horse,* or *head.*

When we ask for a PLURAL, it means more than one. For example, *cat* pluralized is *cats.*

MAD LIBS® is fun to play with friends, but you can also play it by yourself! To begin with, DO NOT look at the story on the page below. Fill in the blanks on this page with the words called for. Then, using the words you have selected, fill in the blank spaces in the story.

Now you've created your own hilarious MAD LIBS® game!

DOWNHILL SKI RACE

PLURAL NOUN _____

VERB _____

NOUN _____

ADJECTIVE _____

VERB ENDING IN "ING" _____

NOUN _____

PLURAL NOUN _____

NOUN _____

PART OF THE BODY _____

PLURAL NOUN _____

ADJECTIVE _____

PLURAL NOUN _____

NOUN _____

NOUN _____

NOUN _____

MAD☺LIBS®
DOWNHILL SKI RACE

From the moment the downhill _____ leave the gates until the
PLURAL NOUN

second they _____ across the finish line, the ski race is a/an
VERB

_____-pounding experience! The skiers must navigate a/an
NOUN

_____ demanding course: from _____ over
ADJECTIVE   VERB ENDING IN "ING"

giant mounds of _____, known as "moguls," to maneuvering around
NOUN

plastic _____ planted in the snow to create a more challenging
PLURAL NOUN

_____. If that isn't tough enough, the racers have to combat the
NOUN

elements—the _____-chilling cold, the blinding snow
PART OF THE BODY

_____, and the _____ winds racing up to 100
PLURAL NOUN   ADJECTIVE

_____ per hour. Only the results of a downhill _____ are
PLURAL NOUN   NOUN

predictable. It seems that year after year the same team wins this _____.
NOUN

Must be something in their _____!
NOUN

MAD LIBS® is fun to play with friends, but you can also play it by yourself! To begin with, DO NOT look at the story on the page below. Fill in the blanks on this page with the words called for. Then, using the words you have selected, fill in the blank spaces in the story.

Now you've created your own hilarious MAD LIBS® game!

TRAITS OF ATHLETES

ADJECTIVE _____

NOUN _____

ADJECTIVE _____

NOUN _____

NOUN _____

PLURAL NOUN _____

ADJECTIVE _____

PLURAL NOUN _____

PLURAL NOUN _____

PLURAL NOUN _____

NOUN _____

ADJECTIVE _____

ADJECTIVE _____

NOUN _____

NOUN _____

PLURAL NOUN _____

MAD LIBS®
TRAITS OF ATHLETES

A/An _____ survey of both men and _____ winter-game
       ADJECTIVE   NOUN

athletes reveals some very _____ statistics:
                      ADJECTIVE

1. 43 percent are ambidextrous. The right _____ always knows
                                 NOUN

   what the left _____ is doing.
                 NOUN

2. 93 percent set impossible _____ for themselves and then
                       PLURAL NOUN

   achieve these _____ goals.
                 ADJECTIVE

3. 47 percent count their calories and eat well-balanced _____—
                                     PLURAL NOUN

   observing the recommended allowance of fruit and _____.
                                   PLURAL NOUN

4. Slightly over 50 percent play musical _____, the most popular
                             PLURAL NOUN

   being the piano, violin, and percussion _____.
                                NOUN

5. 73 percent have a/an _____ sense of timing and
                         ADJECTIVE

   _____ eye-to-_____ coordination.
  ADJECTIVE   NOUN

6. 94 percent never drink hard _____ or smoke _____.
                       NOUN   PLURAL NOUN

MAD LIBS® is fun to play with friends, but you can also play it by yourself! To begin with, DO NOT look at the story on the page below. Fill in the blanks on this page with the words called for. Then, using the words you have selected, fill in the blank spaces in the story.

Now you've created your own hilarious MAD LIBS® game!

FIGURE SKATING

PLURAL NOUN _____

ADVERB _____

PERSON IN ROOM (FEMALE) _____

NOUN _____

NOUN _____

ADJECTIVE _____

ADJECTIVE _____

ADJECTIVE _____

NOUN _____

VERB _____

ADJECTIVE _____

NOUN _____

NOUN _____

NOUN _____

ADJECTIVE _____

NOUN _____

PLURAL NOUN _____

NOUN _____

MAD LIBS
FIGURE SKATING

As a crowd of more than 19,000 _____ filed into the _____
                                  PLURAL NOUN   ADVERB

designed auditorium, _____ , our _____-skating
                           PERSON IN ROOM (FEMALE)   NOUN

champion, went through her warm-up _____. For the first time in
                                         NOUN

her _____ life, the champion felt frightened and _____.
       ADJECTIVE   ADJECTIVE

As the music began, the champion took a/an _____ breath,
                                                  ADJECTIVE

smoothed the ruffles of her _____, and started to _____.
                                 NOUN   VERB

Just as she feared, when it came time for her most _____ jump, a
                                                        ADJECTIVE

triple _____, she lost her balance and landed with a thump on her
           NOUN

_____. She stood up bravely, brushed the ice off her _____,
    NOUN   NOUN

and finished her _____ routine. The crowd gave her a five-minute
                     ADJECTIVE

standing _____. Even though she realized she had lost the competition,
             NOUN

she knew she had won the hearts and _____ of every _____
                                        PLURAL NOUN   NOUN

in the auditorium.

From WINTER GAMES MAD LIBS® • Copyright © 2005 by Penguin Random House LLC.

MAD LIBS® is fun to play with friends, but you can also play it by yourself! To begin with, DO NOT look at the story on the page below. Fill in the blanks on this page with the words called for. Then, using the words you have selected, fill in the blank spaces in the story.

Now you've created your own hilarious MAD LIBS® game!

RULES FOR A SNOWBALL FIGHT

ADJECTIVE _____

VERB ENDING IN "ING" _____

NOUN _____

PLURAL NOUN _____

PLURAL NOUN _____

NOUN _____

PLURAL NOUN _____

PART OF THE BODY _____

NOUN _____

PLURAL NOUN _____

PLURAL NOUN _____

ADVERB _____

ADJECTIVE _____

NOUN _____

PLURAL NOUN _____

ADJECTIVE _____

NOUN _____

NOUN _____

The _____ winter games committee does not recognize snowball

ADJECTIVE

_____ as an official _____. Nevertheless, it has

VERB ENDING IN "ING"   NOUN

established rules and _____ for the athletes who want to throw

PLURAL NOUN

icy _____ at each other.

PLURAL NOUN

- Contestants can toss only one _____ at a time and from a

NOUN

  distance not less than 25 _____ away.

PLURAL NOUN

- Aiming at a/an _____ is not permitted. If anybody

PART OF THE BODY

  is hit below the _____, that person automatically wins.

NOUN

- Loading a snowball with heavy _____ or solid _____

PLURAL NOUN   PLURAL NOUN

  is _____ forbidden. Snowball tampering will result in

ADVERB

  _____ penalties or rejection from the _____.

ADJECTIVE   NOUN

- All _____ must wear _____ gear that protects

PLURAL NOUN   ADJECTIVE

  their eyes, as well as their _____ and _____.

NOUN   NOUN

MAD LIBS® is fun to play with friends, but you can also play it by yourself! To begin with, DO NOT look at the story on the page below. Fill in the blanks on this page with the words called for. Then, using the words you have selected, fill in the blank spaces in the story.

Now you've created your own hilarious MAD LIBS® game!

A WINTER GAME BROADCAST

CELEBRITY (MALE) _____

NOUN _____

NOUN _____

PLURAL NOUN _____

PLURAL NOUN _____

PERSON IN ROOM (MALE) _____

NOUN _____

NOUN _____

PLURAL NOUN _____

NOUN _____

PLURAL NOUN _____

NOUN _____

ADVERB _____

NOUN _____

PLURAL NOUN _____

SAME PERSON IN ROOM (MALE) _____

ADJECTIVE _____

MAD LIBS®
A WINTER GAME BROADCAST

"Hi, we're broadcasting live from the American compound here at the ski

village. Unfortunately, my cohost, _____, has laryngitis and has

CELEBRITY (MALE)

lost his _____. He'll be back with us as soon as his _____ returns.

NOUN   NOUN

Now to breaking _____! Sadly, we've learned that less than twenty

PLURAL NOUN

_____ ago, _____ , America's best _____

PLURAL NOUN   PERSON IN ROOM (MALE)   NOUN

skier and favorite to win the giant slalom, suffered a life-threatening

_____ when he plummeted 300 _____ down the side of

NOUN   PLURAL NOUN

a/an _____. According to the latest hospital _____, he broke

NOUN   PLURAL NOUN

his _____, but doctors are hopeful he'll heal _____ and be

NOUN   ADVERB

back on his _____ by the end of the year. Our fervent _____

NOUN   PLURAL NOUN

go out to _____ and his entire _____ family."

SAME PERSON IN ROOM (MALE)   ADJECTIVE

MAD LIBS® is fun to play with friends, but you can also play it by yourself! To begin with, DO NOT look at the story on the page below. Fill in the blanks on this page with the words called for. Then, using the words you have selected, fill in the blank spaces in the story.

Now you've created your own hilarious MAD LIBS® game!

SNOWBOARDING

PLURAL NOUN _____

NOUN _____

PLURAL NOUN _____

PLURAL NOUN _____

PLURAL NOUN _____

ADJECTIVE _____

ADJECTIVE _____

NOUN _____

PART OF THE BODY _____

NOUN _____

PLURAL NOUN _____

VERB _____

NOUN _____

NOUN _____

PLURAL NOUN _____

ADJECTIVE _____

VERB ENDING IN "ING" _____

PLURAL NOUN _____

MAD☺LIBS®
SNOWBOARDING

Most of us have watched snowboarding spring up before our very

_____. In its short history, _____-boarding has cemented
　　PLURAL NOUN　　　　　　　　　　　　　　NOUN

itself into the _____ of sporting _____ around the world. Its
　　　　　　　PLURAL NOUN　　　　　　　　PLURAL NOUN

simplicity appeals to men and _____ of all ages. All you need to
　　　　　　　　　　　　　　　PLURAL NOUN

snowboard is a/an _____ boot, a relatively short _____
　　　　　　　　　ADJECTIVE　　　　　　　　　　　　　　ADJECTIVE

board, athletic _____, and a willingness to break a/an
　　　　　　　　　NOUN

_____. I am a high-school _____ who has won several
PART OF THE BODY　　　　　　　　　NOUN

_____ in snowboarding competitions. Many of my closest friends
PLURAL NOUN

say I eat, drink, and _____ snowboarding. I admit to practicing morning,
　　　　　　　　　VERB

noon, and _____, but it paid off last week when I was invited to
　　　　　　NOUN

qualify for the team in the freestyle _____. This is where I can shine.
　　　　　　　　　　　　　　　　NOUN

I'm the best at inverted _____, which are _____ because
　　　　　　　　　　　PLURAL NOUN　　　　　　　ADJECTIVE

you're upside down while _____. Excuse me, I'm going now. I
　　　　　　　　　　　VERB ENDING IN "ING"

can't wait to hit the fresh _____ out on the slopes!
　　　　　　　　　　　PLURAL NOUN

MAD LIBS® is fun to play with friends, but you can also play it by yourself! To begin with, DO NOT look at the story on the page below. Fill in the blanks on this page with the words called for. Then, using the words you have selected, fill in the blank spaces in the story.

Now you've created your own hilarious MAD LIBS® game!

BOBSLEDDING GLOSSARY

PLURAL NOUN _____

ADJECTIVE _____

ADJECTIVE _____

NOUN _____

PLURAL NOUN _____

NOUN _____

NOUN _____

NOUN _____

NOUN _____

PLURAL NOUN _____

PLURAL NOUN _____

NOUN _____

VERB ENDING IN "ING" _____

ADJECTIVE _____

VERB _____

NOUN _____

PLURAL NOUN _____

NOUN _____

MAD LIBS®
BOBSLEDDING GLOSSARY

The name "bobsledding" comes from the early racers bobbing their

_____ back and forth to gain the most _____ speed.
  PLURAL NOUN   ADJECTIVE

Here are some _____ phrases to provide a better understanding of
                    ADJECTIVE

this high-speed _____.
                     NOUN

Bobsled: a large sled made up of two _____ linked together. There
                                              PLURAL NOUN

are two sizes, a two-person _____ and a four-_____ sled.
                                  NOUN   NOUN

Brakeman: the last _____ to leap onto the _____. He/she
                            NOUN   NOUN

applies the _____ to bring it to a stop. The brakeman must have
                PLURAL NOUN

very strong _____.
               PLURAL NOUN

Driver: the front _____ in the bobsled is responsible for
                          NOUN

_____ . The driver's _____ goal is to maintain
  VERB ENDING IN "ING"   ADJECTIVE

the straightest path down the track.

Pushtime: the amount of time required to _____ a/an _____
                                                    VERB   NOUN

over the first 50 _____ of a run.
                       PLURAL NOUN

WH: abbreviation for "what happened?" Usually said when the _____
                                                                      NOUN

crashes!

MAD LIBS® is fun to play with friends, but you can also play it by yourself! To begin with, DO NOT look at the story on the page below. Fill in the blanks on this page with the words called for. Then, using the words you have selected, fill in the blank spaces in the story.

Now you've created your own hilarious MAD LIBS® game!

SNOWMAN-BUILDING

ADJECTIVE _____

NOUN _____

NOUN _____

ADJECTIVE _____

NOUN _____

ADJECTIVE _____

PLURAL NOUN _____

PART OF THE BODY (PLURAL) _____

NOUN _____

COLOR _____

NOUN _____

PLURAL NOUN _____

ADJECTIVE _____

NOUN _____

NOUN _____

ADJECTIVE _____

NOUN _____

NOUN _____

MAD LIBS®
SNOWMAN-BUILDING

Question: What kid hasn't loved the _____ thrill of building a/an
                                      ADJECTIVE

_____ man?
       NOUN

Answer: Kids who live where the _____ never stops shining.
                                            NOUN

Nevertheless, snowman-building is one of the most _____
                                                        ADJECTIVE

competitions at the winter games. Each team is given several hundred pounds

of powdered _____ to mold and shape into what they hope will be the
                  NOUN

most _____ snowman anyone has ever laid _____ on.
          ADJECTIVE   PLURAL NOUN

This year's winner was so adorable that everyone wanted to throw their

_____ around him and hug his _____. They
PART OF THE BODY (PLURAL)   NOUN

used a bright _____ _____ for his nose, two shiny
                   COLOR   NOUN

_____ for his eyes, and a/an _____ _____ on
 PLURAL NOUN   ADJECTIVE   NOUN

his head for a hat. In addition, they put a corncob _____ in his mouth
                                                          NOUN

and tied a/an _____ scarf around his neck. Their prizewinning
                   ADJECTIVE

_____ quickly became the talk of the _____.
      NOUN   NOUN

MAD LIBS® is fun to play with friends, but you can also play it by yourself! To begin with, DO NOT look at the story on the page below. Fill in the blanks on this page with the words called for. Then, using the words you have selected, fill in the blank spaces in the story.

Now you've created your own hilarious MAD LIBS® game!

FACE-OFF

NOUN _____

NOUN _____

ADJECTIVE _____

NOUN _____

NOUN _____

NOUN _____

ADJECTIVE _____

NOUN _____

ADJECTIVE _____

NOUN _____

NOUN _____

PLURAL NOUN _____

ADVERB _____

PLURAL NOUN _____

PLURAL NOUN _____

ADJECTIVE _____

NOUN _____

PLURAL NOUN _____

MAD LIBS®
FACE-OFF

If you're seeking fame and _____ as a hockey player, you may want to
                              NOUN

give it a second _____. Hockey is not a sport for the _____
                   NOUN   ADJECTIVE

of heart! You put your _____ in danger the moment you enter the
                        NOUN

rink and skate onto the _____. Hockey is a game of vicious
                         NOUN

_____ contact. To be a/an _____ hockey player you have to
 NOUN   ADJECTIVE

keep your _____ in perfect shape, you have to be lean and
           NOUN

_____, and you can't afford one extra ounce of _____ on
 ADJECTIVE   NOUN

your _____. Hockey attracts the most volatile _____.
      NOUN   PLURAL NOUN

These fans can become _____ physical and throw soda _____,
                       ADVERB   PLURAL NOUN

large sticks and _____, and even _____ coins onto the
                  PLURAL NOUN   ADJECTIVE

ice. You can see why hockey is considered the most physical _____ of
                                                             NOUN

all the _____ at the winter games.
         PLURAL NOUN

MAD LIBS® is fun to play with friends, but you can also play it by yourself! To begin with, DO NOT look at the story on the page below. Fill in the blanks on this page with the words called for. Then, using the words you have selected, fill in the blank spaces in the story.

Now you've created your own hilarious MAD LIBS® game!

DOGS AND SLEDS

PLURAL NOUN _____

PLURAL NOUN _____

NOUN _____

PART OF THE BODY _____

ADVERB _____

NOUN _____

NOUN _____

PLURAL NOUN _____

PLURAL NOUN _____

NUMBER _____

ADJECTIVE _____

PLURAL NOUN _____

NOUN _____

NOUN _____

PLURAL NOUN _____

NOUN _____

NOUN _____

Of all the winter _____, dogsled racing is my favorite. Watching
PLURAL NOUN

these beautiful four-legged _____ courageously pull the sled across
PLURAL NOUN

the frozen _____ tugs at my _____ strings. The rules
NOUN   PART OF THE BODY

for dogsled racing are _____ simple—the first team to cross the
ADVERB

finish _____ wins the _____. A dogsled team consists of 14
NOUN   NOUN

Siberian _____, each weighing approximately 50 _____
PLURAL NOUN   PLURAL NOUN

and each able to pull _____ times its weight. These beautiful and
NUMBER

_____ dogs are trained to respond to the shouted _____
ADJECTIVE   PLURAL NOUN

of their _____. The driver stands on a/an _____ at the rear
NOUN   NOUN

of the sled and guides the dogs with verbal _____ and, if necessary,
PLURAL NOUN

a crack of his _____. Dogsled races are proof positive why a dog is
NOUN

thought of as man's best _____.
NOUN

From WINTER GAMES MAD LIBS® • Copyright © 2005 by Penguin Random House LLC.

MAD LIBS® is fun to play with friends, but you can also play it by yourself! To begin with, DO NOT look at the story on the page below. Fill in the blanks on this page with the words called for. Then, using the words you have selected, fill in the blank spaces in the story.

Now you've created your own hilarious MAD LIBS® game!

THE LODGE

NOUN _____

NOUN _____

NOUN _____

ADJECTIVE _____

PLURAL NOUN _____

NOUN _____

ADJECTIVE _____

NOUN _____

NOUN _____

VERB ENDING IN "ING" _____

PART OF THE BODY _____

NOUN _____

NOUN _____

PLURAL NOUN _____

PLURAL NOUN _____

NOUN _____

ADJECTIVE _____

PLURAL NOUN _____

MAD LIBS
THE LODGE

A/An _____ away from home is most important to a competitive
           NOUN

_____. Athletes should select a lodge recommended by a travel
     NOUN

_____, _____ website, or even relatives or close _____.
     NOUN   ADJECTIVE   PLURAL NOUN

The bedroom should have a king-size _____ with a/an _____
                                          NOUN   ADJECTIVE

mattress to ensure a good night's _____. If possible, there should be a
                                       NOUN

hot _____ to relax those aching muscles after a long day of
         NOUN

_____. Since relaxation is so important to an athlete's
VERB ENDING IN "ING"

_____, the lodge should also provide an indoor swimming
PART OF THE BODY

_____. Other amenities might be a wood-burning _____, a
     NOUN   NOUN

game room stocked with arcade _____, game tables for chess or
                                   PLURAL NOUN

_____, as well as a Ping-Pong _____. Since nutrition is of
PLURAL NOUN   NOUN

_____ significance to athletes, the lodge's restaurant should have a
ADJECTIVE

rating of five _____.
               PLURAL NOUN

MAD LIBS® is fun to play with friends, but you can also play it by yourself! To begin with, DO NOT look at the story on the page below. Fill in the blanks on this page with the words called for. Then, using the words you have selected, fill in the blank spaces in the story.

Now you've created your own hilarious MAD LIBS® game!

SAGE ADVICE

VERB ENDING IN "ING" _____

PERSON IN ROOM _____

ADJECTIVE _____

ADJECTIVE _____

PLURAL NOUN _____

ADVERB _____

PLURAL NOUN _____

ADJECTIVE _____

PLURAL NOUN _____

NOUN _____

ADJECTIVE _____

PLURAL NOUN _____

PLURAL NOUN _____

VERB ENDING IN "ING" _____

NOUN _____

MAD LIBS

SAGE ADVICE

According to the pioneer of downhill _____ ,

VERB ENDING IN "ING"

_____ , "When you ski, your _____ equipment

PERSON IN ROOM   ADJECTIVE

should be the equal of your _____ ability." Remember this sage

ADJECTIVE

advice when buying your first pair of _____. It is _____

PLURAL NOUN   ADVERB

important to take many _____ into consideration before plunking

PLURAL NOUN

down _____ bucks for your _____. Your gender, your

ADJECTIVE   PLURAL NOUN

height, and your _____ are all _____ factors in selecting a

NOUN   ADJECTIVE

pair of _____ that match your skills and _____. It goes

PLURAL NOUN   PLURAL NOUN

without _____ : If you don't have the right skis, you're

VERB ENDING IN "ING"

starting off on the wrong _____.

NOUN

MAD LIBS® is fun to play with friends, but you can also play it by yourself! To begin with, DO NOT look at the story on the page below. Fill in the blanks on this page with the words called for. Then, using the words you have selected, fill in the blank spaces in the story.

Now you've created your own hilarious MAD LIBS® game!

MORE SAGE ADVICE

NOUN _____

NOUN _____

PLURAL NOUN _____

ADVERB _____

ADJECTIVE _____

PART OF THE BODY _____

NOUN _____

ADJECTIVE _____

NOUN _____

ADJECTIVE _____

NOUN _____

PART OF THE BODY _____

ADJECTIVE _____

NOUN _____

NOUN _____

ADJECTIVE _____

NOUN _____

NOUN _____

MAD LIBS®
MORE SAGE ADVICE

Beware! If your skiing equipment isn't top-of-the-_____, you put
                                                    NOUN
your _____ at risk. Here are some important _____ to
         NOUN   PLURAL NOUN
remember:

Ski Boots: Give careful thought to this important piece of equipment. Choose

_____ . Together with ski bindings, these _____
     ADVERB   ADJECTIVE
boots form the link between your skis and your _____.
                                                PART OF THE BODY

Ski Bindings: As far as your safety is concerned, _____ bindings are
                                                        NOUN
the most _____ pieces of _____ in skiing. If you have any
           ADJECTIVE   NOUN
_____ questions, seek the help of a/an _____ professional.
   ADJECTIVE   NOUN

Ski Helmets: Protect your _____ by wearing a/an
                                PART OF THE BODY
_____ ski _____. Helmets absolutely help you avoid a
   ADJECTIVE   NOUN
serious _____ mishap.
          NOUN

Ski Clothing: First and foremost, get yourself some _____
                                                            ADJECTIVE
underwear, preferably thermal, to keep your _____ warm. You will
                                               NOUN
also need a ski _____ to protect your head and ears from extremely
                  NOUN
frigid temperatures.

MAD LIBS® is fun to play with friends, but you can also play it by yourself! To begin with, DO NOT look at the story on the page below. Fill in the blanks on this page with the words called for. Then, using the words you have selected, fill in the blank spaces in the story.

Now you've created your own hilarious MAD LIBS® game!

SLED RACE

NOUN _____

NOUN _____

NOUN _____

PLURAL NOUN _____

NOUN _____

PLURAL NOUN _____

PLURAL NOUN _____

NOUN _____

ADJECTIVE _____

PLURAL NOUN _____

ADJECTIVE _____

NOUN _____

ADJECTIVE _____

NOUN _____

PLURAL NOUN _____

PART OF THE BODY _____

ADJECTIVE _____

PLURAL NOUN _____

MAD LIBS
SLED RACE

Ever since I was in the fifth _____ in school I've dreamed of having
                        NOUN

my own sled. I started delivering the morning _____ on my two-
                                            NOUN

wheeler _____ until I saved enough pennies, nickels, and
                  NOUN

_____ to buy one. It was the smartest _____ I ever made.
PLURAL NOUN   NOUN

Today, I am a champion sled racer with nine first-place _____, seven
                                               PLURAL NOUN

second-place _____, one third-place _____, and four
                PLURAL NOUN   NOUN

_____ ribbons. Although some of my competitors use sophisticated
ADJECTIVE

and aerodynamic _____, I still rely on a/an _____
                        PLURAL NOUN   ADJECTIVE

version of my old sledding _____. Sled racing is relatively simple; the
                                    NOUN

participants line up at the top of a/an _____ hill. When the starter
                                    ADJECTIVE

drops his _____, the competitors climb on their _____ and
                NOUN   PLURAL NOUN

race at break-_____ speed to cross the _____ line
            PART OF THE BODY   ADJECTIVE

ahead of the other _____.
            PLURAL NOUN

MAD LIBS® is fun to play with friends, but you can also play it by yourself! To begin with, DO NOT look at the story on the page below. Fill in the blanks on this page with the words called for. Then, using the words you have selected, fill in the blank spaces in the story.

Now you've created your own hilarious MAD LIBS® game!

SKI JUMPING

NOUN _____

NOUN _____

ADJECTIVE _____

NOUN _____

PLURAL NOUN _____

NOUN _____

ADVERB _____

NOUN _____

ADJECTIVE _____

NOUN _____

NOUN _____

PLURAL NOUN _____

PART OF THE BODY _____

NOUN _____

PART OF THE BODY _____

VERB ENDING IN "ING" _____

PLURAL NOUN _____

PLURAL NOUN _____

MAD LIBS®
SKI JUMPING

Whether you're a/an _____ seated in the stands or a/an _____
                     NOUN   NOUN

watching on television, the _____ beauty of ski jumping is
                            ADJECTIVE

dramatically apparent. What compares to a skier taking flight, soaring into the

crystal-clear _____, against a background of blue _____
              NOUN   PLURAL NOUN

with _____-capped mountains looming _____ in the
     NOUN   ADVERB

distance? But _____ jumping doesn't shortchange you on thrills.
              NOUN

There's _____ drama in every jump. You can't help but sit on the
        ADJECTIVE

edge of your _____ and hold your _____ as conflicting
             NOUN   NOUN

_____ race through your _____ . Will the skier
PLURAL NOUN   PART OF THE BODY

break the world _____? Will he or she break a/an
                NOUN

_____ ? Minutes later, the crowd is
PART OF THE BODY

_____ at the top of their _____ and you have
VERB ENDING IN "ING"   PLURAL NOUN

your answer. You've got a world champion on your _____.
                                                 PLURAL NOUN

MAD LIBS® is fun to play with friends, but you can also play it by yourself! To begin with, DO NOT look at the story on the page below. Fill in the blanks on this page with the words called for. Then, using the words you have selected, fill in the blank spaces in the story.

Now you've created your own hilarious MAD LIBS® game!

SPEED SKATING

NOUN _____

ADVERB _____

NOUN _____

PLURAL NOUN _____

PART OF THE BODY (PLURAL) _____

NOUN _____

VERB ENDING IN "ING" _____

NOUN _____

NOUN _____

PLURAL NOUN _____

PLURAL NOUN _____

ADVERB _____

NOUN _____

PART OF THE BODY _____

COLOR _____

MAD LIBS®
SPEED SKATING

A speed-skating _____ goes by so _____ that if you blink
                        NOUN   ADVERB

a/an _____, you might miss the race. In every competition, skaters
          NOUN

not only race against their fellow _____, they also challenge the
                                      PLURAL NOUN

_____ of the clock. They know a fraction of a/an
PART OF THE BODY (PLURAL)

_____ can be the difference between not only winning but
        NOUN

_____ a record. Consequently, skaters worship at the
VERB ENDING IN "ING"

shrine of speed. When racing, they skate bent over, angled toward the ice, with

one _____ behind them, pressed firmly against their _____,
          NOUN   NOUN

to eliminate being slowed down by wind resistance. They even wear skintight

_____ to improve their speed. And, as you can tell from their trim,
PLURAL NOUN

muscular _____, skaters are _____ weight-conscious. An
            PLURAL NOUN   ADVERB

extra ounce of _____ strikes terror in a skater's
                        NOUN

_____ . To say speed skaters are neurotic is like calling a
PART OF THE BODY

kettle _____!
            COLOR

MAD LIBS® is fun to play with friends, but you can also play it by yourself! To begin with, DO NOT look at the story on the page below. Fill in the blanks on this page with the words called for. Then, using the words you have selected, fill in the blank spaces in the story.

Now you've created your own hilarious MAD LIBS® game!

THE LUGE

ADJECTIVE _____

PLURAL NOUN _____

PLURAL NOUN _____

NOUN _____

NOUN _____

PLURAL NOUN _____

PLURAL NOUN _____

NOUN _____

PART OF THE BODY (PLURAL) _____

NOUN _____

NOUN _____

NOUN _____

PART OF THE BODY (PLURAL) _____

ADJECTIVE _____

PLURAL NOUN _____

ADJECTIVE _____

NOUN _____

MAD LIBS
THE LUGE

Although the _____ luge is thought to be relatively new, it's actually
          ADJECTIVE

one of the oldest of all winter _____. It was a favorite activity of
                    PLURAL NOUN

kings, queens, and _____ in the eighteenth century. The word comes
            PLURAL NOUN

from the French _____ for sled. The luge travels at a/an
            NOUN

_____-threatening speed, often exceeding 75 _____ per
   NOUN   PLURAL NOUN

hour. Luge athletes become virtual flying _____ from the moment
                        PLURAL NOUN

they step into the _____, lie flat on their _____,
          NOUN   PART OF THE BODY (PLURAL)

and, with their _____ looking up into the sky, push off. As they fly
         NOUN

down the ice-covered _____, they steer the _____ by pressing
           NOUN   NOUN

their _____ against the front runners. Protected only by
  PART OF THE BODY (PLURAL)

a/an _____ helmet, they risk their _____ and are in
     ADJECTIVE   PLURAL NOUN

_____ danger until they speed across the finish _____!
  ADJECTIVE   NOUN

MAD LIBS® is fun to play with friends, but you can also play it by yourself! To begin with, DO NOT look at the story on the page below. Fill in the blanks on this page with the words called for. Then, using the words you have selected, fill in the blank spaces in the story.

Now you've created your own hilarious MAD LIBS® game!

IGLOO-BUILDING CONTEST

ADJECTIVE _____

NOUN _____

PLURAL NOUN _____

ADJECTIVE _____

PLURAL NOUN _____

PLURAL NOUN _____

PLURAL NOUN _____

ADVERB _____

ADJECTIVE _____

PLURAL NOUN _____

NOUN _____

ADVERB _____

NOUN _____

ADJECTIVE _____

ADJECTIVE _____

PLURAL NOUN _____

NOUN _____

ADJECTIVE _____

MAD LIBS®
IGLOO-BUILDING CONTEST

Building an igloo is _____ and fun. A hard field of snow is required to

ADJECTIVE

build a/an _____ with a dome. The first rule is to pack the frozen

NOUN

_____ into _____ blocks of all shapes and

PLURAL NOUN   ADJECTIVE

_____. Large _____ are used as the base of the dome and

PLURAL NOUN   PLURAL NOUN

the smaller _____ go on the top. Then, each block should be smooth

PLURAL NOUN

and angled _____ to make a/an _____ bond with the

ADVERB   ADJECTIVE

other _____. Admittedly, building a/an _____ is

PLURAL NOUN   NOUN

_____ more difficult than pitching a/an _____, but it

ADVERB   NOUN

keeps the _____ air out better than a tent. A well-built, average-

ADJECTIVE

size igloo can accommodate three adults or five _____

ADJECTIVE

_____. Believe it or not, _____-building contests are now

PLURAL NOUN   NOUN

being held all over—wherever the climate is _____.

ADJECTIVE

MAD LIBS® is fun to play with friends, but you can also play it by yourself! To begin with, DO NOT look at the story on the page below. Fill in the blanks on this page with the words called for. Then, using the words you have selected, fill in the blank spaces in the story.

Now you've created your own hilarious MAD LIBS® game!

SKIING DISCIPLINES

PLURAL NOUN _____

ADJECTIVE _____

NOUN _____

PLURAL NOUN _____

ADJECTIVE _____

VERB ENDING IN "ING" _____

PLURAL NOUN _____

ADJECTIVE _____

PLURAL NOUN _____

PLURAL NOUN _____

ADJECTIVE _____

ADJECTIVE _____

ADJECTIVE _____

PLURAL NOUN _____

MAD LIBS
SKIING DISCIPLINES

Skiing comes in different _____, and each has its own
PLURAL NOUN

_____ features offering a different kind of excitement and
ADJECTIVE

_____ for skiers of all _____.
NOUN   PLURAL NOUN

Alpine Skiing: This _____ form of skiing is the most general
ADJECTIVE

_____ discipline and is practiced equally by men and
VERB ENDING IN "ING"

_____.
PLURAL NOUN

Telemark Skiing: This is a/an _____ style of skiing. It uses a turning
ADJECTIVE

technique that is admired by many _____ and mastered by few
PLURAL NOUN

_____.
PLURAL NOUN

Freestyle Skiing: This takes skiing to _____ heights, using skis in
ADJECTIVE

many _____ ways to come up with _____ new
ADJECTIVE   ADJECTIVE

disciplines, jumps, and _____.
PLURAL NOUN

From WINTER GAMES MAD LIBS® • Copyright © 2005 by Penguin Random House LLC.

MAD LIBS® is fun to play with friends, but you can also play it by yourself! To begin with, DO NOT look at the story on the page below. Fill in the blanks on this page with the words called for. Then, using the words you have selected, fill in the blank spaces in the story.

Now you've created your own hilarious MAD LIBS® game!

Q & A WITH A CHAMPION ICE-FISHER

NOUN _____

NOUN _____

PLURAL NOUN _____

PLURAL NOUN _____

NUMBER _____

NOUN _____

NOUN _____

NOUN _____

NOUN _____

ADJECTIVE _____

PLURAL NOUN _____

NOUN _____

PLURAL NOUN _____

NOUN _____

PLURAL NOUN _____

ADJECTIVE _____

NOUN _____

ADJECTIVE _____

MAD LIBS®
Q & A WITH A CHAMPION
ICE-FISHER

Q: How does it feel to win a gold _____ ?
<u>NOUN</u>

A: I'm bursting with _____. It's as if I've won a million _____.
<u>NOUN</u>   <u>PLURAL NOUN</u>

Q: How do you always know there are _____ under the ice?
<u>PLURAL NOUN</u>

A: You don't. You may have to drill more than _____ holes in the
<u>NUMBER</u>

_____ to catch your first _____ .
<u>NOUN</u>   <u>NOUN</u>

Q: What's the most important safety _____ you can give a would-be
<u>NOUN</u>

_____-fisher?
<u>NOUN</u>

A: I always tell them what my _____ grandfather told me: Do not
<u>ADJECTIVE</u>

drill a fishing hole bigger than your waistline!

Q: When you ice-fish, you're battling the _____. How do you
<u>PLURAL NOUN</u>

protect yourself against the _____-chilling cold?
<u>NOUN</u>

A: You have to wear protective _____ or you'll freeze your
<u>PLURAL NOUN</u>

_____. I suggest heavy boots, wool-lined _____, and, of
<u>NOUN</u>   <u>PLURAL NOUN</u>

course, _____-johns are a must.
<u>ADJECTIVE</u>

Q: When is it better to stay in the comfort of your _____ than go
<u>NOUN</u>

fishing?

A: Again, as my grandfather used to say: "If the wind is from the east, fishing

is the least." I've always followed his _____ advice.
<u>ADJECTIVE</u>

MAD LIBS® is fun to play with friends, but you can also play it by yourself! To begin with, DO NOT look at the story on the page below. Fill in the blanks on this page with the words called for. Then, using the words you have selected, fill in the blank spaces in the story.

Now you've created your own hilarious MAD LIBS® game!

AWARD CEREMONIES

ADJECTIVE _____

NOUN _____

PLURAL NOUN _____

PLURAL NOUN _____

NOUN _____

PART OF THE BODY _____

ADJECTIVE _____

NOUN _____

ADJECTIVE _____

PLURAL NOUN _____

ADJECTIVE _____

ADJECTIVE _____

PLURAL NOUN _____

PLURAL NOUN _____

MAD LIBS
AWARD CEREMONIES

By far, the most touching and _____ moments of the games are
                              ADJECTIVE

the _____ ceremonies in which first-, second-, and third-place
         NOUN

_____ are presented to the winning _____. There's hardly
PLURAL NOUN   PLURAL NOUN

a dry _____ in the stadium when the officials shake the athlete's
          NOUN

_____ and place the _____ medal around
   PART OF THE BODY   ADJECTIVE

his/her _____. Perhaps the most memorable and meaningful moment
            NOUN

occurs when the _____ winner is handed a bouquet of
                    ADJECTIVE

_____ and the _____ anthem of his/her country is
  PLURAL NOUN   ADJECTIVE

played. When the song ends, the athletes usually break into _____
                                                                ADJECTIVE

smiles, lift their _____ high in the air, and acknowledge the crowd
                      PLURAL NOUN

by waving their _____.
                   PLURAL NOUN

MAD LIBS®

GRAB BAG MAD LIBS

Mad Libs

An Imprint of Penguin Random House

INSTRUCTIONS

MAD LIBS® is a game for people who don't like games!
It can be played by one, two, three, four, or forty.

• RIDICULOUSLY SIMPLE DIRECTIONS

In this tablet you will find stories containing blank spaces where words are left out. One player, the READER, selects one of these stories. The READER does not tell anyone what the story is about. Instead, he/she asks the other players, the WRITERS, to give him/her words. These words are used to fill in the blank spaces in the story.

• TO PLAY

The READER asks each WRITER in turn to call out a word—an adjective or a noun or whatever the space calls for—and uses them to fill in the blank spaces in the story. The result is a MAD LIBS® game.

When the READER then reads the completed MAD LIBS® game to the other players, they will discover that they have written a story that is fantastic, screamingly funny, shocking, silly, crazy, or just plain dumb—depending upon which words each WRITER called out.

• EXAMPLE (*Before* and *After*)

" _____!" he said _____
        EXCLAMATION   ADVERB

as he jumped into his convertible _____ and
                                              NOUN

drove off with his _____ wife.
                            ADJECTIVE

"_____ **OUCH** _____!" he said _____ **STUPIDLY** _____
        EXCLAMATION   ADVERB

as he jumped into his convertible _____ **CAT** _____ and
                                              NOUN

drove off with his _____ **BRAVE** _____ wife.
                            ADJECTIVE

QUICK REVIEW

In case you have forgotten what adjectives, adverbs, nouns, and verbs are, here is a quick review:

An ADJECTIVE describes something or somebody. *Lumpy, soft, ugly, messy,* and *short* are adjectives.

An ADVERB tells how something is done. It modifies a verb and usually ends in "ly." *Modestly, stupidly, greedily,* and *carefully* are adverbs.

A NOUN is the name of a person, place, or thing. *Sidewalk, umbrella, bridle, bathtub,* and *nose* are nouns.

A VERB is an action word. *Run, pitch, jump,* and *swim* are verbs. Put the verbs in past tense if the directions say PAST TENSE. *Ran, pitched, jumped,* and *swam* are verbs in the past tense.

When we ask for A PLACE, we mean any sort of place: a country or city *(Spain, Cleveland)* or a room *(bathroom, kitchen).*

An EXCLAMATION or SILLY WORD is any sort of funny sound, gasp, grunt, or outcry, like *Wow!, Ouch!, Whomp!, Ick!,* and *Gadzooks!*

When we ask for specific words, like a NUMBER, a COLOR, an ANIMAL, or a PART OF THE BODY, we mean a word that is one of those things, like *seven, blue, horse,* or *head.*

When we ask for a PLURAL, it means more than one. For example, *cat* pluralized is *cats.*

MAD LIBS® is fun to play with friends, but you can also play it by yourself! To begin with, DO NOT look at the story on the page below. Fill in the blanks on this page with the words called for. Then, using the words you have selected, fill in the blank spaces in the story.

Now you've created your own hilarious MAD LIBS® game!

INTERVIEW WITH A ROCK STAR

PLURAL NOUN _____

PLURAL NOUN _____

NOUN _____

COLOR _____

VERB _____

ADJECTIVE _____

NOUN _____

NOUN _____

ADJECTIVE _____

ADJECTIVE _____

NUMBER _____

ADJECTIVE _____

ADJECTIVE _____

ADJECTIVE _____

NOUN _____

VERB _____

MAD LIBS
INTERVIEW WITH
A ROCK STAR

QUESTION: Whatever made you choose the name "The Psycho_____"

PLURAL NOUN

for your group?

ANSWER: All the other good names like the "Rolling _____,"

PLURAL NOUN

"_____ Jam," and " _____ Floyd" were taken.

NOUN   COLOR

QUESTION: You not only _____ songs, but you play many

VERB

_____ instruments, don't you?

ADJECTIVE

ANSWER: Yes. I play the electric _____, the bass

NOUN

_____ , and the _____ keyboard.

NOUN   ADJECTIVE

QUESTION: You now have a/an _____ song that is number

ADJECTIVE

_____ on the _____ charts. What was the inspiration for

NUMBER   ADJECTIVE

this _____ song?

ADJECTIVE

ANSWER: Believe it or not, it was a/an _____ song that my mother

ADJECTIVE

used to sing to me when it was time for _____, and it never failed to

NOUN

_____ me to sleep.

VERB

MAD LIBS® is fun to play with friends, but you can also play it by yourself! To begin with, DO NOT look at the story on the page below. Fill in the blanks on this page with the words called for. Then, using the words you have selected, fill in the blank spaces in the story.

Now you've created your own hilarious MAD LIBS® game!

HAVE I GOT
A GIRAFFE FOR YOU!

PLURAL NOUN _____

PLURAL NOUN _____

PART OF THE BODY _____

NUMBER _____

PLURAL NOUN _____

PART OF THE BODY _____

TYPE OF LIQUID _____

PART OF THE BODY (PLURAL) _____

PART OF THE BODY _____

ADJECTIVE _____

PLURAL NOUN _____

ADJECTIVE _____

ADJECTIVE _____

VERB ENDING IN "ING" _____

NOUN _____

PLURAL NOUN _____

NOUN _____

MAD LIBS
HAVE I GOT
A GIRAFFE FOR YOU!

Giraffes have aroused the curiosity of _____ since earliest times. The
                                        PLURAL NOUN

giraffe is the tallest of all living _____, but scientists are unable to
                                    PLURAL NOUN

explain how it got its long _____. The giraffe's tremendous
                            PART OF THE BODY

height, which might reach _____ _____, comes mostly from
                          NUMBER   PLURAL NOUN

its legs and _____. If a giraffe wants to take a drink of
             PART OF THE BODY

_____ from the ground, it has to spread its
      TYPE OF LIQUID

_____ far apart in order to reach down and lap up the
PART OF THE BODY (PLURAL)

water with its huge _____. The giraffe has _____ ears
                    PART OF THE BODY   ADJECTIVE

that are sensitive to the faintest _____, and it has a/an _____
                                   PLURAL NOUN   ADJECTIVE

sense of smell and sight. When attacked, a giraffe can put up a/an _____
                                                                   ADJECTIVE

fight by _____ out with its hind legs and using its head like a
         VERB ENDING IN "ING"

sledge _____. Finally, a giraffe can gallop at more than thirty
       NOUN

_____ an hour when pursued and can outrun the fastest
PLURAL NOUN

_____.
NOUN

MAD LIBS® is fun to play with friends, but you can also play it by yourself! To begin with, DO NOT look at the story on the page below. Fill in the blanks on this page with the words called for. Then, using the words you have selected, fill in the blank spaces in the story.

Now you've created your own hilarious MAD LIBS® game!

THE OLYMPICS

NOUN _____

PLURAL NOUN _____

ADJECTIVE _____

PLURAL NOUN _____

PLURAL NOUN _____

NUMBER _____

ADJECTIVE _____

ADJECTIVE _____

NOUN _____

ADJECTIVE _____

VERB ENDING IN "S" _____

PART OF THE BODY _____

NOUN _____

ADJECTIVE _____

PLURAL NOUN _____

PLURAL NOUN _____

MAD LIBS
THE OLYMPICS

Every two years, countries from all over the _____ send their best
NOUN

_____ to compete in _____ games and win
PLURAL NOUN   ADJECTIVE

_____. These events are called the Olympic _____, and
PLURAL NOUN   PLURAL NOUN

they started _____ years ago in _____ Greece. When a
NUMBER   ADJECTIVE

winner receives his or her _____ medal at the games, the national
ADJECTIVE

_____ of his or her country is played by a/an _____ band. As
NOUN   ADJECTIVE

the band _____, the citizens of that country put their
VERB ENDING IN "S"

_____ to their chest and join in the singing of their
PART OF THE BODY

national _____. Thanks to television, these _____ events
NOUN   ADJECTIVE

can now be watched by over a billion _____ throughout the world
PLURAL NOUN

every two _____.
PLURAL NOUN

MAD LIBS® is fun to play with friends, but you can also play it by yourself! To begin with, DO NOT look at the story on the page below. Fill in the blanks on this page with the words called for. Then, using the words you have selected, fill in the blank spaces in the story.

Now you've created your own hilarious MAD LIBS® game!

HOME SWEET HOME

NOUN _____

PART OF THE BODY _____

NUMBER _____

NOUN _____

COLOR _____

ADJECTIVE _____

NOUN _____

NOUN _____

PLURAL NOUN _____

NOUN _____

NOUN _____

ADJECTIVE _____

NOUN _____

ADVERB _____

PART OF THE BODY _____

VERB ENDING IN "ING" _____

ADJECTIVE _____

MAD LIBS®
HOME SWEET HOME

Some people are fond of the saying, "Home is where you hang your

_____." Others say, "Home is where the _____
   NOUN   PART OF THE BODY

is." As for me, even though my home is a rustic, _____-story
                                                                            NUMBER

_____ home with a/an _____ picket fence surrounding it,
   NOUN   COLOR

I think of it as my _____ castle. Perched on a/an _____
                        ADJECTIVE   NOUN

overlooking a babbling _____ and surrounded by a forest of huge
                           NOUN

_____, my home offers me _____ and tranquility. Each
   PLURAL NOUN   NOUN

and every _____ I look forward to coming back to my _____
              NOUN   ADJECTIVE

home, where my faithful _____ will _____ greet me by
                            NOUN   ADVERB

wagging its _____ and _____ all over
                PART OF THE BODY   VERB ENDING IN "ING"

me. I just love my home _____ home.
                            ADJECTIVE

MAD LIBS® is fun to play with friends, but you can also play it by yourself! To begin with, DO NOT look at the story on the page below. Fill in the blanks on this page with the words called for. Then, using the words you have selected, fill in the blank spaces in the story.

Now you've created your own hilarious MAD LIBS® game!

INTERVIEW WITH A COMEDIAN

NOUN _____

ADJECTIVE _____

ADJECTIVE _____

NOUN _____

NUMBER _____

PLURAL NOUN _____

NOUN _____

VERB _____

VERB _____

PLURAL NOUN _____

PLURAL NOUN _____

ADJECTIVE _____

NOUN _____

MAD LIBS®
INTERVIEW WITH A COMEDIAN

QUESTION: Were you always a stand-up _____?

NOUN

ANSWER: No. I had many _____ jobs in my _____

ADJECTIVE   ADJECTIVE

lifetime. I started out as a used _____ salesperson, and then for

NOUN

_____ years, I sold ladies' _____.

NUMBER   PLURAL NOUN

QUESTION: When did you discover you were a funny _____

NOUN

who could make people _____ out loud?

VERB

ANSWER: It was in school. The first time our teacher had us do show and

_____, I made the _____ in my class laugh so hard

VERB   PLURAL NOUN

they fell out of their _____.

PLURAL NOUN

QUESTION: How would you describe your _____ act?

ADJECTIVE

ANSWER: I am a thinking person's _____.

NOUN

MAD LIBS® is fun to play with friends, but you can also play it by yourself! To begin with, DO NOT look at the story on the page below. Fill in the blanks on this page with the words called for. Then, using the words you have selected, fill in the blank spaces in the story.

Now you've created your own hilarious MAD LIBS® game!

MOVIES SHOULD BE FUN

PLURAL NOUN _____

ADJECTIVE _____

PLURAL NOUN _____

NOUN _____

ADJECTIVE _____

NOUN _____

NOUN _____

PERSON IN ROOM (MALE) _____

A PLACE _____

ADJECTIVE _____

PERSON IN ROOM _____

PERSON IN ROOM _____

ADJECTIVE _____

PLURAL NOUN _____

PART OF THE BODY (PLURAL) _____

MAD LIBS®
MOVIES SHOULD BE FUN

In recent years, there have been too many disaster movies in which tall

_____ catch on fire, _____ dinosaurs come to life,
PLURAL NOUN   ADJECTIVE

and huge _____ attack people in the ocean, making you afraid to
           PLURAL NOUN

get out of your _____ in the morning. Movie fans ask why we
                  NOUN

can't have more _____ pictures like *It's a Wonderful*
                    ADJECTIVE

_____, *Gone with the* _____, or *Mr.*
     NOUN   NOUN

_____ *Goes to (the)* _____. These films
PERSON IN ROOM (MALE)   A PLACE

made you feel _____ all over. These same fans also ask why we can't have
               ADJECTIVE

more funny films with comedians such as Laurel and _____,
                                                     PERSON IN ROOM

and Abbott and _____. These _____
                 PERSON IN ROOM   ADJECTIVE

performers gave us great slapstick _____ that still makes our
                                      PLURAL NOUN

_____ ache from laughing.
PART OF THE BODY (PLURAL)

MAD LIBS® is fun to play with friends, but you can also play it by yourself! To begin with, DO NOT look at the story on the page below. Fill in the blanks on this page with the words called for. Then, using the words you have selected, fill in the blank spaces in the story.

Now you've created your own hilarious MAD LIBS® game!

COOL IT

PLURAL NOUN _____

ADJECTIVE _____

NOUN _____

ADJECTIVE _____

NOUN _____

NOUN _____

NOUN _____

NOUN _____

ADJECTIVE _____

VERB ENDING IN "ING" _____

NOUN _____

ADJECTIVE _____

NOUN _____

VERB _____

MAD LIBS
COOL IT

Weather plays an important part in our daily _____. What is
<u>PLURAL NOUN</u>

weather, anyway? According to _____ scientists, who are known as
<u>ADJECTIVE</u>

meteorologists, weather is what the air is like at any time of the _____.
<u>NOUN</u>

It doesn't matter if the air is cold, hot, or _____, it's all weather. Weather
<u>ADJECTIVE</u>

changes from hour to _____, from day to _____, from
<u>NOUN</u> <u>NOUN</u>

season to _____, and from year to _____. Daily changes in
<u>NOUN</u> <u>NOUN</u>

weather are caused by _____ storms _____
<u>ADJECTIVE</u> <u>VERB ENDING IN "ING"</u>

across the earth. Seasonal changes are from the earth moving around the

_____. When the vapors in _____ clouds condense, we
<u>NOUN</u> <u>ADJECTIVE</u>

have _____ and snow. Whether you like it or not, weather is here to
<u>NOUN</u>

_____.
<u>VERB</u>

GOING TO TOWN

LAST NAME _____

ADJECTIVE _____

PLURAL NOUN _____

ADJECTIVE _____

PERSON IN ROOM _____

PLURAL NOUN _____

PLURAL NOUN _____

ADJECTIVE _____

NOUN _____

NUMBER _____

VERB ENDING IN "ING" _____

ADJECTIVE _____

ADJECTIVE _____

ADJECTIVE _____

NOUN _____

NOUN _____

MAD LIBS® is fun to play with friends, but you can also play it by yourself! To begin with, DO NOT look at the story on the page below. Fill in the blanks on this page with the words called for. Then, using the words you have selected, fill in the blank spaces in the story.

Now you've created your own hilarious MAD LIBS® game!

MAD LIBS®
GOING TO TOWN

THE ART SCENE

Today the _____ Gallery presents a series of _____
            LAST NAME   ADJECTIVE

landscape paintings and still-life _____ by the _____ artist
                                        PLURAL NOUN   ADJECTIVE

_____. These beautiful _____ will be on exhibition for
 PERSON IN ROOM   PLURAL NOUN

the next three _____.
                  PLURAL NOUN

MUSIC

Tonight marks the _____ debut of the all-_____ choir of
                       ADJECTIVE   NOUN

_____ great _____ voices. This _____
    NUMBER   VERB ENDING IN "ING"   ADJECTIVE

ensemble will present _____ renditions of such _____ children's
                           ADJECTIVE   ADJECTIVE

songs as "Twinkle, Twinkle, Little _____" and "Old MacDonald Had
                                        NOUN

a/an _____."
          NOUN

MAD LIBS® is fun to play with friends, but you can also play it by yourself! To begin with, DO NOT look at the story on the page below. Fill in the blanks on this page with the words called for. Then, using the words you have selected, fill in the blank spaces in the story.

Now you've created your own hilarious MAD LIBS® game!

THE THREE MUSKETEERS

ADJECTIVE _____

PLURAL NOUN _____

ADJECTIVE _____

NOUN _____

ADJECTIVE _____

NOUN _____

NOUN _____

PLURAL NOUN _____

NOUN _____

PERSON IN ROOM _____

PLURAL NOUN _____

ADJECTIVE _____

NOUN _____

NOUN _____

PLURAL NOUN _____

NOUN _____

MAD LIBS®
THE THREE MUSKETEERS

There is no more rousing story in _____ literature than *The*
<u>ADJECTIVE</u>

Three _____. This _____ romance by the
<u>PLURAL NOUN</u>   <u>ADJECTIVE</u>

great French _____, Alexandre Dumas, tells the story of
<u>NOUN</u>

D'Artagnan, a/an _____ young _____ who
<u>ADJECTIVE</u>   <u>NOUN</u>

arrives in 17th-century Paris riding a/an _____ with only three
<u>NOUN</u>

_____ in his pocket. Determined to be in the service of the
<u>PLURAL NOUN</u>

_____ who rules all of France, he duels with Athos, Porthos,
<u>NOUN</u>

and _____, three of the king's best _____.
<u>PERSON IN ROOM</u>   <u>PLURAL NOUN</u>

Eventually, these swordsmen and D'Artagnan save their _____
<u>ADJECTIVE</u>

king from being overthrown and losing his _____. Over the years, *The*
<u>NOUN</u>

Three Musketeers has been made into a stage _____, two
<u>NOUN</u>

motion _____, and even a Broadway _____.
<u>PLURAL NOUN</u>   <u>NOUN</u>

MAD LIBS® is fun to play with friends, but you can also play it by yourself! To begin with, DO NOT look at the story on the page below. Fill in the blanks on this page with the words called for. Then, using the words you have selected, fill in the blank spaces in the story.

Now you've created your own hilarious MAD LIBS® game!

SNOW WHITE

PLURAL NOUN _____

PLURAL NOUN _____

ADJECTIVE _____

ADJECTIVE _____

NOUN _____

NOUN _____

NOUN _____

ADJECTIVE _____

ADJECTIVE _____

PLURAL NOUN _____

NOUN _____

COLOR _____

NOUN _____

PART OF THE BODY _____

ADVERB _____

MAD LIBS
SNOW WHITE

One of the most popular fairy _____ of all time is *Snow White*
PLURAL NOUN

and the Seven _____. Snow White is a princess whose
PLURAL NOUN

_____ beauty threatens her stepmother, the queen, who wants to
ADJECTIVE

be known as the most _____ lady in the _____.
ADJECTIVE   NOUN

Snow White is forced to flee from the _____ in which she lives and
NOUN

hide in the nearby _____. Once there, she is discovered by
NOUN

_____ animals who guide her to the _____ cottage of
ADJECTIVE   ADJECTIVE

the seven dwarfs. The dwarfs come home from digging in their mine and

discover Snow White asleep in their _____. The dwarfs take care
PLURAL NOUN

of her until a prince, who has traveled the four corners of the _____
NOUN

in search of Snow _____, arrives and gives her a magical
COLOR

_____ on her _____, which miraculously brings her
NOUN   PART OF THE BODY

back to life. Snow White and the prince live _____ ever after.
ADVERB

MAD LIBS® is fun to play with friends, but you can also play it by yourself! To begin with, DO NOT look at the story on the page below. Fill in the blanks on this page with the words called for. Then, using the words you have selected, fill in the blank spaces in the story.

Now you've created your own hilarious MAD LIBS® game!

MAGIC, ANYONE?

PLURAL NOUN _____

ADJECTIVE _____

ADJECTIVE _____

NOUN _____

NOUN _____

NOUN _____

NOUN _____

ADJECTIVE _____

PART OF THE BODY _____

PLURAL NOUN _____

ADJECTIVE _____

NOUN _____

ADJECTIVE _____

NOUN _____

PART OF THE BODY (PLURAL) _____

PART OF THE BODY _____

PLURAL NOUN _____

MAD LIBS®
MAGIC, ANYONE?

_____ of all ages enjoy watching _____ magicians
   PLURAL NOUN   ADJECTIVE

perform their _____ tricks. Every man, woman, and _____
                  ADJECTIVE   NOUN

loves to see a magician pull a/an _____ out of a hat, saw a live
                                      NOUN

_____ in half, or make a huge _____ disappear into
   NOUN   NOUN

_____ air. Audiences love when magicians perform sleight of
  ADJECTIVE

_____ with a deck of _____, a/an _____coin, or a
 PART OF THE BODY   PLURAL NOUN   ADJECTIVE

silk _____. The greatest of all magicians was the _____
     NOUN   ADJECTIVE

Harry Houdini, who was able to escape from a locked _____ even
                                      NOUN

though his _____ were tied behind his _____
     PART OF THE BODY (PLURAL)   PART OF THE BODY

and his feet were wrapped in iron _____.
                         PLURAL NOUN

MAD LIBS® is fun to play with friends, but you can also play it by yourself! To begin with, DO NOT look at the story on the page below. Fill in the blanks on this page with the words called for. Then, using the words you have selected, fill in the blank spaces in the story.

Now you've created your own hilarious MAD LIBS® game!

THE BIG GAME

PLURAL NOUN _____

PERSON IN ROOM _____

NOUN _____

LAST NAME _____

PLURAL NOUN _____

A PLACE _____

PLURAL NOUN _____

A PLACE _____

PLURAL NOUN _____

NOUN _____

ADJECTIVE _____

ADJECTIVE _____

NOUN _____

NOUN _____

NOUN _____

VERB _____

ADJECTIVE _____

MAD LIBS®
THE BIG GAME

To be read with great enthusiasm!

Hello there, sports _____! This is _____,
PLURAL NOUN   PERSON IN ROOM

talking to you from the press _____ in _____ Stadium,
NOUN   LAST NAME

where 57,000 cheering _____ have gathered to watch (the)
PLURAL NOUN

_____ _____ take on (the) _____
A PLACE   PLURAL NOUN   A PLACE

_____. Even though the _____ is shining, it's a/an
PLURAL NOUN   NOUN

_____ cold day with the temperature in the _____ 20s. A
ADJECTIVE   ADJECTIVE

strong _____ is blowing fiercely across the playing _____ that
NOUN   NOUN

will definitely affect the passing _____. We'll be back for the opening
NOUN

_____-off after a few words from our _____ sponsor.
VERB   ADJECTIVE

MAD LIBS® is fun to play with friends, but you can also play it by yourself! To begin with, DO NOT look at the story on the page below. Fill in the blanks on this page with the words called for. Then, using the words you have selected, fill in the blank spaces in the story.

Now you've created your own hilarious MAD LIBS® game!

THINGS TO DO
THIS WEEKEND

LAST NAME _____

ADJECTIVE _____

PLURAL NOUN _____

PLURAL NOUN _____

NOUN _____

ADJECTIVE _____

NOUN _____

ADVERB _____

NOUN _____

ADJECTIVE _____

PLURAL NOUN _____

PERSON IN ROOM _____

ADJECTIVE _____

NOUN _____

ADJECTIVE _____

ADJECTIVE _____

NOUN _____

NOUN _____

ADJECTIVE _____

FILM

_____ Theaters offers a/an _____ program of foreign
LAST NAME   ADJECTIVE

_____ never before seen in American _____. The first film to
PLURAL NOUN   PLURAL NOUN

be shown will be *Henry and the* _____. This is the _____
NOUN   ADJECTIVE

love story of a man and his _____. It will be shown _____
NOUN   ADVERB

until the end of the _____.
NOUN

STAGE

Appearing in our _____ theater for the next three
ADJECTIVE

_____ is _____, that very _____
PLURAL NOUN   PERSON IN ROOM   ADJECTIVE

star of stage, screen, and _____. He/she will be appearing with
NOUN

our _____ repertory company in nightly performances of
ADJECTIVE

William Shakespeare's _____ comedy, *A Midsummer Night's*
ADJECTIVE

_____. Tickets can be purchased now at the _____
NOUN   NOUN

office by telephone, fax, or _____ card.
ADJECTIVE

MAD LIBS® is fun to play with friends, but you can also play it by yourself! To begin with, DO NOT look at the story on the page below. Fill in the blanks on this page with the words called for. Then, using the words you have selected, fill in the blank spaces in the story.

Now you've created your own hilarious MAD LIBS® game!

SCENE FROM A HORROR PICTURE

ADJECTIVE _____

PART OF THE BODY _____

PLURAL NOUN _____

NOUN _____

ADJECTIVE _____

PLURAL NOUN _____

EXCLAMATION _____

NOUN _____

PART OF THE BODY _____

PERSON IN ROOM _____

NOUN _____

NOUN _____

PART OF THE BODY _____

ADJECTIVE _____

VERB _____

ADVERB _____

NOUN _____

NOUN _____

To be read aloud (preferably by live people):

Actor #1: Why did we have to come to this _____ old castle?
ADJECTIVE

This place sends shivers up and down my _____.
PART OF THE BODY

Actor #2: We had no choice. You know all the _____ in town
PLURAL NOUN

were filled because of the _____ convention.
NOUN

Actor #1: I'd have been happy to stay in a/an _____ motel.
ADJECTIVE

Actor #2: Relax. Here comes the bellboy for our _____.
PLURAL NOUN

Actor #1: _____! Look, he's all bent over and has a big
EXCLAMATION

_____ riding on his _____. He looks just like
NOUN   PART OF THE BODY

_____ from that horror flick *Frankenstein*.
PERSON IN ROOM

Actor #2: No. I think he's my old _____ teacher from _____
NOUN   NOUN

school.

Actor #1: I'm putting my _____ down! I'm not staying in this
PART OF THE BODY

_____ place. I'd rather _____ in the car!
ADJECTIVE   VERB

Actor #2: You're worrying _____.
ADVERB

Actor #1: Really? Look at the bellboy. He has my _____ in one hand,
NOUN

your _____ in the other, and his third hand . . . His *third* hand?
NOUN

Ahhhhh!

MAD LIBS® is fun to play with friends, but you can also play it by yourself! To begin with, DO NOT look at the story on the page below. Fill in the blanks on this page with the words called for. Then, using the words you have selected, fill in the blank spaces in the story.

Now you've created your own hilarious MAD LIBS® game!

IN THE GOOD OLD SUMMERTIME

_____ PLURAL NOUN

_____ PLURAL NOUN

_____ ADVERB

_____ VERB ENDING IN "ING"

_____ ADJECTIVE

_____ NUMBER

_____ PART OF THE BODY

_____ PLURAL NOUN

_____ NOUN

_____ PLURAL NOUN

_____ TYPE OF LIQUID

_____ NOUN

_____ ADVERB

_____ PLURAL NOUN

_____ PLURAL NOUN

_____ NOUN

_____ NOUN

_____ NOUN

_____ NOUN

MAD LIBS®
IN THE GOOD
OLD SUMMERTIME

Many selective _____ prefer the Summer Olympics to the
                    PLURAL NOUN

Winter _____. They respond _____ to such swimming
           PLURAL NOUN   ADVERB

and _____ competitions as the hundred-meter _____
        VERB ENDING IN "ING"   ADJECTIVE

-style race, the _____-meter _____-stroke race, and, of
                     NUMBER   PART OF THE BODY

course, the diving contests in which _____ dive off a high
                                           PLURAL NOUN

_____ and do triple _____ in the air before
        NOUN   PLURAL NOUN

landing in the _____. Equally fascinating are the track and
                   TYPE OF LIQUID

_____ events in which _____ conditioned _____
    NOUN   ADVERB   PLURAL NOUN

compete for gold _____. They compete in such exciting events as
                    PLURAL NOUN

the 1,500-_____ race, the hundred-_____ dash, the ever-
               NOUN   NOUN

popular _____ vaulting, and, last but not least, throwing the hammer,
            NOUN

the javelin, and the _____.
                         NOUN

MAD LIBS® is fun to play with friends, but you can also play it by yourself! To begin with, DO NOT look at the story on the page below. Fill in the blanks on this page with the words called for. Then, using the words you have selected, fill in the blank spaces in the story.

Now you've created your own hilarious MAD LIBS® game!

GOOD MANNERS

NOUN _____

NOUN _____

NOUN _____

VERB _____

PART OF THE BODY _____

ADVERB _____

NOUN _____

NOUN _____

NOUN _____

NOUN _____

PART OF THE BODY (PLURAL) _____

NOUN _____

ADJECTIVE _____

ADVERB _____

MAD LIBS
GOOD MANNERS

1. When you receive a birthday _____ or a wedding
   NOUN

   _____, you should always send a thank-you _____.
   NOUN   NOUN

2. When you _____ or burp out loud, be sure to cover
   VERB

   your _____ and say, "I'm _____ sorry."
   PART OF THE BODY   ADVERB

3. If you are a man and wearing a/an _____ on your head
   NOUN

   and a/an _____ approaches, it's always polite to tip your
   NOUN

   _____.
   NOUN

4. When you are at a friend's _____ for dinner, remember, it's
   NOUN

   not polite to eat with your _____, take food from
   PART OF THE BODY (PLURAL)

   anyone else's _____, or leave the table before everyone else.
   NOUN

5. When meeting your friend's parents, always try to make a/an

   _____ impression by greeting them _____.
   ADJECTIVE   ADVERB

MAD LIBS® is fun to play with friends, but you can also play it by yourself! To begin with, DO NOT look at the story on the page below. Fill in the blanks on this page with the words called for. Then, using the words you have selected, fill in the blank spaces in the story.

Now you've created your own hilarious MAD LIBS® game!

TV GUIDANCE
PICK OF THE WEEK

NOUN _____

ADJECTIVE _____

NUMBER _____

PLURAL NOUN _____

PLURAL NOUN _____

NOUN _____

PART OF THE BODY (PLURAL) _____

ADJECTIVE _____

PERSON IN ROOM (FEMALE) _____

NOUN _____

PART OF THE BODY _____

PLURAL NOUN _____

ADJECTIVE _____

ADJECTIVE _____

PERSON IN ROOM _____

NOUN _____

NOUN _____

MAD LIBS
TV GUIDANCE
PICK OF THE WEEK

THURSDAY, 8:00 P.M. "My Adventures as a Foreign _____."
NOUN

This is an exciting and _____ made-for-TV movie that takes place
ADJECTIVE

during the time of World War _____. We give it a rating of three
NUMBER

_____.
PLURAL NOUN

FRIDAY, 7:30 P.M. "Happy _____."
PLURAL NOUN

When an old high-school _____ welcomes him with open
NOUN

_____ and throws him a/an _____ party, this puts
PART OF THE BODY (PLURAL)   ADJECTIVE

_____, his former _____ friend, into a bad state of
PERSON IN ROOM (FEMALE)   NOUN

_____.
PART OF THE BODY

SATURDAY, 10:00 P.M. "Where Have All the _____ Gone?"
PLURAL NOUN

This _____ thriller, by the _____ director _____,
ADJECTIVE   ADJECTIVE   PERSON IN ROOM

is about a Manhattan _____ searching for a missing person in a
NOUN

small _____.
NOUN

MAD LIBS® is fun to play with friends, but you can also play it by yourself! To begin with, DO NOT look at the story on the page below. Fill in the blanks on this page with the words called for. Then, using the words you have selected, fill in the blank spaces in the story.

Now you've created your own hilarious MAD LIBS® game!

GOOD HEALTH TO ONE AND ALL

ADJECTIVE _____

ADJECTIVE _____

VERB ENDING IN "ING" _____

PART OF THE BODY (PLURAL) _____

PLURAL NOUN _____

PLURAL NOUN _____

NOUN _____

PLURAL NOUN _____

PLURAL NOUN _____

NOUN _____

PLURAL NOUN _____

PLURAL NOUN _____

ADJECTIVE _____

PLURAL NOUN _____

ADJECTIVE _____

ADJECTIVE _____

A/an _____ fitness revolution is taking place. Today, millions of
ADJECTIVE

people are doing all kinds of _____ exercises such as jogging, walking,
ADJECTIVE

and _____ to get their _____ in shape and
VERB ENDING IN "ING"   PART OF THE BODY (PLURAL)

develop their _____. Many go to gyms and health _____
PLURAL NOUN   PLURAL NOUN

to work out by punching a/an _____, lifting _____, or
NOUN   PLURAL NOUN

performing aerobic _____. In the past _____
PLURAL NOUN   NOUN

people have become very weight conscious. They have learned what

_____ they should and should not eat. They know it's healthy to eat
PLURAL NOUN

green _____ and _____ fruit. They also know to avoid
PLURAL NOUN   ADJECTIVE

foods high in _____ and _____ fats, especially if they
PLURAL NOUN   ADJECTIVE

want to lead a long and _____ life.
ADJECTIVE

MAD LIBS® is fun to play with friends, but you can also play it by yourself! To begin with, DO NOT look at the story on the page below. Fill in the blanks on this page with the words called for. Then, using the words you have selected, fill in the blank spaces in the story.

Now you've created your own hilarious MAD LIBS® game!

WHY DO SKUNKS SMELL?

NOUN _____

ADJECTIVE _____

PLURAL NOUN _____

A PLACE _____

PLURAL NOUN _____

ADJECTIVE _____

NOUN _____

VERB ENDING IN "ING" _____

PART OF THE BODY _____

PART OF THE BODY (PLURAL) _____

PART OF THE BODY (PLURAL) _____

ADVERB _____

COLOR _____

PART OF THE BODY _____

PART OF THE BODY _____

MAD LIBS

WHY DO SKUNKS SMELL?

Surprisingly, a skunk is a friendly _____ who can make a/an
                                        NOUN

_____ household pet. But what makes these _____
ADJECTIVE   PLURAL NOUN

smell to high (the) _____? The skunk has scent _____
                     A PLACE   PLURAL NOUN

that contain a/an _____ -smelling fluid. When attacked, the skunk
                   ADJECTIVE

aims this smelly _____ at its enemies. But the skunk does give
                  NOUN

warning before _____. It raises its _____ first, or
                VERB ENDING IN "ING"   PART OF THE BODY

stamps its _____ so that you can run away as fast as your
            PART OF THE BODY (PLURAL)

_____ can carry you. The most _____ recognizable
PART OF THE BODY (PLURAL)   ADVERB

skunk is the one with a/an _____ line on its _____ and
                            COLOR   PART OF THE BODY

another one between its _____ and its ears.
                         PART OF THE BODY

MAD LIBS® is fun to play with friends, but you can also play it by yourself! To begin with, DO NOT look at the story on the page below. Fill in the blanks on this page with the words called for. Then, using the words you have selected, fill in the blank spaces in the story.

Now you've created your own hilarious MAD LIBS® game!

FAMOUS QUOTES FROM THE AMERICAN REVOLUTION

NOUN _____

NOUN _____

COLOR _____

PART OF THE BODY (PLURAL) _____

NOUN _____

PLURAL NOUN _____

VERB ENDING IN "ING" _____

NOUN _____

PLURAL NOUN _____

PLURAL NOUN _____

ADJECTIVE _____

NOUN _____

Nathan Hale said: "I regret that I have but one _____ to give for
                                                    NOUN

my _____."
    NOUN

William Prescott said: "Don't fire until you see the _____ of their
                                                        COLOR

_____."
PART OF THE BODY (PLURAL)

Patrick Henry said: "Give me liberty or give me _____."
                                                      NOUN

Paul Revere said: "The _____ are _____."
                          PLURAL NOUN   VERB ENDING IN "ING"

John Hancock said: "I wrote my _____ large so the king could read it
                                    NOUN

without his _____."
              PLURAL NOUN

Thomas Jefferson said: "All _____ are created equal. They are
                              PLURAL NOUN

endowed by their creator with certain _____ rights and among these
                                          ADJECTIVE

are life, liberty, and the pursuit of _____."
                                          NOUN